**"Ahab!" Elijah thundered,
"Hear my words!"**
Ahab raised himself erect on the
throne. The room was held in rapt
surprise. Elijah's eyes flashed at the king.
His mighty voice reechoed from the
walls. "Ahab! As the Lord God of Israel
lives, before whom I stand, there shall be
neither dew nor rain."
Ahab hesitated a moment, stunned by the
outburst. In that moment Elijah wheeled
and strode from the throne room, past the
startled guards, and toward the outer
doors.
"Take him! Guards! Seize him!" Ahab
stood as he shouted the order.
And for three years Israel baked under
a rainless sky.

ELIJAH

William H. Stephens

LIVING BOOKS
Tyndale House Publishers, Inc.
Wheaton, Illinois

Fourth printing, Living Books edition, April 1983

Library of Congress Catalog Card Number 76-1325
ISBN 0-8423-4020-3, Cloth
ISBN 0-8423-4023-8, Living Books Edition
Copyright © 1976 by Tyndale House Publishers, Inc.
Wheaton, Illinois
Printed in the United States of America

Preface

THREE MEN LOOM very large in Israel's history: Moses, Elijah, and Ezekiel. The first is well-known, the last two are mysterious, but Elijah is the most enigmatic of the three. He bursts on the scene, already a giant, and we know next to nothing about his origins. He is at once a phenomenal hero and a curious quitter. He was unmovable during Baal's greatest strength, yet he ran after Baal's back-breaking defeat.

Much of the answer to this strange, fiery, lonely prophet is found in a study of his adversary: Baalism. The story is harsh. Baalism was a sensuous and cruel religion, yet its appeal to sex and power captivated the minds of the Israelites. Baalism almost overwhelmed the land. Israel came as close to religious annihilation during Elijah's day as she did during the Babylonian captivity.

Elijah's story needs to be told today. The parallels between ninth-century B.C. Israel and twentieth-century A.D. America are striking. The current emphasis on economic power by large corporations and wealthy men, along with the sex orientation that runs throughout our society from advertising to side street pornography, together call for Elijah's story to be told. Perhaps we can learn from his, and from Israel's, experience.

Some scenes in *The Mantle* will shock those men and women who love the biblical text, men and women after my own heart. Yet I could not leave out those scenes that reveal Baalism for what it was. In no other manner could Elijah's story be told, nor could the parallels to our day be made. The scenes are not fabrications; they are true to the nature of Baalism, uncovered through eight years of research in books both musty and new, in libraries of several cities. Almost every incident actually occurred in similar fashion in religions closely related to Phoenician Baalism. Every description of idols and rituals is true to history. Elijah truly fought a giant.

I have been true, as well, to the biblical record, and have tried to tie together what we know with what legitimately might have been. In this process of historical fiction Elijah's story will, I hope, help us grapple with the revelations God gave the world through that great prophet.

Who knows? Perhaps new prophets will rise above this day.

William H. Stephens
Nashville, 1976

Chapter One

THE PALACE WAS BUILT on the highest point of the hill of Samaria. Jezebel could see the sea from the courtlike roof. She came here during those rare moments when she could be alone, for the view refreshed her. Sea was home.

A slight breeze blew in from the Great Sea to tease Jezebel's purple robe, which hung to her ankles in three short, overlapping tiers. Light gusts gave an occasional glimpse of ornate silver ankle clasps.

A beautifully embroidered outer girdle gripped her midriff. Jezebel's beauty was fragile but striking. She easily could become fleshy. Her coal black hair, arranged high on her head and crowned with a tiara, made her round face appear a bit longer. Soft features, combined with an olive-colored complexion without the slightest hint of roughness from the sun, belied a brilliant, scheming mind. Thin, well-groomed eyebrows outlined large and expressive eyes, which she further accented by using a silver probe to draw black antimony powder along the edges of her eyelids. She had practiced using her eyes all through her younger years.

Now, when the trust of a man was important she would make them as deep and lustrous as a gazelle's.

Jezebel pulled her mantle closer around her shoulders. Spring was only just beginning to stir, and the breeze still held some chill. The view of the Great Sea from her parapet was striking. She looked west, down the Vale of Barley. The sea glistened just over a range of hills in the distance. Home. How she longed to see the white sails against the rock harbor, the wind filling them as they put out to sea. But destiny put her here. And Melkart was destiny.

Five years had gone by since her marriage to Ahab. Two kings had arranged the marriage. Ahab's father, Omri, king of Israel, was one of them. The other was Ethbaal, king of Phoenicia, her own father. She often relived that moment, horrible and grand, when she first learned of the alliance.

Ethbaal had asked her to stroll with him along the walkway on top of Tyre's city wall. She had no idea what he was to announce. They had said little, Jezebel enjoying just being with her father. She remembered the tinkling sound made by the tiny bells that lined the edge of his robe. He was short, not much taller than she. Jezebel had inherited his eyes, but, being a woman, she knew better how to use them. Ethbaal's were less controlled, more apt to burn unchecked with the fierce conviction that nearly always dominated his speech.

"Jezebel." He called her name softly. They stopped walking and he pointed out to sea toward three ships that approached the city. She looked at him quizzically. "Jezebel, those ships. Where do you suppose they have been?"

"Why, to Egypt, I suppose."

"Yes, to Egypt, and farther than Egypt. And what do you suppose was their cargo?"

Jezebel hid her irritation at the childhood quiz. "The dyed cloths and artwork of our country."

"Yes." Ethbaal's eyes glowed with pride. "And colored glass, jewels, perfume, embroidery, and our beautiful bronze cups. We have much to offer the world. Look around you, Jezebel. What do you see?" His arm swept in an arc to take in the city walls.

"Well," Jezebel began hesitantly, not knowing his purpose. "I see a beautiful city, built on a rock off the coast. I see ships and harbors, and the Lebanon mountains. What do you want me to say?"

"I want you to see the lifeblood of Phoenicia, Jezebel. We are rich from trading our own wares, but our greatest asset is our ships and the men who sail them."

"Father, I am proud of our courageous sailors. Every Phoenician knows of their travels."

"Look deeper, Jezebel. You are too much the idealist."

"You, of all people, should appreciate an idealist, father. Are not all priests idealists?"

"Tempered with reality, my dear. I did not become king by being idealistic."

Jezebel shuddered. She had heard how Ethbaal assassinated Phoenicia's king and usurped the throne. Now he was both high priest and king.

"What I want you to learn is the importance of trade with the world. We have the greatest navy in the world. If we use it well we can bring even more riches to Tyre. Jezebel, have your tutors taught you of the past alliance between Solomon of Israel and our own brilliant King Hiram?"

"Yes, and of Solomon's wisdom, too."

"When you can align yourself with one who is brilliant, that too is a mark of wisdom."

Jezebel began to understand the significance of the walk. Her smile faded. "What are you telling me, father?"

"I am telling you that Israel controls the main trade routes to the East, to the great cities of Damascus, Riblah, Emesa, Hamath, Aleppo, Charchemish, Haran, and Nineveh. That, my dear, is a prize to be won."

Blood drained from Jezebel's face. She leaned against a wall abutment to control her rising impulse to faint. Her response, after a strained moment, began in a whisper, but her voice rapidly regained its strength. "Father, do you mean to use me to seal an alliance with Israel?" Her strength faded then and she buried her face in her hands.

"Jezebel. Jezebel, my dear." Ethbaal's voice grew soft.

Tenderly, he pulled her to him. "Hear me out. I will not force you to go against your will."

Jezebel raised her head slowly. She touched her eyes with her handkerchief to keep the tears from streaking her makeup. "All right, father."

"My dear, Omri is a brilliant man. He has established Israel and has conquered Moab. The country is gaining strength and its borders no longer are marauded by petty kings. His accomplishments are discussed in many great cities of the world."

Ethbaal released his daughter and stood beside her, looking out toward the sea. He glanced at her after a moment in a vain attempt to read her thoughts. Then he continued.

"Omri has a son called Ahab, a man older than you by twelve years, who already has demonstrated his prowess as a soldier and a leader of men. I have met him. He is as hard as the mountains of his country. He grew up before Omri gained the throne and helped his father conquer the land. His blood is strong." He smiled and laid his hands on Jezebel's arm. "I know you well, my dear. You will never be happy with a weak man. I assure you that this man Ahab is not weak. You will like him."

Jezebel turned around to face the sea. Ethbaal wisely remained silent, leaving her to her thoughts. She had hoped to marry a king from Mesopotamia or Asia Minor, richer countries both in culture and wealth, but as she pondered Ethbaal's words she could think of no really good reason for her desire. Israel, though, seemed so lacking in social graces. And their religion! In the name of Melkart, what did their Yahweh god have to offer? Still, to be part of a growing country might be an exciting life.

"Father?" She spoke without looking at him. "Has the alliance already been settled?"

"Only discussed, Jezebel."

"Then you can make two stipulations for me?"

"And what might they be?"

"Ahab must have wives already."

"Of course. Several. I don't know how many."

"I must be his queen if I go."

"If that were not the case, the alliance would be of only limited value to Phoenicia. I have insisted already on that term. Omri readily agreed, for the alliance is as much to Israel's benefit as to ours. What is your other request?"

"I must be free to take priests with me and to worship Melkart and Asherah as I choose."

Ethbaal laughed. "My dear. All marriage alliances of which I am aware carry that stipulation. Then you will be satisfied with the arrangement?"

Jezebel turned to face her father. A mischievous glint flashed in her eyes. She placed her hand teasingly on her abdomen. "Only if Ahab is the man you say he is."

"That, my fair daughter," Ethbaal laughed, "is something you may observe soon for yourself."

"He is coming to Tyre?" Jezebel exclaimed.

"Yes. He must be as near as Carmel now, and he is a fast charioteer. He should be here sometime tomorrow."

A thrill of excitement passed through her, but priding herself on her maturity, she suppressed her emotion until she could see her proposed husband.

She had felt immediate confidence in Ahab. He was a man, of course, with the normal pride and foolishness of a man, but in the five years of their marriage he had been all the man she could have hoped for.

Ahab was not really handsome, but his rugged, virile features appealed to her. He had not grown up a prince, with a prince's soft life. As her father had said, he was as hard as Israel's hills. Her favorite mental picture of him was as she had first seen him, climbing down from his chariot, the folds of his robe still tucked into his waistcloth. His muscled frame supported a large, bearish head. Dust from the road clung to his hair and beard. She had watched his arrival from a palace window and remembered thinking whimsically, "Can't the son of a king find a cleaner way to ride?"

By the time Ahab had been introduced to her he had washed and put on a clean scarlet robe with an outer garment of purple, tasseled along its edges. She remembered feeling the hardness of his palms and thinking how seldom she had felt callouses on a man's hands.

Almost a year had passed before the wedding, but the months had been busy. Preparations for her move to Samaria as well as the wedding itself had made every day exciting.

It seems a long time ago, Jezebel thought. She turned from the parapet to look at the road that approached from the northeast. She could see as far as the hills from which she had gained her first glimpse of Samaria's white limestone walls. She had commented to Ahab how much the architecture reminded her of Phoenicia.

"Certainly," he had answered. "Phoenician stonemasons supervised the construction."

The only approach to Samaria was that road, which curved from the east, but the only gate was on the west wall. With a smile Jezebel recalled her surprise at seeing no gate as they approached the city. The road ran against the high north wall. The party had followed it around to the west side, there to enter the city where the hill dropped in a severe slope from the roadway. Jezebel had marveled at the military forethought of Ahab's father, but such protection would be uppermost in the mind of a king who had gained his kingdom as a soldier.

Jezebel first felt herself to be a queen at that moment she entered the gate. Riders had gone ahead of them to announce their arrival. As the gates swung open to the royal pair, the roar of excited crowds burst into deafening cheers. A cedar-lined box affair, curtained with silk and supported by poles borne on men's shoulders—three to each end—was ready to taxi Ahab and his bride.

An orchestra of flutes, pipes, lyres, and cymbals quickly formed in front of them, their music moving the crowd to chant psalms to Ahab. Women shouted their approval of Jezebel as she passed near enough for them to become aware of her beauty and gracefulness. Children, aided by the women, spread leaves in the path of the procession. A bandy-legged, potbellied merchant ran to the taxi to force a gift into Jezebel's hands. It was a beautifully wrought box of perfume. She waved back at him, but he was lost in the crowd. Small children waved and shouted their hellos as the procession passed, and they giggled as Jezebel returned their waves.

The throng lined the street all the way to the palace, shouting all the way. The line closed behind them and merged in a solid mass until the press of bodies reached to the shops on each side of the street. The weak gave way to the stronger, who shoved ahead to gain yet another glimpse of their lovely new queen, and they followed with shouts until the procession disappeared through the large oak gates into the palace courtyard.

The thrill of that procession had dwarfed even the real marriage procession of a few days later, because it had marked for Jezebel her acceptance by the people of the city. *How much*, she wondered now as she looked out across the haze to the sea, *can I count on that kind of reception by all of Israel?*

Jezebel had matured during the five years she had been Ahab's wife. She had thought a great deal. She had pondered the future carefully. During those days she had come to love the Vale of Barley. It was beautiful in the springtime, and even now the water from winter rains flowed easily west, gathering the waters of smaller wadis in its lazy move to the sea. Later, the leaves and clusters of vineyards on either side of the Vale would become so thick that the light-colored earth would be obscured. Farther west, across the row of little hills, oak forests clustered in patches on the Plain of Sharon. The beauty of the Vale of Barley, though, was not the strongest reason for her love of the valley. It spoke to her. In her musings the Vale, which moved gently to the sea, came to symbolize a union of Israel and Phoenicia. Perhaps, in years to come, the union would be more than an alliance.

Jezebel had come to appreciate the bounty of the land. Israel was wealthy in food. The finest grapes and grain to come from the sweat of men's brows came from Israel, along with wool and olive oil, dates and pomegranates, and the healing balm from the hills of Gilead. Phoenicia, with all her wealth, could grow little produce. Ethbaal was right. Israel held great possibilities for Phoenicia, and Phoenicia for Israel. *But more than that, dear father,* Jezebel thought, *our countries belong together, wed as I am wed to Ahab.*

Before Jezebel turned to go, she stared briefly at a large new tomb at the foot of the hill of Samaria. She had learned to love Omri, even enough to call him father. She would miss him, but the period of mourning was over. There was work to be done. Baal must become Israel's God if the combining of the countries was to work. Israel's Yahweh was too weak. Melkart, the God of Power, and Asherah, the Goddess of Fertility, must capture the heart of Israel.

Her first step was to be a long conference with Ahab. The time would come at dinner tonight.

The largest room in Ahab's palace was the banquet hall. Scores of persons gathered in the enormous, cedar-lined room for their meals. High-ranking priests, allied to various gods who had been imported along with wives chosen by Ahab or Omri for political reasons, sat discreetly aloof from cults other than their own. Jehu, Ahab's general, and his staff, court visitors, favorites, and royalty all occupied their given places at the king's table. Lounge couches on which the diners reclined as they ate protruded at right angles from long, low oak tables. The lounge couches were of the finest cedars of Lebanon, hand-rubbed to a glossy finish, part of an enormous wedding gift from Jezebel's brother, Baal-azar II, who since then had succeeded his father as king of Tyre, Phoenicia's ruling city. The couches of the royal house and of the highest priests of Yahweh were inlaid intricately with ivory.

Court servants busily plied their ways among the tables, offering breathtaking fare. Roast goose, roast gazelle, mutton, tender calf steaks, all especially prepared with fine Arabian spices, loaves of piping hot bread, fig cakes, raisins from the groves of Israel, pomegranates, olives, cheeses, saltwater fish, melons, vegetables, and the world's finest wines were offered the diners. The tables were served in order of protocol, but even the last table served had no cause for complaint.

Jezebel had arranged for the table she shared with Ahab to be set a short space apart from the guests. Ahab knew by the arrangement that a discussion was in the offing, for by now he had learned his queen's tactics. Nevertheless, he did not object.

Jezebel, wise in the ways of men, waited until Ahab had done with his boasting of the day's work and of his wise decisions. *A man must talk of his exploits or he will become angry with an unlistening wife,* she thought patiently. She waited and listened carefully, for her request was too important to be refused due to bad timing.

With an ear keen to detect the proper time to change the conversation, Jezebel realized that Ahab was repeating incidents he already had explained. She shifted on the lounge chair and held her wine goblet between her hands. "Ahab, I have been reading the chronicles of Israel's kings."

"Really? What did you learn?" Ahab's excitement at Jezebel's interest in his country was apparent.

"I was reading of Jeroboam's policies. He really was a very good king."

"Yes," Ahab agreed. He stroked his bushy, well-trimmed beard. "Of course, he was the man of the hour when Israel rebelled against the rule of Solomon's son Rehoboam. It helps to have your people solidly behind you."

"I was interested in his act of setting up places of worship in Bethel and Dan as rivals to the Temple at Jerusalem." She feigned ignorance. "Why did he feel such a policy was necessary, Ahab?"

"He could do nothing else. The priests taught the traditional belief that only a descendant of David could be the legitimate ruler over Yahweh's people. Since Jeroboam was not a son of that house, he could hardly encourage his people to go to Jerusalem where they would hear such teaching. Also, Jeroboam wanted to break the feeling of kinship between the peoples of Israel and of Judah. He had to make the annual pilgrimage to Jerusalem unnecessary."

Jezebel smiled. "Then," she asked, "if people worship the same god they finally will become one people?"

Ahab glanced at her furtively, the importance of her discussion becoming apparent to him. He answered warily, "I suppose that is true."

"Ahab, how many Israelites worship Yahweh?"

"I couldn't say. Most of them, I think."

"But don't they worship other gods, too?"

"Jezebel," Ahab said irritably, "why ask me questions when you already know the answers? Tell me what you want to say."

"Very well. We have talked many times of the benefits both Israel and Phoenicia receive from the alliance of our countries. Would not the alliance be better sealed if our people became one?"

"No doubt that is true, and I know where you are leading me. But why should not Phoenicia accept Yahweh instead of Israel accepting Melkart?"

"Really, Ahab. There are several reasons and you know them as well as I do. Your people serve baals of every description alongside Yahweh. They have their baals of the valleys, baals of streams, baals of trees and groves, baals of hills and mountains. Why not add Baal-Melkart to the group? He is not much different from the baals they worship now, except that he is infinitely stronger. Your people will accept him easily, but the Phoenicians never will accept your Yahweh with his austere demands."

Ahab's face furrowed. He wished that a priest of Yahweh could answer Jezebel for him. He agreed, though, that the priests were too narrow and the prophets impossible. Jezebel, he knew, was partly right and partly wrong, but he was not schooled in religion as she was. How could he say what was right?

"I don't believe in making any god angry, Jezebel," he responded, "and for myself, I have strong allegiance to Yahweh. Besides, I hope someday to strengthen the relations between my country and Judah. Your plan would not help in that respect."

"I don't ask you or any of your people to stop their worship of Yahweh. I only ask that you allow those who wish to do so the chance to worship in a temple to Melkart."

Ahab raised his bushy eyebrows, a flush of color coming to his neck. Carefully, he set his goblet on the table and turned to Jezebel. "You are asking my permission to build a temple to Melkart?" His voice was harsh.

Jezebel was momentarily taken back by Ahab's directness. She raised her wineglass to her lips to gain time to think. Quickly, she decided that a straight answer would be wise. "Yes."

Ahab put his hand to his own goblet and turned it slowly on its base. A moment passed in silence. "Why should I grant your request, Jezebel?" he finally asked.

Jezebel's lips formed into a thin line. She answered carefully, her eyes wide and deep. "Because Melkart is strong, very strong, and he can help Israel, and . . ." She paused, leaning toward Ahab, gazing at him until her silence forced him to look at her. ". . . and you, Ahab. He can help you."

"Yahweh can help me," Ahab answered fiercely.

"Your Yahweh has done well for you, my king." Jezebel's voice was soft and sincere. Her lips were moist from the wine. She leaned forward and spoke intently. "But Yahweh is a god of the hills, Ahab. Melkart is the God of Power. He can help you anywhere. And his Goddess, Asherah, can make the cattle of your land multiply, and your vineyards, and your grain fields." As she spoke, she waved her goblet in an arc as though to take in the whole land.

Ahab chuckled. "A Phoenician goddess? What has she done to make farmlands of the mountains of Phoenicia?"

"Asherah is called by many names," Jezebel dodged.

Ahab looked questioningly at her. "Like what?"

"Like Ishtar of Assyrian lands, Atargatis of Syria, Isis of Egypt, and Aphrodite of Mesopotamia." She paused between each name to let the silence emphasize each one.

"All of them are the same as Asherah?"

"Only the gods know for sure, but they seem the same to

me. Don't you see, Ahab? The most powerful nations and the richest worship the Goddess of Fertility."

Ahab, distressed at his inability to answer Jezebel and yet intrigued at the veiled promise of wealth, thought, *The affairs of state and war are nothing compared to the wit of a woman.* He shrugged his shoulders. "Who am I to talk of gods?"

"But you do believe they give their aid to men." Jezebel stated rather than asked the question.

Ahab answered wearily, "Yes, I'm sure they do. But I am not sure how much or how little."

"If they help little they can but harm little. On the other hand, you may do well to enlist the aid of such a powerful God as Melkart."

"The prophets of Yahweh say Israel is to serve only Yahweh."

"Come, Ahab. You do not even believe that yourself, and how many of your people believe it? I doubt that even Yahweh is as jealous as your prophets claim."

Ahab was silent, preferring to ignore the subject, but Jezebel intended to press her advantage. "Ahab, please, you will grant my request, won't you?"

Ahab raised his goblet and drank deeply of the Sorek wine, his eyes studious. He stared at the dark liquid, swirling it slowly. "All right, Jezebel. You may or may not be right about Melkart's strength, but you are surely right about the worship of Baal drawing our people together. You may have your temple."

Jezebel smiled.

He looked at her, his eyes hardening. Then, reaching to her couch, he grasped her wrist and squeezed. Jezebel's wine swirled over the brim and onto the polished floor. He spat his words through clenched teeth. "But hear me, my queen." His sudden violence sent a chill to shake her body. "You are not to interfere in any way with the worship of Yahweh. Is that understood?"

Surprised, Jezebel tried to draw back, but Ahab's grip only tightened.

She quit struggling. "Yes, Ahab, I understand."

Ahab slowly released his grasp. He spoke deliberately. "I'm sorry I hurt you. But be sure of this. I meant what I said."

Obviously shaken, Jezebel touched her hair. The movement restored her composure. She smiled and sipped her wine. The conversation completed, they finished their meal in silence.

Ahab pushed his plate away. "Are you finished, my dear?"

Jezebel returned her goblet to the table and rose slowly. Every eye followed the royal couple until their departure was complete. When the door closed behind them the tables began to empty. Following perfect protocol, those seated nearest the king led the exit as others followed in order. The room became a sea of moving color. Brilliant flowing robes, flashing jewels, and embroidered linen moved toward the exit.

The room was empty now, but still it boasted the luxury of soft, colorful cushions, Oriental rugs, and linen tablecloths. Flames flickered in oil lamps, some on the tables, others attached to the walls. Servants came to salvage the remaining food, which would find its way to their own tables, or go to fatten animals in the royal courtyard, or to prolong the miserable lives of beggars for a few more hours.

Chapter Two

Jezebel sat erect in her throne chair, today more confi-
dently a queen than yesterday. Meor-baal's arrival in her
conference room would herald a new day for Israel. He
would be here soon.

The queen's throne chair occupied a wall opposite a window which, guarded by a heavy bronze lattice, opened to
the palace courtyard. The clinking of metal and an occasional snort of a horse accompanied by men's grunts
drifted into the room.

It was the window rather than the throne chair that
dominated Jezebel's conference room. On each side stood
a statue. One was of Melkart, Phoenicia's Baal-god, his
stern, bloodthirsty eyes looking out from a bearded face.
Clad only in a turban and a loincloth, he rested a battle-
ax on one shoulder. The other figure was Asherah, whose
fertility rituals dominated the worship of Baal. She stood
immodestly cupping a breast in each hand, her naked
body blatantly inviting men to engage in the fertility rituals
of her cult.

Jezebel enjoyed her free moment of meditation as she

waited for Meor-baal's arrival. She was excited. Melkart's stony eyes returned her stare, and the stirring within her breast was his promise of blessing. In her musings, she imagined a conquering army. She saw Ahab's command booth set up on a hill overlooking the battleground. Hundreds of chariots raced across the valley floor, their drivers cracking whips over the heads of their sweating horses, shouting curses from dirt-streaked faces, wheels churning dust so that the earth itself joined their ranks. Bowmen lined the base of the hill in two rows, the bottom row kneeling to allow their standing companions to shoot simultaneously. At a shout, a hail of arrows darkened the sun like a cloud. Spears and copper shields caught the sun and reflected it on leather-vested, bearded men, awaiting with taut muscles the command to charge. Israel, led by Ahab and inspired by Melkart, would sweep over little Judah like a flood. Edom's mountain fortresses would fall. Bedouin sheiks would offer tribute. The walls of Damascus would shatter under the battering ram of Israel.

Asherah smiled, and Jezebel dreamed of the herds and flocks of Gilead and Bashan. She saw them multiply and become sleek. Waving fields of wheat and barley covered the valleys and plains of the land. Huge vineyards made the terraced hillsides invisible with their foliage. And Israel's young men and women grew strong and fair. Israel one day would belong to Melkart and Asherah, and then the dreams would come true.

A rap at the door broke the queen's reverie.

"Enter," she responded.

A doorman appeared. "Meor-baal awaits outside, my queen."

"Show him in."

The doorman stood aside to allow the young man to enter the room, then closed the door behind him.

Meor-baal was dressed in a simple white linen robe, bound at the waist with a scarlet girdle, his turban circled with a matching cloth. "My queen." He spoke with dignity as he bowed.

"Meor-baal, a chariot and supplies are being made ready

for you at this moment. You will proceed with all haste to Tyre and present yourself to my brother. Baal-azar will aid you in gathering a complement of priests. You are familiar with the temple at Byblos. Go there if you must. I want you to bring back with you the best qualified men you can find."

Meor-baal smiled. His heavy mustache dominated his beardless face. "It will be with the greatest pleasure, Queen Jezebel. How many do you want?"

"Four hundred."

A wrinkle appeared on Meor-baal's forehead, then quickly disappeared. "Four hundred?"

"Yes." Jezebel enjoyed his surprise for a moment before she continued. "A temple will be built here and another at Jezreel. They must be staffed. I also want several teams of two, a prophet and a priest, strong enough to suffer the rigors of travel. They will go from village to town to set up shrines and altars. In addition, you will arrange for efficient engineers, stonecutters, masons, woodcarvers, and carpenters to plan and erect the temples." Jezebel pulled a scroll from beside her and extended it to Meor-baal. "Here are your credentials. The scroll also contains a detail of my requests. Everything else you need is in the chariot that awaits you. Now go, and may Melkart bless you, my priest."

Meor-baal bowed and, without a word, strode in long steps from the room. The journey would take, he supposed, two days. His sandals shuffled easily on the stone steps as he descended to the courtyard. He stopped at the chariot long enough to tuck the folds of his robe into his girdle, then he mounted and took the reins from the handler. The chariot was of leather rather than bronze, frail but swift. The two-horse team, both bays, responded with a lurch to Meor-baal's shout and passed through the palace gates at a brisk trot. The leather tires whispered against the basalt rock pavement as Meor-baal guided his team through the city's streets until, once outside Samaria's walls, they gathered speed.

Meor-baal settled his team to a steady lope, guiding them

north toward Ibleam. He mused about the trip. From Ibleam, which he should reach in time for a late lunch, he would turn northwest to follow the Carmel range to the garrison of Megiddo.

The trip was uneventful, crossing one wadi after another as he moved north, then riding the shoulder of Carmel under a gray sky.

Night came early under the overcast. Guards were closing Megiddo's gates as Meor-baal began his ascent up the steep incline to the fortress. When the guards saw his approach, they held the huge iron-hinged oak gates partly open. One of the guards called to the sentries posted on the wall. Meor-baal stopped and, with the guards watching closely, produced the scroll from his robe. At the sight of Jezebel's seal, the guards heaved to open the gates wider, and Meor-baal drove his horses through the first gate of the chariot fortress.

Inside the second gate, a leather-vested soldier climbed into Meor-baal's chariot and reached for the reins. At his grunt and snap of the wrist, the team moved between rows of horse stables and chariot stalls.

Meor-baal watched in amazement. "So this is one of Solomon's chariot cities?" he mused. "He was a great king, indeed." Speaking more directly to his guide, he asked, "How many chariots, my friend?"

"One hundred fifty," the guide replied without looking from the lane. "And four hundred fifty horses."

They continued at a slow trot past rows of stone hitching-posts, each separated from the next by a stone manger, then crossed a courtyard and halted before a large house.

"Come," the guide grunted. "Our captain will give you food and lodging. I will present you to him."

Meor-baal stepped gratefully from the chariot. His legs felt a bit wobbly as his feet touched the ground after his long ride.

Drizzle fell all during the night and Meor-baal slept well to the gentle sound. By sunrise the overcast had begun to break. By midmorning, with Meor-baal well on his way, white, fluffy, cheerful clouds spotted the sky. The priest was grateful for the fresh horses the captain had given him. His journey would go faster than expected.

The smell of the Great Sea greeted his nostrils. Were it not for a low ridge of hills near Carmel he would be able to see the water. Mount Carmel rose majestically from the valley floor to thrust its headland out into the sea like the battering ram of a conquering army. The mountain caught the sea rains first, as their clouds passed east, and so remained green throughout the year. Vineyards and orchards covered its slopes, separated by bare rocks from thick brush and forests at its summit. "Truly you are a home of the gods!" Meor-baal whispered in awe. "Ah, and the day is near, Yahweh of Israel, when Baal will end the contest for this great mountain and banish you to the wastelands of the desert."

The young priest reined up to slow his horses, pondering whether to take the time to visit the shrines of Melkart and Asherah at Carmel's summit. Then, thinking better of his schedule, he returned his team to the journey with a snap of the reins. Carmel would have to wait.

Late in the afternoon the walls of Tyre appeared, rising out of the sea itself. Were it not for the white clouds in the background the dark stone walls of the island city would have been hard to see. The western sun cast shadows from the south port's fortifications across a convoy of Egyptian trading vessels anchored in the harbor. He felt proud. Melkart had been good to Tyre.

Meor-baal turned his team onto one of the causeways that connected the island with the mainland. With obvious familiarity, he drove his horses through the flat stone streets to the palace of Baal-azar and reined up at the entrance.

From one of the square parapets that stood on each side of the sealed gates, a guard called for him to identify himself.

Meor-baal called back, "I bear a personal message from Queen Jezebel of Israel to her brother, the great King Baal-azar of the Phoenicians."

The guard spoke to someone whom Meor-baal could not see, then called back, "Drive your team just inside the gates and halt them." At those words, the huge oak gates swung outward. Meor-baal snapped his reins and stepped his sweating team the few paces inside, where a massive chain barred further progress. A heavy-bearded, leather-vested soldier stood waiting. His conical cap indicated his captain's rank. He stretched an open hand toward the young priest. "Your credentials."

Meor-baal handed him a small, tightly-rolled scroll. It was sealed with wax, into which Jezebel had pressed her official seal. The captain barked a command and a mustached young man stepped into the chariot.

"Leave your chariot and team to this man's care and come with me," the captain directed.

Meor-baal handed the reins to the mustached one and followed the captain, who strode briskly across the courtyard to a flat-roofed house. Inside, he turned to Meor-baal. "What are you called?"

"Meor-baal."

"You are not an Israelite?"

"No, I am from Byblos. I was born from a sacred union in the temple of Baal." Meor-baal continued with obvious pride. "My mother was a zonah, and of course I do not know who my father was. Now I am a priest of Baal serving my Queen Jezebel."

The stony, disinterested features of the captain's face melted. The son of a temple prostitute was sacred, especially one so young who already was such an important priest. He bowed, his sword clinking on the stone floor.

Rising to his feet, the captain announced softly, "Hot water and fresh clothing will be brought to you. I will have two men serve you during your stay. In the meantime, I will arrange an interview with the king."

The heat rose in shimmering waves from the sandy road. Meor-baal's eyes, and those of his prophet companion, ached by day's end, though they had become accustomed to the reflection of the summer sun from the hot earth. A chariot would be welcome, but in the interest of their cause he and his friend had agreed to Jezebel's request that they travel on foot. A prophet on foot impressed the people as being more dedicated than one who rode in a chariot. He could wish, however, that he had been assigned to visit the villages of northern Samaria above the Jezreel Valley. It was cooler there. But at least their itinerary led them occasionally to the sea where they could find some relief from the heat.

"There's Dor," the prophet announced, pointing to a white-walled village obscured by the golden wheat that covered the plain.

"A welcome sight. First we wash our feet, then some cool wine."

The two companions quickened their pace.

Several elders sat at the entrance of the gate. The old men, venerated by tradition, witnessed business transactions and gave advice to the residents of the city. Often they sat in judgment in disputes. They watched the pair approach the gate. Both Meor-baal and the prophet were dressed simply. Their robes, once white, had grayed during their journey, despite several washings. Their legs were bare and deeply tanned, the folds of their robes pulled up and tucked into their leather waistbands. Cloths were attached to their small turbans to hang down the backs of their necks for protection against the sun. The two looked much alike, except that the prophet had a full beard that made him look older than the priest.

The prophet walked a pace or two ahead of Meor-baal, and the two of them stopped in front of the elders. The prophet placed his hands on his hips and stared at the older men until, by his silence, he commanded their full attention.

"We will speak here, at this spot, at sunset," he announced in a deep-throated voice. Then, to maintain an air of mystery, he turned and walked away. Meor-baal followed without speaking.

The elders stared after them. "A prophet," one surmised aloud.

"Yes," another agreed. "I have heard travelers speak of many prophets visiting many cities, but they are not the prophets of Yahweh."

Several heads nodded. One wizened elder, his white beard thin with age, countered in the shrill voice of the aged, "But we do not *know* they are not Yahweh's prophets."

Heads nodded again.

The elder continued. "If they are of Yahweh, we must hear their words. If they are not of Yahweh, what harm can come from one evening of listening? We can expel them tomorrow."

Bearded faces turned from one another and, one by one, the elders struggled to their feet and left in different directions to announce the appointment.

Meor-baal and the prophet did not appear until exactly at sunset. Already, a crowd of men had gathered.

The prophet whispered to the young priest. "Look at them, and think of all the other villages where our brothers are working tonight. We cannot fail, Meor-baal."

"You will do well, my friend," Meor-baal answered.

A stone stairway led from the gate to the top of the city wall. The prophet mounted high enough to be seen easily by the crowd. He turned to face them, his long robe blowing softly in the evening breeze.

Just as he was about to speak, a voice called out from the crowd, "Whose prophet are you?"

The prophet smiled and spread his arms. "I am a prophet of the people," he answered. "Your prophet."

Meor-baal listened with concern. The crowd very well could become antagonistic.

"Are you not a prophet of Baal?" the voice called out.

The prophet answered quickly to cut off any attempt from the mob to join the derision of the voice, and he spoke as deeply and as powerfully as he could. "Let me tell you why I call myself a prophet of the people." The crowd responded uneasily. Some shuffled, but he was allowed to continue.

"The true God wants his people to be happy and well fed. He wants them to enjoy the bounty of the earth and the pleasures of life. Can you imagine the goodness of a god who would see his people struggle from the rise of the sun until its setting and reap barely enough harvest to exist? Can you imagine a god who places good things in the earth and then rations them out in small amounts? I speak by the authority of a God who offers men the bounty of the earth. This is why I call myself a prophet of the people."

The crowd seemed willing to listen, though he had not directly answered the heckler's question. The prophet's voice rose in tone and confidence. He told of the richness of their land. He praised the strength of their young men. He spoke in soothing tones of the beauty of their women. Gradually, very gradually, he injected the name of Baal. When he sensed a resentment growing against him, he resorted to humor. He played the mob as an angler would a fish, gradually bringing it under his control, until the mob became an audience. All the while he grew bolder.

The prophet's beard jerked in the flickering light, following the movement of his chin. The oil lamps cast a gigantic shadow on the wall behind him. The crowd, half hypnotized by his speaking, began to feel that the shadow represented the size of the prophet's soul.

He told of the need for men to share in the creation of life with Baal. Yahweh, he said, was the god of the hills, of the nomad, of the sheepherder, of the tent dweller, not the god of the fertile plain and the walled city. Do not neglect the god of the hills when you travel through the hills, but neither neglect the Baal-god Melkart when you are in his domain.

The audience hung on his words. He made them laugh occasionally. He spoke thoughts they had not heard before. "After all," the prophet cried, "look at pitiful Judah. What is her wealth compared to Israel's? Are not her people more faithful to Yahweh than you are yourselves? Remember Solomon! Did he not grow in power and wealth as he brought hundreds of foreign women to his harem, and with them their gods? Yahweh must be weak to permit such a thing, or else he really does not care! And look at Phoenicia, and Damascus, and Assyria, and the Hittites. Look at the kingdoms across the sea. Are they weak? Could not Melkart make of Israel as strong a nation as those countries?"

The prophet's voice flowed on. The crowd grew larger. "Why, Baal was the God of this land before you Israelites came here. Don't you know he claims it? Do you suppose he will give you food in plenty and good crops when you neglect him for another god?" The prophet told of wheat fields and olive groves and orchards and produce and cattle and sheep beyond compare. He described a land rich beyond their imaginations. "Do you know where this land is?" he asked. "Right here! Baal-Melkart will make your land richer than your dreams if you will serve him."

In terms that rang of the sound of battle, he told of Melkart's record of war victories. "Was ever there a God like Melkart? Why, he was the God who brought you from Egypt, not Yahweh, for Baal wanted you to serve *him* on this soil, *his* soil.

"And Melkart has a consort, Asherah, beautiful beyond compare! It is she who is the Goddess of Fertility, and she wants her people to share in the rituals of the fertile land. Ah! Any god can ask you to give of your flocks and produce at his altars, but this goddess understands men and asks them to help her make the land fertile. How? Why, there are women who have dedicated their lives to serve Asherah. With them, you will gain the blessing of fertility, for yourselves and for your land."

The prophet, now in subdued tones, told of the willingness of these women to serve their goddess.

The crowd listened with astonishment. The young men's muscles grew tense and fever grew in their loins. Fathers thought how such a thing might help bring abundance to the tables of their families. Childless men thought that perhaps Asherah would bless their homes with children if they sought her help. Older men thought of the ease of lying with such women.

As the prophet spoke, Meor-baal mixed with the crowd and whispered to the young men that sacred prostitutes waited for them at the high places and in the sacred groves about the city. Young men looked at one another wide-eyed. Some of them slipped away quietly.

"All day tomorrow," the prophet was saying, "the priest of Melkart and Asherah will be at the altar on the hill just beyond the city. Bring your offerings to him and be blessed, so that your spirits may mingle with the sweet savor and rise to the sky. Melkart and Asherah will receive you as one of their own, and their blessings will come to you."

And on the morrow they would come. Old men. Young men. Widowers. Childless couples. Luckless farmers. They would come to the altar in search of their dreams. And Baal would gain a foothold in the city of Dor.

Abinadab was intrigued by the events of the evening. The loanmaker stood behind the crowd, dressed in finer clothing than most of his townsmen. He regarded the promises made by the Baal prophet as absurd, but the sermon was fine entertainment. Soon, though, the crowd itself caught his notice. Here were people he knew, people caught up in the message to the point of rapture. The power of the prophet so to control people fascinated him. Control over people. Surely the prophet had some secret he could share. Perhaps it was the secret of the Baal religion.

He did not go to the sacred grove. Instead, he waited until the men scattered in their lustful fervor, then he bade the two servants of Baal to his home to talk.

The discussion was held in the room of Abinadab's home where he conducted his business. It was a special room he had built onto his house, with walls of thick, heavy stone and two sets of doors for added protection. Some of the wall-stones were hollow, known only to him, to serve as hiding places for the money he used for lending. Wooden shelves fixed at the top of each wall held scrolls and broken pieces of pottery—ostraca—on which he scratched records of his transactions. Cloaks and other collateral dominated three-fourths of the shelving.

Meor-baal and the prophet reclined comfortably on Persian rugs and large pillows that covered most of the floor. Abinadab sat with his back against more pillows behind a low table. He faced his guests.

"You spoke of Asherah tonight," he began. "I want to hear more of her consort, the Melkart you say is so powerful."

Meor-baal gestured for the prophet to answer.

"Melkart is the God of Tyre. He also is the God of Power. I need not tell you how well he has won his place among the gods. He now is most honored by us, the Phoenicians. Asherah is the Goddess of Fertility, but she works best for those who worship her and Melkart together. The God of Power works in harmony with the lovely Asherah."

"Yes. Lovely and promiscuous," Abinadab answered.

"If the gods do not copulate, how can the earth yield its fruit? And will men who till the earth not be more productive if they copulate with Asherah's chosen zonahs? Will not the earth follow the example?"

"Perhaps. I know little of such things. But tell me of Melkart. He never has fought a battle, at least none that I can recall. From whence comes his power?"

Meor-baal smiled. "You think like most of the world, friend Abinadab. Melkart has fought many wars for many kings, but you are right that he has not fought for Tyre. Real power comes through commerce, not through war. Melkart has blessed Phoenicia through commerce."

"Ah, I thought you might say that. I am interested."

"In power?"

"In power. In wealth. Yes, why should Melkart not aid me? I have a good mind. I know the people of Dor. And our region is good, especially in grain and wine."

"Our Queen Jezebel wants very much for Israel and Phoenicia to be united in commerce. Israel is rich in produce. But your way of doing things, the way people live in this country, does not lend itself well to real commercial power. If you truly will learn from Melkart, you may be of service to Jezebel's plans. But you must be willing to change."

"In what way?"

"Your small landowners impede commerce. The people toil each year for a small crop, only a small part of which is available for purchase by small-time merchants, who then must sell to large caravans, who then must take the produce to Phoenicia or Egypt. Some of your farmers do well, some do not. The land is not used wisely. Those who do not farm well should not farm at all. They should do something else."

"The ancient laws of Israel decree that every family of Israel should keep his land forever," Abinadab responded.

"That is not the way of Melkart. You cannot have power if you allow the land to remain so divided."

"What are you doing with those cloaks piled on top of your shelves?" the prophet interrupted.

"They are collateral for loans."

"Do not the laws of Israel require that you return them each night to the owners, so they will have warm cover for the cold nights?"

Abinadab did not lower his eyes, to the surprise of the prophet. It was a good sign. Perhaps this man was strong. "Yes," the moneylender answered. "The ancient laws require that. But to do so diminishes the cloak's value as collateral. So long as the people who owe me money are warm at night, they do not repay quickly. When they are cold I get my money back, and they do not quibble so much about the interest I charge."

"So you break the ancient laws of Israel when they suit your purpose, but you loudly protest, as you did a moment ago, when you see no need to break the law."

Abinadab swallowed but answered quickly. "Yes, I suppose that is true. But land is more sacred in Israel than cloaks. It is a greater law."

"The choice is yours. You can have power measured by the value of cloaks or by the value of fields."

"I see your point."

"One more thing," the prophet continued. "How do you keep the people from taking you before the elders who sit at the gate?"

"They do take me sometimes."

"And how do you retain their cloaks, then?"

Abinadab again spoke firmly. "The elders are friends of mine."

"You bribe them?"

"No." His voice rose in anger. "I have never bribed an elder. I would not bribe a judge of my people."

"Then how do they rule in your favor?"

"They know my point of view. They are convinced, as I am, that a cloak is poor collateral when it can be picked up each night at sundown."

"And how did they come to agree with you so fully?"

"They have become my friends. We talk at parties and in one another's homes. We attend religious functions together. I give them gifts on special occasions. They are my friends."

The two Baal servants glanced at each other. "Why don't you be honest with yourself?" they chided their host. "You *are* bribing the elders. Admit it, and Melkart will show you the way to power."

Abinadab leaned forward. "You sit as my guests in my house and dare accuse me of dishonesty?"

Meor-baal laughed. "Don't be angry, Abinadab. We only seek to clarify our meaning. I fear that your worship of Yahweh has dulled your senses. You really don't believe Yahweh's teaching that men should not accumulate wealth at the expense of the poor or weak, but you cannot tear away from the laws of Israel. So you hover between one view and the other. You strain Yahweh's laws enough to satisfy your business needs, but not so much that you break away from them completely. The result is that you remain a very small fish compared to what you could be."

"All right. I will listen to what Melkart teaches."

The priest sat up and pointed his finger at Abinadab.

"First, let me hear you admit that your friendship with the elders and your gifts to them are a form of bribery."

Abinadab stared at Meor-baal for a moment. Then he spoke in a low tone. "All right, I suppose it is a form of bribery."

"Now," the priest responded, "we are getting somewhere."

"Whose cloaks are these?" the prophet asked.

"They belong to men of Dor. Baana, Shammah, several others."

"And if you did not keep them each night they would not pay you well?"

"That is a fact."

"Then you could claim the cloaks by default."

"Yes. But what do I want with cloaks? It is more profitable to lend money than to sell cloaks."

"But suppose you allow the owners to keep their cloaks at night and they do not pay on time. Would that not put them in a difficult position toward you?"

"Certainly."

"You said you had a fine mind. Let Melkart come into your mind. Think like Melkart. Think like the God of Power. Lie back and think. We will be silent."

The priest and the prophet lay back on their pillows. Abinadab watched them, his brow furrowed in surprise. He sat for a moment staring at them. Then he murmured, "I don't know how Melkart thinks. That's why I asked you to come."

"Lie down," the prophet ordered.

Abinadab pulled the pillows from behind his back and arranged them on the rug. He lay down on his side, facing the two guests.

"Lie on your back," the prophet said.

He shifted to his back.

"Now think. Think about what you said. Think about the power you have now. Think how you can use that power to get what you want."

Abinadab lay quietly. For some minutes he could not focus on the subject. His thoughts for so long had been on the securing of loans, most of them small, and the proper handling of his business affairs.

It was a statement of Meor-baal's, an interruption of his reverie, that sparked his mind. In the dead quiet Meor-baal spoke slowly, with heavy precision: "Those men who dashed madly in their lust worship fertility. They pray for its increase. They wish for power, too, and worship it. But all they need do to worship fertility is to turn their bodies loose. To worship power, they must do more. Power will not come to the man who but worships it, only to the man who exercises it. You gain power through action." It was Meor-baal's only interruption through the entire night, but Abinadab caught the words as though they were hung in the air at that point in his destiny by Melkart himself.

He rolled the words and tasted them in his mind. Faces formed, faces of men who owed him money, faces whose eyes could not see as far as his, faces who had other possessions that, accumulated, meant power to the man who accumulated them. There was Baana, the happy one, whose wife was known for her figcakes and her barren womb. There was Shammah, Baana's close friend, who lost his wife some months ago, and whose two daughters were almost of marriageable age.

The faces paraded before his vision, all of them men who owed him money. A plan began to form. As a gesture of good will to the discovery of Baal by Dor's citizens, he would return each cloak to each man, and he would offer them extra money to buy oxen, more tools, better seed, and storehouses for the produce that would come from the newly-blessed fields. Their fields would be his collateral. He would foreclose immediately if any could not pay. The first foreclosure would be hard, but he would do it. He would be strong.

Chapter Three

Zebul's fleshiness was apparent even under his copious priestly garments. His thick, short-fingered hands protruded from huge sleeves, and deep-set eyes peered from shallow caves over puffed cheeks. His heavy beard and long hair covered most of his face and neck. He was a man who had grown confident through years of leadership, for he had come to believe that he really was a cut above the average man.

His garments were regal. He wore a blue robe, woven without a seam, bordered with blue, purple, and scarlet ornamentation in the design of pomegranates alternated with tiny golden bells. The bells made tinkling sounds as Zebul occasionally shifted his weight from one foot to the other. A vest covered the robe from under his arms to his waist. The vest, scarlet like the ornaments, was interwoven with gold thread. It was held at the waist with a matching girdle. Across his chest was a breastplate, opulently adorned with jewelry. His turban was of simple white linen, pinned at the front with a large jewel that designated his high office. The real high priest in Jerusalem wore in place of such a jewel a gold plate inscribed, "Holiness to the Lord." Zebul conceded this single difference in dress out of practical deference to the people, who believed there was only one true high priest of the Hebrews.

He was brooding. Bad enough to be relegated to a seat below the priests of Baal at the king's table, but to be threatened with expulsion altogether was horrendous beyond words. Zebul was the highest ranking priest in Israel. In fact, he conducted himself as though he indeed were Israel's high priest in spite of his Judean counterpart. He had risen to his present position because he had a knack both for the mechanics of the priesthood—which functions he carried out with great efficiency—and for the machinations of politics.

Zebul stood in the shade of the city wall and looked down the north side of the hill of Samaria. He gazed intently at the progress of building the great temple, but he took little notice of the workmen's efforts. He was wrestling toward a decision. The worship of Baal had spread throughout Israel like the heat of the sirocco wind. The past year had seen altars built to Melkart and holy places built to Asherah all over the land.

His problem was not moral. He had long since given up such bounds on his personal ambition. In fact, his nearness to holy things never had touched the emptiness of his soul, an emptiness he long ago had accepted simply as a part of life.

Zebul's nervousness was evident, if one could see him well in the shadow of the wall. He had a quirk of rubbing his knuckles against his ring. Leaning against the city wall, he weighed the course of Israel's future and tried to consider the facts objectively. He could see two courses of action.

The first course called for great personal sacrifice, but quite conceivably he could be well rewarded eventually. Should he cast his lot unequivocally with the Yahwists and intrigue against Jezebel? If Baalism were defeated, he would be in an enviable position of leadership, provided that he could outwit Jezebel, Meor-baal, and other intelligent minds of the opposition long enough to survive.

The building being raised below him represented the other alternative. The temple walls rose imposingly to the sky. *Strange irony,* Zebul thought, *that the Phoenicia that lent stonemasons to Solomon to build the magnificent Temple to Yahweh in Jerusalem should lend others now to build this temple to Baal.*

The Phoenicians indeed were brilliant in the use of stone. Straight level trenches had been cut into the sloping hillside to receive the foundation stones. Before the walls had begun to rise, the arrangement of stones resembled two long, parallel stairways joined by stone fences on each end. The entrance was at the south end, nearest the city wall. The main floor would extend level to the back of the temple. The hollow space beneath, created by the slope of the hill, was designed for priests' quarters.

Zebul often had come to watch the building's progress, as roughly squared stones were hauled on donkey-drawn carts from a nearby limestone quarry to the workmen, who marked them with red chalkline, square, and plumbline to exactly the required size and texture. Already the stones had hardened to a glaring white. Two huge obelisk columns were being raised on either side of the entrance by a system of ropes. Once erected, they would join the fertility of the earth to the goddess of the heavens who gives so bountifully to men.

Strange how the gods fight, Zebul thought. *Each claims to give the same gifts to men—happiness and prosperity. Yahweh could learn something from Baal.* He smiled at the thought. *Why should men choose to live austere and holy lives to receive Yahweh's blessings when they have the same promises from Baal, who demands only sacrifices and the consort of beautiful women?*

He paused and reflected, caressing his ring more rapidly. Funny how lust is so integral a part of religion. A religion often is rejected or accepted simply because of its view of sex. He chuckled. "Is truth then bound up in sex?" he asked himself aloud.

Zebul had not forgotten his history learned from the chronicles of the kings. The Israelites never really had followed Yahweh faithfully for very long at a time. The baal-gods of the brooks and valleys and hills and trees always had claimed their fancy. People, after all, follow the god of the time. Occasionally there is a certain temper, a certain indescribable mood that permeates the air, causing men to become conscious of their wrongdoings and ready to respond to the prophet's challenge. At other times, though, the prophet's efforts influence only a few. Those few may keep the name of their god alive, barely, but the prophet's sweeping influence must await that changing, undefined, and completely unpredictable and independent mood. Zebul watched a dust devil swirl near the temple, as though its movement would reveal to him the mood of his time.

That the name of Yahweh would remain alive was no question to the astute Zebul. The schools of prophets, the priests, the elaborate laws and ritual that were woven into the very fabric of Israel's society all were insurance enough for such confidence. Whether Yahweh worship would revive and become aggressive during *his* lifetime was the question. Baalism held the day. Its aggressiveness appealed to young people and encouraged their natural rebellion against inherited values. Its rituals were even more elaborate and much more sophisticated than those of Yahweh worship, a difference that men—especially young men —often mistake for depth.

Zebul walked slowly past the work project, carefully avoiding the debris of construction. Below the new temple, the road had been widened from a footpath to a lane that was able to accommodate carts traveling in opposite directions. He liked to think among the king's grapevines in the valley, but the plants were not yet high. Zebul wished for the beauty of climbing vines that would arch overhead to form a passageway when summer came. Then the green of the leaves would be offset by the dark color of the Sorek grapes. He passed through the vineyard toward his second choice for seclusion, the pink-blossomed oleanders growing next to the wadi.

With his stubby hand, Zebul brushed the dirt from a large rock. He clapped his hands to rid them of the dust and sat down, arranging his robes carefully. The little wadi rushed with springtime water, gathering from even smaller tributaries as it made its way to the Great Sea. *To make as much difference to the sea*, he thought, *as the words of Yahweh's servants make to Israel.*

The big priest rested fat forearms on fat thighs. His rich robe drooped apronlike between his legs as he continued his analysis, which gradually was evolving into a decision. He stared at the water, reading its story. The people of his day looked on religion as serious, but they smiled at the deprecations of the prophets. If the people only would become angry, perhaps the prophets would have some chance of success, but a tolerant, dismissing smile, that is devastating.

His fingers worked their way through the heavy beard to scratch an itching on his cheek. His conclusion was well considered. *Yahwism is swimming upstream. All of the currents of the world flow against it.* He stood and turned toward the temple above him. From the valley its wall towered more imposingly than ever. He straightened to announce his decision to himself, an announcement that never passed his lips but nonetheless resounded in his mind: *I shall not give my life to a doomed cause.*

His decision made, he turned to follow the wadi upstream to a road that wound to the city wall. This way back was longer, but less an exertion than the way he came. He gained the road and turned south toward the city, mulling over his future as he went. He would not openly repudiate his Yahweh religion, but he would not oppose Baalism. As he accepted Baal alongside Yahweh, he would in turn be accepted again as a favorite by the court. Such was his hope.

An ancient olive grove, sloping down into the valley, grew on the right side of the road. As he approached and continued alongside it, a rustle of leaves and branches followed him. His first thought was of bandits, but surely bandits would not operate so near the capital. Being the lone traveler on the road and his size making flight impractical, he stopped and slowly turned to face the gnarled trees. When whoever was there saw his high office of priesthood, he would be left alone.

"Who's there?" he called.

A purple-robed figure appeared and approached him. "Hello, priest of Yahweh," the woman said. Her face was unveiled and heavy with cosmetics, her eyebrows heavily outlined, her raven hair pulled back tightly away from her face and covered on the crown of her head with a conical cap. She no longer was a young woman, but her heavy makeup hid that fact well. Her skin appeared smooth and her features soft. A silk robe outlined rather than hid her body. "You are a large man to be on foot." Her smile and openness kept her from seeming a stranger. "Come, rest a moment and refresh yourself."

Zebul looked up and down the road, unconsciously twitching his ring.

The woman laughed, but comfortably. "No one will see you talking here with a foreign woman. We can sit there." She pointed to a gnarled, smooth-skinned olive tree. "A shallow valley behind the tree will hide us from the road. Come, the rest will do you good."

Zebul nervously attempted to turn and go, but the woman laced her arms about one of his. He could feel her breast as she squeezed gently. "A stranger becomes lonely for someone to talk with."

She led the way, her small hand clutching his forearm. He followed her and, once out of sight of the road, relaxed. They sat on the soft grass below the tree. The woman waited until the priest became settled, then sat next to him. Her forwardness was obscured by her gracefulness. She gradually shifted her body in the most natural manner until she touched him. Zebul, thoroughly aroused for the first time in months—his wife was almost a stranger to him—recalled his earlier thought about the lust of men and decided to leave the morals to another day. He turned toward her, and she was ready to respond. Her kiss brought to the surface emotions he long had suppressed and he swirled in a vortex of colors and sensations that blotted out everything but the fulfillment of his passion.

Some moments later, the zonah drew on her robe. "Please, priest of Yahweh, a payment for Asherah." Zebul felt for his coin purse, then realized that he had not brought it with him. Slowly, he drew the ring from his finger, held it out in his hand, gazed at it a moment, and let it slip from between his fingers to the grass. He turned toward the road. The woman laughed softly.

The road was empty. No one had seen him, but he hastened his pace. Every leaf of every tree and bush, every pebble in the road, every anemone that grew profusely in the fields turned itself into eyes and stared at him. The loud rasp of locusts screamed out to him the story of his seduction. The soft rustling of the wind echoed the woman's soft laughter.

Zebul plodded along the city wall. His stomach felt hollow and uneasy. A lump formed in his throat and crowded its way to his chest. He shook his head violently to scatter the guilt that crowded around him. His thoughts teased him. "I have known men to come smiling from a zonah and continue their work with added vigor. Why should such a feeling of regret haunt me?" he whispered softly to himself. He reached to his turban to straighten the jewel that had become twisted out of place.

In the weeks that followed, Zebul regretted the incident, yet at times he longed to feel the embrace of the zonah again. Alternately the affair turned in his mind, first the awfulness of desecrating himself as a priest of Yahweh, then the joyful thrill of fulfilling himself as a man. He reproved himself frequently, yet he could not help but outline in his imagination the figures of women he knew. His concourse with the sacred prostitute became a catalyst that more and more often tempted him to give vent to his sexual feelings. He could not reconcile the feelings with his Yahweh religion. In light of his decision to compromise with Baalism, the act, he reasoned, should not continue to bother him, but he found that the morals he had repeated piously so many times really had become a part of him. To solve the problem, he gradually learned to ignore his previous convictions. All the while, he kept his conflict within himself. Since he never had been a zealous priest, his friends detected no difference in his manner.

In due time, the temple to Baal was completed. Priests from the Phoenician cities of Byblos, Tyre, and Sidon were present for the dedication. Zebul watched the occasion, in company with several other priests, from the walkway atop the city wall. Ahab had made an early token appearance but had not returned since. Several speeches were made throughout the day, the longest by Jezebel. He could not hear her distinctly, but he had been aware of her voice raised at times to its full intensity, and he had seen her wave her arms vigorously.

As the day passed toward evening Zebul became aware of new preparations. Word spread that the spring worship of Asherah, delayed until now because of the temple construction, would be held in the evening. In front of the two obelisk columns that Zebul had watched workmen erect some time earlier was an altar on which the Baal priests would sacrifice a young calf. Standing in the doorway to the temple was a huge statue of Melkart, similar to the smaller one Jezebel had placed next to the window in her room. Gradually the crowd dispersed to prepare itself for the evening rituals, until only Baal-priests were left to make the court area ready for the festival.

Zebul left with his friends, but he declined their invitation to dine together. He went instead to his home, determined to carry out a plan to disguise himself and attend the rituals that night. He had intended to stay away, but while on the walkway he thought he caught a glimpse of the zonah he had met by the roadside. The memory of their meeting aroused a passion he could not ignore.

His first plan to trim his beard and hair had to be rejected after more careful thought. He would not be able the next day to explain his changed appearance. His girth made disguise difficult, but he finally decided that the simple wool robe and camelhair mantle of a tent dweller would be best. Such simplicity was in marked contrast to the fine clothing and many accessories he usually wore.

The flickering oil lamps cast eerie, dancing shadows around the courtyard. From where he stood on the perimeter the statue of Melkart appeared larger than he had imagined it to be. He purposely arrived late, and the ritual of sacrifice already had begun. The two officiating priests were dressed in skins and had on animal masks, one like the head of a horned bull, the other like a goat. A line of men and women, each couple holding a baby, grew longer.

The priests produced a lamb, a perfect specimen, and laid it on the altar. Expertly, one of them slit veins and arteries so that the blood drained quickly. Then he cut the lamb in what appeared to Zebul's practiced eye to be a prescribed and symbolic manner. Next, a bull calf was burned on the altar, its stench permeating the atmosphere of the temple area. The line of parents began to move then. The priests circumcised one baby after another, each time handing back to the parents their screaming offspring, newly dedicated to Melkart. Most of the boy babies should have been circumcised earlier by Yahweh's priests, yet the parents had chosen to wait for the dedication of Melkart's temple. Zebul felt a pang of jealousy. The choice was significant.

Under the towering statue of Melkart an orchestra of flutes, harps, lyres, trumpets, drums, and cymbals filled the air with music. They began with a loud clash at the moment the sacrifices began, then rose in crescendo to a mighty forte as the smoke of the burned calf rose to Melkart, whose home was the sky. The music softened to a mellowness, accentuated with the soft beat of drums and easy clashing of cymbals while the line of babies passed. When the last child had been dedicated the orchestra stopped playing. The only sound left was the soft shuffle of sandals as young parents left the courtyard and as Baal priests came from the temple to gather around the altar.

As if on signal, suddenly there came from the orchestra a rapid pounding of drums, followed by a resounding clash of cymbals. The priests then screamed in full-bodied unison: "Our God is Baal-Melkart, our Judge, and none is above him! The heavens rain oil, and the wadis run with honey!" The pounding of drums immediately resumed and the priests began to dance around the altar. They began with little more than a slow run, but as the orchestra joined the drums and the music became more intense they ran more frantically. They twisted their bodies; their faces became contorted; they circled, jumped, and shouted. Some beat themselves with leather thongs, while others offered their backs to be thrashed by brother priests.

The music continued all the while. The steady thumping of the drums and the clashing of cymbals added a monotonous, intoxicating rhythm. Soon, several young men joined the priests around the altar. Others began to recite chants to Baal. Women dashed around the orchestra to kiss Melkart's statue; others went into ecstatic trances to join the dancing men.

Soon the entire courtyard was bedlam. Screaming men and women, their eyes glazed in ecstatic trance, twisted their bodies into unbelievable contortions. Mantles and robes, normally prized beyond other possessions, fell to the ground to be trampled unnoticed in the dust. Partners were chosen, with no consideration of Israel's moral traditions, while the unattended, newly-circumcised babies cried from the outskirts of the court area. Eyes became transfixed on the bodies of partners. Each man and woman watched the stomach muscles of the partner. The dancing became more and more sensual. Untouching bodies gyrated toward each other and retreated, toward and retreated, again and again, until the space separating them closed.

Zebul watched like a zombie. Already men and women lay around the base of the altar, the obelisks, the temple wall, anywhere to escape the pounding of feet, and openly engaged in the holiest ritual of Asherah.

Nowhere in the throng did Zebul see the zonah he sought. Thinking she might be in the temple, the fat priest circled the court to work his way to the entrance, stepping around lovers who hardly knew each other. An occasional female arm reached toward him, and he glanced to its source each time to see a woman as fat as he, or old, or maimed, none of them able to engage in the wild dancing, but each aroused to passions that cried out for satisfaction.

The inside of the temple was lighted more brightly than the courtyard. Zebul paused to look around. The walls were niched at several points, into which were placed alternating statues of Asherah, her organs emphasized in the crudest fashion, and Melkart.

Zebul's desire subsided at the sight of the excessive crudity. Even in his most private and sensual thoughts he never had imagined such scenes. In an attempt to deify sex, the statues only emphasized how insatiable was the sexual appetite.

In the center of the room was a statue of Asherah, cast in the exact pose as the one in Jezebel's chamber. As Zebul gazed at it, he was startled by a voice at his side. "Well, priest of Yahweh, have you laid aside your robes to join us?"

Zebul looked at the woman made familiar by his dreams. "Am I so easily recognized?"

"Oh, probably not by most." She smiled and tilted her head a bit. "But then I have seen you before without your robes." She laughed lightly.

Zebul frowned. "I have not forgotten." Then, deciding to change the subject, "Why such a large open room?"

"Are you so ignorant of the traditions of Asherah? Every woman devoted to Baal must pay her homage to her goddess for the gift of fertility. One time in her life she must bring a pallet and find her place in the temple. Any stranger who comes to the city may enter the temple and look until he finds a woman to his liking. She must go outside with the first man who chooses her. She can refuse no one. The payment she receives goes into the temple treasury." She paused and smiled, ". . . to join your ring."

Zebul ignored the thrust. "Perhaps she would be fortunate and not be chosen by anyone."

"Is the body of man and woman so unfortunate as that? No, my fat priest, that indeed would be most unfortunate, for she cannot leave once she enters the temple until her debt is paid. I knew a crippled woman in Byblos who remained in the temple for three years. Her family fed her faithfully until finally a maimed warrior viewed her with compassion."

Zebul shuddered.

"And now, you have come to find me. I am glad that I pleased you. Your gift was extravagant." The woman moved toward him.

"No," Zebul blurted. "I have changed my mind." He backed away.

The zonah looked at him, surprised. She shrugged and went to bow before the statue of Asherah.

Zebul breathed hard as he watched her go. She easily could have aroused him if she had tried. He watched the woman bow and rise again and again before Asherah. She muttered chants in rhythm. As he watched, he saw her shiver as though a shock thrilled through her. She rose to her feet. With arms outstretched and eyes glazed she began the whirling dance that had possessed the mob outside. Hypnotized by the statue, she danced as though possessed by a demon, her shrieks answering Melkart and Asherah as they called to her to move faster and faster, to whirl, to dance, faster and faster, harder and harder, her shrieks accenting each touch of a foot to the floor. Sweat poured profusely until her clothing was plastered to her thrashing body. Saliva flowed from her mouth to run down her chin. Zebul watched the movement of her body, but it no longer held interest for him, his appetite seared by the wild abandon he witnessed.

As he opened the door to leave he was greeted by a din even greater than before. Being a bit higher than the courtyard, he could see well. A young man, naked and brandishing a sacrificial knife from the altar, danced the most frenzied dance he had seen yet. A large crowd gathered around him as the youth's wide-mouthed and continuing scream filled the air. His body was covered with dirt, some of it clotted with blood that flowed from self-inflicted cuts over his body. As he swung the knife wildly in his orgiastic dance, fresh cuts appeared. The crowd clapped in rhythm and priests led the people in chants to Baal. The young man's screams were so loud now that they echoed from the city wall and down the valley. His arms and legs flew so wildly that Zebul could hardly tell the limbs apart.

Suddenly the youth stopped dead still and erect. Then, with a scream that startled even the ecstatic crowd, he grasped his organ and castrated himself. He threw the knife over the heads of the crowd and it clanked harmlessly against a stone. Screaming violently, with blood streaming down his legs, he darted up the hillside. The crowd parted to give him room, and then followed him until he crumpled at the foot of the city wall.

Two Baal priests caught him under his shoulders and held him up toward the crowd. One raised his hand and shouted, "A new priest, a new holy man! One who has dedicated himself to the service of Baal! Behold him! He will wear the clothes of a woman and live with us in the temple." With the announcement, other priests hurried to help carry the young man to the temple quarters where they would care for him until his recovery, then give him a place to serve in the temple.

Zebul did not follow the crowd back to the courtyard but made his way toward the city gate. Out of sight of the throng, he stopped against a tree and retched. Then, weakly, dazed with disbelief, he turned toward the city gate.

Chapter Four

PALE AND DISHEVELED, Zebul made his way along the stone streets to his home. His sandals shuffled unevenly on the basalt floor as he moved through the darkness to his room. He dropped his clothes on the floor, slipped quickly into a robe, and fell onto his bed. He lay stunned, his eyes open and unblinking.

His mind drifted for some time, rejecting the incidents of the evening. Gradually, though, sensibility returned. With monotonous accuracy the events ran through his mind. He tried to shake free from the haunting pictures of gyrating bodies and incense smoke, from the feverishly amorous arms and the zonah and the wild-eyed young man. Exhausted and almost asleep, he repeatedly jerked to consciousness with the shriek of the youth or the shrill of instruments and pounding of drums resounding in his ears.

Sometime before dawn the nightmare of sounds and voices and orgy gave way to bits of Scripture he had recited so many times throughout his life. Passages from the sacred scrolls of the Law, which he had memorized routinely, rose in his subconcious mind. At times he awoke and sat up in bed to look around the room. Each time, some familiar object jarred him back into the world of the present.

By dawn Zebul was praying, but not in the monotonous manner he had possessed during the execution of his public duties. He prayed passionately. For the first time in his life he gained a feeling for the words of the Law and an understanding of their true meaning. His sensibilities shaken to the core, the genius of Yahweh religion broke on him like the new dawn.

The Law of Moses, the covenant which God had made with Israel, the bits of sermons Zebul had heard from the lips of prophets whom he had considered trite and fanatical swirled in his mind. For the first time in his life, he saw the teachings of Yahwism against the backdrop of the world as it existed beyond the confines of the Temple. In his mind, the words rebounded from the walls of the marketplace, swirled in the wind of the threshing floor, filled the houses of the common people, hung in the air with the dust over the trading caravans, and permeated the atmosphere along with the sweet smell from the wine-press. For the first time, he saw the prophets and other religious leaders as men bound to their time, yet ahead of their time, creating an ever-increasing tension to force men to rise above their petty selfishness to things higher and more noble. Gradually, he came to see Baalism as a weight to be cast off, as a shackle that bound men to the past, as a stick for the strong and a drug for the weak.

Zebul sat up once more, shook off the stupor of sleep, and, still aching with exhaustion, struggled from his bed. He made his way to an intricately inlaid chest. He opened the lid and fumbled through brightly colored robes and stacked them to one side. Near the bottom he found a simple white traveling robe. He threw it to the bed, along with a white cloth with which to cover his head.

He crossed the room to a table and poured water from an earthenware, narrow-necked jug into a basin. Lowering his heavy body to a stool, he bathed himself as quickly as his tired muscles would allow him.

Revived by the cool water, he began to feel a new kind of excitement. He was nearly dressed when he realized that he no longer felt the old familiar emptiness. His brow furrowed; he became aware that for the first time in his life he felt excited about being alive.

Infused with the new vitality, Zebul obtained a bronze chariot and a single horse to pull it. With an easy trot, he circled the city wall toward the north-south highway.

As he passed near the Baal temple, he could not avoid a glance toward the courtyard, though now it was repulsive to him. The area was littered with forgotten clothing torn by dancing feet and half buried under the dust.

An idea burst into his mind. He reined his horse and lashed the lines to a tree. Not bothering to sidestep the already trampled garments, he made his way to the altar in front of the free-standing obelisk columns. The ashes from the sacrifice of the night before had not yet been removed. He looked around for a container. Surely, among all this debris of clothing, there would be a clay jar. Finding none, he bent over, puffing from the exertion, and picked up a closeknit wool robe. He held it at one end with both hands and snapped it vigorously several times. Dirt from the trampling feet of the night before flew from it. He laid it carefully on one side of the altar and scooped ashes with his bare, fat hands until a heap several inches high lay on the cloth. Gathering the corners of the robe together carefully so as not to spill the contents, he made his way back to his chariot.

Soon he was on the highway leading to Bethel. The road curved around Mount Ebal, steep, rocky, and barren, boasting only a few stunted olive trees and, higher up, prickly pear. Beyond Ebal rose the twin mountain of Gerizim, not quite as high but equally bare. From these two mountains Joshua had carried out Moses' instructions that when the conquering Israelites had crossed the Jordan going west into the Promised Land they should build an altar to Yahweh. Joshua assembled the people in the pass between the mountains, near the well Jacob had dug four centuries earlier, their multitudes flooding up the hillsides. A representative from each tribe, six on each mountain, climbed above the mass of the people to shout in unison the Curses and the Blessings of the Law. Thundering from Mount Ebal, resounding in the natural theatre, Zebul could imagine the scene:

> *Cursed is the man who makes any graven or molten image.*
> *Cursed is he that sets light by his father or his mother.*
> *Cursed is he that removes his neighbor's landmark.*
> *Cursed is he that makes the blind to wander out of the way.*
> *Cursed is he that perverts the judgment of the stranger, fatherless, and widow.*
> *Cursed is he that lies with his father's wife, or any manner of beast, or with his sister, or with his mother-in-law.*
> *Cursed is he that smites his neighbor secretly.*
> *Cursed is he that takes reward to slay an innocent person.*
> *Cursed is he that confirms not all the words of this law to do them.*

After each pronouncement, the people responded loudly, "Amen!" Their voices blended together in a gigantic fury of sound, so awesome in its enormity that the very earth below them vibrated with the wave.

After the sound of the curses had died away, there came equally strong voices from Mount Gerizim, trumpeting the Blessings of the Law:

> *If you harken diligently to the voice of Yahweh your God, and do his commandments, then Yahweh your God will set you on high among the nations of the earth, and all these blessings shall come upon you:*

> Blessed shall you be in the city, and in the field.
>
> Blessed shall be the fruit of your bodies, and the fruit of your ground, and the fruit of your cattle, the increase of your cows, and the flocks of your sheep.
>
> Blessed shall be your basket and your kneading trough.
>
> Blessed shall you be when you come in, and when you go out.
>
> Your enemies that rise up against you shall flee before you seven ways.
>
> Yahweh shall command the blessing upon you in your storehouses, and in all that you set your hand to, and he will bless you in the land he gives you . . .
>
> All the people of the earth shall see that you are called by the name of Yahweh . . .
>
> Yahweh shall open unto you his good treasure, the heavens to give the rain to your land in his season, and to bless the work of your hand. . . .

Zebul never had thought seriously about the Curses and the Blessings of the Law. Now, the moral codes of the two religions standing in such stark contrast, he realized in a new way: *Yahweh promises the same fertility that Baal promises!*

The teachings went over in his mind as he continued his journey past the city of Shechem and, finally, Shiloh. Bethel lay ahead, its white walls glistening in the afternoon sun. The journey had been hard on the soft Zebul, but the beauty of the city revived his spirit.

Zebul spotted a tree just off the road and he guided his horse to it. He secured the reins, took the cloth of ashes from the floor of the chariot, and squatted under the protection of the tree. From the opened cloth he applied the ashes to his skin, starting with his sandaled feet, working up his legs to his body, his arms, his clothes, and finally his face, beard, and hair. He would meet Ahijah as an Israelite in mourning, penitent and despairing.

He remounted his chariot and snapped his horse to a fast trot. Once through the gates of Bethel he guided his chariot carefully through the streets, which were paved with wide, flat stones. The sharp sound of hooves and the harsh grating of wheels made the air heavy with activity. Faces turned to gaze at the strange, fat figure, but he moved too fast for a crowd to gather. He made his way along remarkably well-drained streets lined with strongly constructed buildings to the simple house of Ahijah. He was tired, and prayed that Ahijah would be at home.

The priest reined his horse to a stop and, still holding the reins in one hand, dismounted his chariot. His knock was answered by an old man dressed in a worn robe of the kind more prosperous Israelites used as underclothing. From a leaden face, heavily veined and with prominent cheekbones, peered eyes that were entirely out of keeping with the frail body that housed them. They held the piercing look of alertness and determination. Zebul glanced at the stringy whiskers and thin hair and had the impression that the beard once had been full and flowing from a craggy face. The hair had disappeared from the old man's thin arms and his skin was incredibly wrinkled. He stood without speaking, looking quizzically at the ash-covered Zebul.

"I am Zebul, priest from Samaria, high priest of Israel. I have come to talk with Ahijah."

"I am Ahijah. What brings you to me in mourning clothes?" The old prophet either did not recognize the priest or he believed him to be an imposter.

"My message is long and I am tired. I beg your hospitality for the night."

Ahijah, puzzled but accustomed to a lifetime of unusual requests, stepped outside and closed the door. "Come with me. We will settle your horse first."

The old man, supported by a staff, led the way around the house to the small courtyard behind, closed the high gate, and watched as Zebul fumbled to loose the horse from its trappings. Obviously, the fat man was not accustomed to the task.

Ahijah pointed to a manger. Zebul acknowledged by slapping the horse lightly on the rump and watched as he plodded toward the feed.

Ahijah gestured to the back door and led the way. The sandals of both men shuffled on the hard earth, one because of age, the other from fatigue.

Inside, Ahijah finally spoke. His tone was cold. "I recognize you now. You really are Zebul, who fancies himself high priest of Israel. I did not believe it was you in those ashes." He spoke with obvious contempt. "You must know how many times I have denounced you as an opportunist. Why do you now come to me? Did you think to trick me with your ashes?"

Zebul looked at the old prophet, whose voice was surprisingly vigorous for his age. "What you have said of me is true, but that is behind now. You see a different person from the priest you denounced."

Ahijah's brows furrowed, but he said nothing.

"That is why I have come to you."

"I will give you the benefit of the doubt. Your humility is impressive."

Ahijah motioned the priest to a stool by a rough-hewn table. Zebul sat down. The old man brought a large, narrow-necked earthen jar and some towels. "Cleanse away those ashes," he commanded.

As Zebul wiped the soot from his body, he began. "These ashes are from the altar of Melkart."

Ahijah glared.

"Hear me, Ahijah." Zebul started his story, relating in detail his struggle with himself and the events of the night before. While he talked the aged Ahijah brought a pot from a brazier and set it on the table. Seating himself opposite the priest, he broke a loaf of bread in two and handed half of it to Zebul. Both men dipped their bread into the pot of broth and ate.

Ahijah, who had kept abreast of the development of Baal worship, listened intently to Zebul's story, then finally asked, "Why do you come to me? To ask advice or to seek consolation?"

Zebul replied gravely. "I came to you because you are the most respected leader of the prophets of Yahweh. You must do something to turn Baalism from the land."

"What do you think I have been doing all my life?"

"But something new and different is called for. A better organized battle must be fought."

Ahijah did not answer at once. His wrinkled face tightened in exasperation. Finally he spoke. "I am old. Sheol will claim me before the battle is hardly begun."

"I am a priest," Zebul countered, "not a prophet. I cannot say what to do, but something must be done, Ahijah. You must think of something."

"I have prophesied for many years. I have learned that calling men back to Yahweh is like waging war. What happens to me does not matter, but if I were to die while leading the battle my death would be counted as a victory for Baal."

Zebul lowered his head, his hands clasped together on the table before him. He was silent for a moment, then looked hard at Ahijah. "Then your task must be to select a leader the other prophets will follow and respect."

Ahijah shook his head. He placed his staff into a mortar joint to keep it from sliding on the floor, grasped the side of the table with his other hand, and rose laboriously from his stool. He turned away from Zebul and walked to a window that looked out onto the tiny courtyard. He was glad he was old and soon would leave the strife of a prophet's life. The scourge that promised to come, he knew, would be greater than any he had known. He leaned tiredly on the window sill. *Sixty years of prophesying*, he thought, *and what difference had it made?* He had witnessed the downfall of the enemy, Philistia, only to watch the rise of Syria, an enemy far more formidable. Spiritual warfare was no different. One battle succeeded another. In the flame of his youth he had pictured a spiritual progress of Israel to a higher plane, but no such transformation had taken place. The occasional revival of interest in Yahweh religion inevitably was followed by a relapse into pagan rituals. *Preaching is like throwing a pebble into a pool,* he thought, *a small splash, ripples that gradually subside, and the glassy surface returns. Why bother to cast the pebble?*

He turned and stared at Zebul, who met his gaze. A smile started faintly at the corners of his mouth. Perhaps the ripples had touched the life of this fat, once-pompous priest before they subsided. The old prophet spoke slowly. "No man can appoint a leader for prophets." He paused and shuffled back to the table. "But perhaps God does have a man."

"I will search for him. He must be found."

Ahijah lowered himself onto the stool beside the table and chuckled disdainfully. The intensity of the old man's gaze made the priest uneasy. "You latecomers to the battle amuse me." He spoke slowly. "To which prophet do you propose to offer the job?"

Zebul's fat jowls quivered as he started to speak, then he thought better. He shook his head in exasperation. Faintly he answered, "There must be something I can do."

Ahijah's face softened. "Zebul, there is something you can do." He paused. "But searching for the particular prophet God may choose to challenge Baal is a waste of time."

Zebul frowned. The old prophet seemed stronger and more alert. "You priests must learn something about prophets," the old man continued, speaking with more zest. "Duties are not assigned and rotated as with you. What do you suppose would be the result if you were to choose the wrong man to lead?" Without giving Zebul a chance to answer, he continued. "Your recent experience has made you painfully aware of the seriousness of this challenge to Yahweh."

Zebul nodded.

Ahijah's hands were clenched so tightly that his knuckles were white. "Your concept of Yahweh is too small. Don't you think he knows what is happening?" He paused to allow Zebul to catch the full import of the question. "Hear me, my priestly friend. Yahweh knew long years ago that such a crisis would arise. You may be sure that God has been preparing a prophet to meet the occasion. When the time is ripe, he will appear, and you can be sure that God will do his work in a manner different from that which you, or I, or any other priest would have chosen."

Zebul sat quietly for a moment, studying the wizened face of the old prophet. He adjusted the towel on his wide shoulders as he rose. Standing over the prophet, he finally asked simply, "You are so certain?"

The answer was solemn. "I am certain."

It was the kind of country you would expect a prophet to come from. The Jordan River separated it from the rest of Israel, both geographically and culturally. Its people raised sheep and cattle, most of them partly nomadic. They looked with condescension on the settled farmers west of the Jordan who, they believed, claimed to be Yahwists but could not refrain from sacrificing to the fertility baals for good crops.

The mountain range rose precipitously from the exuberant growth of the tropical Jordan Valley. From the valley, the cliffs rose from limestone and changed to black volcanic mass at the top.

The land was high, open, and extensive. Large, rolling plains rose again and again into rocky hills and gradually dissolved into the great eastern desert. The hills were wild and rugged, covered with clumps of forests. It was a country of solitude that was broken occasionally by dashing mountain streams whose valleys were haunted by fierce beasts.

In the north lay the grasslands of Havoth-Jair. The land was spotted with occasional clumps of black Bedouin goathair tents. The rude stone villages were small and anonymous, each one about like the rest, catering to the nomadic families who moved from the heights during the summer to the gorges and valleys during the winter. The people were wild and unkempt compared to the farmers west of the river.

It was dusk on the farmlands of the west, but night had come already to the Jordan Valley as Elijah approached the Bethshean ford. The valley was made wider here by the intrusion of the Valley of Jezreel from the west where it cut through the Samarian hills. Bethshean sat in the mouth of the valley, on a low hill some five hundred feet above the valley floor. She was the principal city of the rich valley plain, the chief marketplace of the region for its corn, balsam, flax, and dates. The water was shallow enough here in the wider valley, and the Jordan's constant tangle of thorns was broken, to provide a crossing point. The ford was deserted now; dusk was a time to be inside with one's family.

Elijah started through the water. He had the appearance of the stern land of his birth. As he slowly cut through the current, his bulky muscles rippled under thick hair that covered almost all of his body. Long, unkempt black locks fell in complete disarray over his broad, thick shoulders. His large, square-jawed head was set on a short, stout body that was sunbaked to a pecan brown. The piercing gaze from his dark eyes announced a frightening confidence in himself and his mission. Elijah used his appearance to advantage, though he did so subconsciously. The wild look came into his eyes and face without conscious effort when he preached—even when he thought of the apostasy of Israel. He was a fanatic to his unsympathetic audiences, a hero to other prophets. His voice was strong, with a shocking quality that sent his opponents into shells of restrained anger. He was loved by his admirers, disdained and mocked by those he antagonized, and feared by both for his unpredictable intrusions into public places. Often after he appeared at an assembly or party, the people would slowly leave, unable to shake the pall cast by his attack. His guerrilla tactics were disconcerting and rudely effective.

The water covered Elijah's wide leather belt and fought with his short, coarse tunic. He held his heavy black wool mantle high to keep it from getting wet.

Once across the river, Elijah climbed the road to Beth-shean. The gatekeeper already had begun to lock the huge oak gates. At the prophet's request to enter, the keeper responded with sullen acquiescence. He dared not curse a prophet. Elijah entered with a nod of thanks and made his way along Bethshean's basalt streets, his sandals whispering softly on the black stones.

Rejab's house was simple but solidly constructed of square limestone blocks. Only a single door and no windows opened to the street. From the courtyard in the rear, outside stairs led to the flat roof. One small room constituted the second story, set to one side of the roof, to accommodate visitors. The downstairs area consisted of a large room. On one side was a raised platform for sleeping and family activities. Small square stools were placed around the walls of the room for the seating of guests. A large clay pan sat on the floor near one wall. In winter it was filled with coals and covered with a board and a heavy piece of goathair material. Thus arranged, it furnished enough heat to make the room comfortable. A back door to the large room opened onto a courtyard that was walled around with sun-dried brick.

Elijah grasped the iron knocker and rapped. A slight breeze blew down from the Valley of Jezreel.

The door opened almost immediately. A wide smile spread over Rejab's face as he recognized his old friend. "Welcome, Elijah." Rejab grasped the prophet warmly, kissing both cheeks. He was older than the prophet by some years and rather fat, but he moved with ease.

Rejab gushed with excitement. "Come in, come in, my friend the prophet." He hustled Elijah inside and scuttered across the room, his fluttering light robes outlining his ponderous belly. He placed a cushion on the seat of an oak stool and another one upright against the wall to form a back. "Here, sit here, my friend. Miriam!" he called to his wife, who already had seen Elijah and was at that moment greeting him with short bows and exclamations.

"Sit! Sit!" Rejab jabbered.

Elijah gratefully settled into the cushions. He had traveled for two days and a night without resting for more than moments at a time.

Miriam rushed to him with a figcake and a cup of wine.

"Yes, yes," Rejab gushed incessantly. "Perfect for the weary traveler. You are a joy to me, Miriam. Take it, Elijah, and refresh yourself."

Elijah drank gratefully, more refreshed by the antics of his host than by the food. The joviality of Rejab offered temporary escape from the somber realities of his past musings. The medicine was good.

Rejab joyfully told the story of the day. A Bedouin tribesman was crossing the Jordan at the place where Elijah made his ford. His camel stumbled in the swift water and went completely under, not a humorous event at all to the camel or its owner. Rejab's description of the naked man diving into the water to cut the camel's load loose and get the animal to shore, Elijah thought, could not have been nearly so funny as Rejab's story made it seem.

Rejab enjoyed his own storytelling immensely. As he talked, his stomach joggled with his laughter, making him look as though he was bouncing on the little stool. He gestured widely in his talk, and his voice sometimes rose to shrills.

Miriam interrupted Rejab only momentarily with her call to dinner. Throughout the meal of hot broth and bread, which the men dipped with their fingers into the large pot of dense liquid, Rejab continued his hilarity. That Elijah was quiet did not bother the host. Elijah often was quiet.

Finally Elijah interrupted. "Rejab, tell me what you know about the Baal temple at Samaria."

The smile, which appeared to be etched permanently into Rejab's face, faded quickly. "Have you heard of the dedication?"

"Yes."

"That is all I know. It took place two nights ago. The city was paralyzed all the next day. The people say it does not matter. They can serve both Yahweh and the baals. I am just a poor merchant. I do not know of such things. All

I know is that after the prophets of Melkart speak the people I trade with are less scrupulous and more cunning in their deceit." Rejab gripped the crude goblet of wine with both hands. He swirled the liquid and gazed at it thoughtfully. "There is something else, Elijah."

"What else?"

"Word has come from Obadiah that Jezebel intends to make Melkart and Asherah the official gods of the court."

Elijah's jaws clenched. When he rose from his seat, Rejab felt a tinge of fear. Elijah turned the goblet up and finished its contents with a gulp. He clenched the empty cup tightly, a wild look in his eyes, his muscles tense. Then slowly he relaxed and set the cup on the table.

"That is what I feared, Rejab. May Yahweh reward you for your kindness. I must retire, and I will leave before you arise in the morning. I shall not bother you."

"You shall bother us," Rejab objected. "I shall not interfere with your mission, but you shall not go on an empty stomach. You can serve Yahweh better if you are strong. When shall you leave?"

"I must be in Samaria when Ahab sits on his throne. I leave at the beginning of the last watch before dawn. I shall run the distance."

"It's twenty miles, Elijah."

"I shall run the distance," the prophet repeated.

Rejab looked askance at his guest. Difficult as the trip surely would be, uphill much of the way, he knew Elijah would do as he said. "Then you will need your strength all the more. When you arise, your food will be ready."

Elijah grasped Rejab by both shoulders and kissed his cheek. "You are the best of men, Rejab."

The moon was dark in the early hours before morning, and Miriam needed lamplight to see. She laid bramble twigs and thorns in the outdoor oven and lit the tinder with fire from the lamp. She fanned it with her breath until it blazed, then threw dried pieces of dung into the flames for fuel. By the time Elijah roused, the breadcakes were ready to serve. Rejab left tracks on the dew-covered ground as he approached with a large goatskin, the head hole and three legs tied, the other left open to serve as a spout. He filled Elijah's cup with wine. They ate silently.

Elijah set his cup on the flat rock that served as an outdoor table. "I must go, Rejab." He kissed them both. "Good-bye, Miriam." The gate to the courtyard closed behind him. For a moment Rejab and Miriam listened to their friend's rapid gait, then the sound faded away and they were alone again.

Chapter Five

Obadiah was a full head taller than Elijah, but not so powerfully built. His slender frame was robed immaculately, his beard trimmed to a thin line and a short goatee. His mustache matched the thin line of his beard. He wore no head covering, but his finely combed hair was held neatly in place with a headband. A blue matching sash stood out in restful contrast to the whiteness of his robe. His complexion was soft, yet deeply colored from the sun, his forehead high with a prominent vein in the center. He stood with an air of confidence; his eyes indicated a quick mind. He was in control of all of the royal possessions and he administered them with talent. Ahab's confidence in him was apparent, for often he was consulted on matters completely outside of his appointed function.

Elijah spoke in a low, urgent voice. His penetrating eyes matched the intensity of his words.

"Elijah, what you ask is too dangerous. I cannot do it."

"You must do it. I must see Ahab."

"He will have you in stocks in the marketplace."

"He would not arrest a prophet."

Obadiah shook his head imploringly. "Elijah, Ahab has given a great deal of authority over the court to Jezebel. He will order your arrest because she would want it done."

"Then I shall not let myself be caught."

"How can you be so certain?"

"Ahab has made certain that his palace guards are loyal to the faith of Israel, hasn't he?"

"Yes."

"They will allow me to escape. Before Ahab can alert others, I will be on my way to the Jordan."

"Why can't you simply give me a message to take to him?"

"You know that is a foolish question, Obadiah."

"Yes. You are determined then?"

"I know what I must do."

"All right. I will get you to him. But I must find a robe to cover you. The guards would not let you enter like that, even with me."

With a robe covering his hairy body and with hair and beard freshly combed, Elijah walked beside Obadiah. They passed through the courtyard amid an occasional greeting by workmen and servants who had no reason to question Obadiah's selection of companions. At the palace entrance Obadiah simply nodded to the guards.

Inside the palace proper the two men crossed a large entry hall. Their footsteps echoed on the stone floor of the cavernous room. They stopped at the double doors to the throne room, blocked by the guards' crossed spears.

"Obadiah," one cautioned, "our regrets, sir, but your name is not on the roster to see the king today."

Obadiah spoke softly. "It is Elijah who would see Ahab."

Elijah loosened the rich robe to reveal his prophet's garb underneath. The guards looked, glanced at each other, and hesitated, uncertain.

"The Lord God Yahweh has given me a message to speak before Ahab. You would not strive against Yahweh." Elijah spoke softly but with command, as though he, not Ahab, were regent.

The senior guard regained his composure quickly. "We

are servants of Yahweh, Elijah, and admirers of your courage, but we also are soldiers in the king's command. You cannot enter unless summoned. Why do you not simply request an audience?"

Elijah shrugged the robe from his shoulders. Standing silent only for a moment, his eyes searched theirs. "Yahweh has summoned me. That is enough." With a hand on each spear he wrenched them from the doors, quickly threw the latch, and shoved the double doors aside. They crashed loudly against the wall as the burly prophet walked quickly toward the throne. Ahab looked up, puzzled. Elijah stopped a few paces away from the gold-inlaid throne.

The court attendants looked at Ahab in anticipation. The guards quickly followed Elijah and grasped each arm. The king hesitated, surprised. Then he regained his demeanor.

"The hairy one," he said. "You must be Elijah."

"I am."

Ahab gestured to the guards to release him. "You are foolish to come into my presence unannounced."

"Kings rise and fall by the word of Yahweh. I am his prophet. It is you who should be afraid."

"I am being tolerant of you, Elijah. Speak what you will say and leave my presence."

Elijah pointed his finger at Ahab. "Ahab, what does my name mean?"

The king spoke with amused condescension. "Elijah means 'Yahweh is God,' a fitting name for his prophet, I suppose."

"You will learn the truth of my name, Ahab."

Elijah turned and moved toward the door, then stopped midway between it and the throne. He turned and looked at Ahab. The king sat, now composed, looking at the prophet with a slight smile. Elijah turned to face the king directly. He raised his arm slowly and pointed a finger straight ahead. With all the fierce power he could force from his ample lungs, Elijah screamed, "*Ahab, hear my words!*" The attendants jumped with a start as the sound echoed through the hall. Ahab raised himself erect on the throne. The room was held in rapt surprise. Elijah's eyes flashed at the king. His scream echoed again from the walls. *"Ahab! as the Lord God of Israel lives, before whom I stand, there shall be neither dew nor rain these years, but according to my word!"*

Ahab hesitated a moment, stunned by the outburst. In that moment Elijah wheeled and strode from the throne room, past the startled guards, and toward the outer doors.

"Take him! Guards! Seize him!" Ahab stood as he shouted the order. Guards mobilized and attempted to obey. Elijah broke into a run. The guards at the outer door turned toward the commotion.

"It's Elijah! Stop him!" a guard shouted toward them. The guards made a halfhearted attempt to appear loyal, but they allowed Elijah to slip by them. The prophet, his legs pounding furiously, leaped to a chariot that was passing through the gates. The driver turned, but Elijah's powerful hand on his shoulder forced him to the floor of the chariot. "Stay there!" Elijah barked. Yelling and snapping the reins, he sent the horses careening through the streets toward the city gates.

The street cleared at the sound of Elijah's powerful screaming. Mothers huddled their children toward the shops; dogs scampered under carts; and men, out of the way, looked to see what the commotion was about.

The chariot charged through the gates, slowing only enough to turn to the right to circle the wall. Ahab would have archers on the city walls where the road circled around the city to the east. He shoved the reins into the hands of the crouching driver and leaped from the slowed chariot. He landed on his shoulders and rolled to his feet, stumbled, and began to roll down the hill that sloped steeply toward the south.

The palace was in an uproar. The guards, usually efficient to a fault, fumbled, trying to look fierce and businesslike, but each one, loyal to Yahweh, was glad to see Elijah escape.

Ahab was in a rage. He had sent archers to the city walls overlooking the road that passed along its base, but he knew Elijah was too shrewd to escape by such an obvious route.

He returned to the throne room. As he mounted his throne, Jehu was announced.

"Send him in immediately."

Jehu entered, dressed in conventional robe and waist-girdle rather than uniform. He was lean and wiry, taller than Ahab. His shoulders were broader but not so thick as the king's, his muscles sinewy rather than bulging. Veins stood out prominently on his arms and hands. His hair reached only halfway down his neck and was held tightly in place with a headcloth; his beard was short and well trimmed. He did not like Ahab, but the thought of disloyalty never had occurred to him. He walked in long strides to the throne and knelt on one knee.

"At your service, sir. The courier informed me of the event as I left my quarters."

"Then," Ahab said grimly, "you know your task. Assign as many men as you think necessary to run Elijah down."

"He will be difficult to catch," Jehu answered as he rose.

Ahab searched him with his eyes, a look of stern understanding hardening the lines in his face. "Of that I am certain. It also occurs to me that no soldier who holds sympathy for him will do much of a tracking job. Had my palace guards been less dedicated to Yahweh he would be facing me now."

Jehu, surprised, stood silent.

"Never mind. Only be careful that the patrol you assign to the task is made up of men who are more confident of Melkart than of Yahweh."

"As you say, my king." Jehu bowed and departed.

Ahab sat in silence. His eyes followed the line of the lotus leaf pattern inlaid along the ivory-covered walls. How much credence could he give to Elijah's threat? The prophet had a strong reputation among the people, but what did that matter? Still, such a threat would be the most foolish of gestures were Elijah not certain that his message was authentic.

Ahab shuddered. The storehouses were empty. In his effort to increase the wealth of Israel, all surplus food had been traded to Phoenicia. Should he stop the caravans now en route to Tyre? Should he take charge of the farmers' silos? Such an act would be an admission that he took Elijah seriously.

The door opened and a guard stepped inside quietly. "King Ahab, my Queen Jezebel awaits your pleasure, sir."

Ahab nodded his approval.

Jezebel entered quickly, leaving her entourage of attendants outside.

"You already have heard?" Ahab asked.

"With such commotion, one needs only one ear, my husband and king."

"I am glad you came. You understand these matters of religion better than I. Come sit beside me."

Jezebel's feet fell quietly on the rich pastel-colored Persian rugs as she made her way to a smaller throne beside Ahab's.

"You really are worried then, Ahab?"

"I am aware of Elijah's reputation."

The color drained from Jezebel's face. The playful smile disappeared. "It was the hairy one who spoke?" She used the epithet with a sense of awe.

"It was Elijah."

"Then you can be sure, Ahab. He does not speak flippantly."

Ahab stared at his queen for a moment. He had not known whether to take the threat seriously or not, but with Jezebel's alarm, all doubt was gone. He spoke slowly.

"I know the ways of men, Jezebel. I can war with kings and armies, but I cannot do battle with gods."

"Then let a god fight a god."

Ahab's brow wrinkled. Jezebel continued. "Evidently Yahweh is angry at what he considers Melkart's invasion of his domain. All you need do is call the priests and prophets of Melkart and have them call on Baal to intervene."

"Since you take the threat so seriously, I truly am concerned. I shudder at the strength Yahweh has shown in the past. I should never have allowed you to build that temple."

"It was a mistake, Ahab, if Yahweh is stronger than Melkart. But if Melkart is stronger, then your decision was wise. Would you not rather serve the stronger of the gods?"

Ahab was silent.

"All right," Jezebel continued, "what are your alternatives?"

"Alternatives?"

"As I see it, you can do one of three things. You can ignore the warning and take the chance of a drought, since Melkart will not help you without your seeking his help. Or you can heed Elijah's threat and banish the prophets and priests of Baal, in which case you will rupture our relationship with Phoenicia and incur the wrath of Melkart."

Ahab frowned. He was not nearly so concerned, however, with incurring Melkart's wrath as with rupturing the treaty with Phoenicia, a matter he could understand better.

"Or you can give Melkart a chance to prove his strength against Yahweh, which will accomplish both our ends."

"Meaning what?"

"The Israelites will embrace Melkart when Yahweh goes down in defeat. Then our two countries will move closer together."

"You have a way of wording the alternatives, don't you?"

Jezebel shrugged. "After all, my dear king, Asherah is the Goddess of Fertility. She assuredly has more power over the rains that fall on the fields than does Yahweh. Yahweh must be foolish indeed to challenge our Baal in such a way."

Ahab smiled, surprised. He had not thought of the contest in such clear-cut terms. He clapped sharply for the door guard. "Send a courier for the wise men of Melkart."

Elijah ran toward a grove of olive trees near the base of Samaria's hill. He caught a gnarled branch to slow his speed, flung himself to the ground, and pressed his ear to the rocky earth. No sound of running horses. He cautiously rose to his knees, his chest heaving, and peered between the dense tangled limbs up toward the city. Sentries moved on the walkway atop the walls, searching in every direction. He could not underestimate Ahab.

Bethel or Jericho would be natural places for him to seek help amid their congregations of prophets. His friends would hide him, but Ahab was certain to seek him there first.

The grove offered only temporary security. He dared not wait even for nightfall. He must escape before Ahab could organize his search properly. The surrounding terrain was too open. He could not long escape a search. *Bethshean,* Elijah thought excitedly. *Rejab will hide me there.*

The plan grew rapidly in Elijah's mind. He would leave the olive grove in a dead run. The guards on the wall would see him head south toward Bethel. When Ahab received word, he would direct his search there, while Elijah circled back toward Bethshean. Obadiah—if he entered the search at all—would consider the prophet's earlier reference to the Jordan as a ploy.

Elijah moved to the edge of the grove, adjusted his mantle into his girdle so to leave his legs and arms as free as possible, and broke into a run across the rocky hillside. He heard a shout and knew he was seen. His powerful legs thrust him with surprising speed over the open space toward a dry wadi. His strides were short, but his legs pumped rapidly. He watched for loose rocks, and with an eye practiced from years of shepherding, his feet landed each step solidly.

Once into the wadi he realized that it was too shallow for adequate protection. A glance toward the wall revealed the excited scurry of guards who obviously knew where he was. He decided to convince them further of his escape to Bethel. With heaving chest, careful to breathe through his nostrils so as not to sear his throat, he ran east, upstream, toward Samaria's north-south road. Once there, he turned south, again knowing that he would be seen.

Within a quarter mile the road turned sharply east around a hill abutment. Elijah rounded the hill, then, out of sight of Samaria, he left the road to climb up a small, upward-rising valley. The steep climb would tire him, but the hill was covered with vineyards and olive groves. He was safe so long as he did not slow his pace. Before the search could be organized effectively, the prophet had to cross the main north-south road that ran along the mountain ridge. It was there he must exercise the greatest care. Then he could make his way carefully down into the Jordan valley.

A wide, merciless ribbon of jungle grew along the riverbank. It was the Pride of the Jordan. The Jordan River coiled and twisted like a sluggish serpent through the center of the tangled mass of thickly-branched and almost leafless juniper trees, bushes, and wild growth. Elijah struggled through canebrakes and rushes along the edge of the Pride, then met the fury of the infinite thorn branches that grabbed at his clothes and scratched his skin. He dropped to his knees and crawled slowly to avoid the sharp thorns, now and then slithering on his belly under dense undergrowth. Even if Ahab's searchers knew where he was, they could not reach him; but he knew the net would tighten quickly. Though Jehu was a Yahwist, he was a loyal soldier and methodically thorough.

Elijah reached the muddy Jordan at last and dropped from a low ledge into the water. It barely covered his knees. His feet sank in the slime and, with each step deeper into the water, the mud sucked at his sandals. At waist depth, he leaned forward to swim at a slight angle upstream in order to offset the current's effort. When his hands touched mud again, he regained his feet and waded toward the rank vegetation of the opposite bank.

He massaged his temples to ease the ache already starting to grow from the fatigue and thirst. His throat felt raspy and harsh. He scooped water into his hands from the Jordan, muddy as it was, and drank slowly, fighting off the impulse to gulp the warm liquid.

He forced himself into the twin jungle of the river's east side. It was not as wide here as on the west side, but every bit as thick. He walked when he could and crawled when he had to, brushing away insects, watching for snakes, listening for larger animals. By the time the jungle abruptly gave way again to canebrake, darkness had come already to the west side of the valley. Elijah stood erect, his hands on the back of his hips, and leaned backward to stretch the ache from his spine. The act helped but little. He plunged haphazardly through the last reeds and onto the greasy bank.

The east bank was a gray marl, covered with the debris of the spring flooding. Dead wood covered with sun-dried and whitened slime lay in a tangled pile against an uprooted tree. Elijah pulled himself onto the ridge road and, ignoring the limestone filth, sat down to watch the shadow of the western mountains climb higher up toward the crest of the eastern cliffs. He could rest for only a few moments, for the deep valley would be dark even with the moon full.

The prophet continued his journey only long enough to find a gravel bar, which would be relatively free of sandfleas and other insects. It would be a miserable enough night at best.

Just as the sun was early in its setting, so it was late in its rising in the Pride of Jordan. Elijah was awake before the sun found its way between the mountains. There was enough light, though, for him to search for figs, apricots, and berries.

As he ate, a sense of uneasiness began to grow within him. More rested and thinking more clearly now, he recalled the excitement of Ahab's court. Ahab knew that Yahweh would not send either rain or the dew that lay each morning like a heavy mist until the prophet of Israel's God announced an end to the drought. The king had no choice but to find God's prophet and force him to end the announced famine. The intensity of the search would grow in step with the drought.

Elijah knelt by the river. He picked up small pebbles and tossed them absentmindedly into the water. He thought of Rejab. Their friendship was known to many people. Rejab's house would be watched. Soldiers would search everywhere. Rewards would be offered, so that no matter where he tried to hide, sooner or later someone would report his presence.

He placed his face on his knees and for a long time remained in the praying posture. Vultures circled overhead, their silence an ominous contrast to the loud call of ravens. The chattering of cranes and swallows, the loud chirp of locusts, and the occassional buzz of a bee went completely unregistered in Elijah's solitude.

Finally he rose. In his inner being the awareness of a message was so strong that the prophet was certain God spoke out loud.

The Brook Cherith would be his home for a time. The wadi was so insignificant that he himself never had explored its narrow recesses. The ravens would feed him. The implausibility of the promise did not occur to him.

The Brook Cherith was not far away. His trip in the main had been correct, except that he should have turned south instead of north after he crossed the river. He retraced his steps along the gravel bank until he came to the ugly marl that marked his crossingpoint of the night before. The valley narrowed even more. Above him the eastern cliffs rose so close, separated from the riverbed by little more than the width of a road, that he could hear the rock pigeons fluttering noisily in and out of the caves that pitted the limestone. The vale was ugly, with mounds of gray sludgy clay and damp sand. Gnarled trees, limbs, and bushes that had been torn from their footings by the spring rains were tumbled together in wild heaps, now covered with white, dried mud. The cobra-like asp was a constant danger, and Elijah was careful to skirt the piles of rubbish and watch for holes in the sand. The dank, rotting vegetation and the oppressive heat of the narrow valley made the air heavy and unpleasant. At times, Elijah was forced into the water by tangled masses of thornbushes to struggle against the swift current.

Finally the prophet arrived at his destination. The Brook Cherith cut a channel from the eastern cliffs and across the narrow plain into the Pride of Jordan. He looked in disbelief. The spring rains long since had dried up. The brook was no more than a dry wadi. He looked up the dry bed that cut such a narrow cleft between two mountain ridges.

The ever-present oleanders caked with dried mud promised a hard fight to anyone who might attempt a journey up the bed.

Could I be wrong? Elijah mused. *Is this where Yahweh would lead me?* He shrugged off the feeling and paused only long enough to drink his fill of muddy water and gather a few wild berries, which he wrapped in his headband and hung at his waist. Then he clambered out of the unsightly jungle, crossed the road and narrow plain, and attacked the forbidding entrance to the wadi.

Progress was slow. The tumbled rocks had to be tested for each step. Tangled masses of debris caused him to climb through thick oleanders and expose himself to possible snakebite. His face was caked with dust. It was in his mouth and clung to his hair. He frequently had to stretch his fingers out hard to keep them from cramping.

Suddenly he was there. A basin of clear water, fed by a tiny stream that trickled from the limestone of the mountain, created a beautiful garden. The water disappeared again from the basin into the limestone to make its way underground through the porous limestone to the Jordan below.

A cave, common in the limestone hills, was close by. Elijah knelt beside the pool of clear water and drank deeply. It was cooler than that of the Jordan, and sweeter. He leaned against a large rock near a stand of oleanders and closed his eyes. His headache was gone and the nightmare of last night drifted from his memory, but he was very tired. He shook his head to stay awake, and leaned forward to untie his sandals. Laying them aside, he walked to the stream and sat with his feet in the water. He had not had his sandals off for two days. He laid his mantle down, loosed his leather girdle, and pulled off his robe. The silt of the Jordan had stuck in the thick hair of his body. He started with his head, washing the silt of two days from his long, tangled hair and beard, and continued until he had bathed himself completely.

His clothes were next. They were even dirtier than he had been. He washed them carefully and hung them on branches to dry, then opened the cloth of berries and ate slowly and tiredly. When he finished he retrieved his clothes, almost dry now, and dressed, walked slowly to the cave, and sank exhausted to its floor.

Chapter Six

Zebul opened the door and looked quizzically at his visitor. His flushed cheeks revealed as much surprise as his eyes. He stepped back from the door and motioned Obadiah to enter.

"Your visit puzzles me."

"Yes. I can see that it does." Obadiah's words were clipped and aloof, a thinly-veiled antagonism evident.

"A glass of wine?"

"Thank you, no."

"Take a chair, then." Zebul motioned to a square-backed chair over which was draped a multi-dyed tapestry.

"I will stand. I have little to say."

The fat priest felt a twitch at the corner of his eye accent his irritation. Righteous Obadiah. How often as high priest he had delighted to bait the governor about his narrow religious views. Now, strangely, he felt an urge to impress the man. "I want you to sit for a few moments. I'm glad you came. There is a matter I wish to discuss."

Obadiah's hesitation revealed his distrust. Still, Zebul's new attitude was curious. He strode to the seat, his well-developed dignity utilized to the greatest degree to show his feeling of detachment.

Zebul waited until Obadiah arranged the folds of his cloak to suit himself, then he spoke. "First, your business."

The Governor's beard jerked in precise movements as he spoke. "I have been instructed to advise you that the seating arrangement has been altered at the king's table." He paused. When he resumed speaking the words were sharp. "Equal tables are to be set for the chief priests of Melkart and of Yahweh. The two of you will occupy places of equal honor."

Zebul did not answer. His unsmiling stare was blank, his face furrowed. The priest turned to the grillwork window, his back to Obadiah, his fingers slowly playing with his new ring. Obadiah watched expectantly, but quietly, determined not to be sucked into some intrigue of Zebul's. When the priest turned his face to his old enemy, his voice was firm. He spoke slowly, with resignation. "I cannot share honors with the chief priest of Melkart."

Obadiah's chin thrust upward and forward, the jerk of his head accented by his stiff and trim goatee. "I think you misunderstood me, Zebul. The queen does not *ask* you to share. I state a fact you will be wise not to question."

"The *queen?*"

Obadiah allowed a moment's silence to accent his answer. "Our King Ahab has given Jezebel full control over matters of religion. What I have just stated to you is her directive."

"I shall not sit at a table equal with the high priest of Melkart."

Obadiah rose angrily to his feet. His words were staccato. "Your intrigues and games bore me, Zebul. I am not an amateur, and I have known you for a long time. Do not pretend with me. I was sick of your whines when you were demoted to a less honorable table, and I am certain that your smiles will be broad at dinner tonight."

Zebul's voice was firm and surprisingly calm. "You may report my decision to Queen Jezebel. I will not . . ."

"Your cheap play for power is foolish, Zebul. You at least have been shrewd in your plays for power before. Let me assure you that you will not be assigned a higher place than the high priest of Melkart."

"Then I shall remain at a lower place."

The two men stared at each other. Obadiah's manner was, to Zebul, natural. His hardlined face was determined, his look of distrust and disgust apparent. His confidence bordered on arrogance. Zebul could not see the twinge of uncertainty, however, inside the governor, for the fat priest's manner was perceptibly changed. Such a shift was difficult for the logically-minded Obadiah to contend with. Zebul's determined answer appeared not to be playful or conniving, but sincere, his manner more resolute.

Zebul broke the silence. "Obadiah, you have every reason not to believe my sincerity in what I want to tell you."

Obadiah reacted with a cold stare. Zebul decided to approach the subject another way.

"I have been to see Ahijah." He detected a slight waver in the governor's attitude. "I do not intend to reveal to you all of the events and personal distress I have gone through to reach my present state of mind, Obadiah, but my interests now are to eliminate the Baal religion from our courts and from our land."

Coldness returned to Obadiah's stare. "It is as I suspected. I only regret that Yahweh does not have a high priest in office who would take your course of action for the right reasons." Disgustedly, he pulled his cloak around his shoulders and started toward the door.

The fat priest moved to block his exit. "Obadiah!" The governor stopped. With all of the dignity of his office evident in his upraised chin and erect posture, he stared again at Zebul with exaggerated patience, as though the priest were an exasperating child on whom discipline would be wasted. "Obadiah." Zebul spoke more evenly. "I do not expect to win."

Obadiah's shoulders relaxed just a bit, and a slight furrow in his brow softened his response. "I can assure you that what you have just stated is undoubtedly correct." He turned from the door. "Such being the case, I don't suppose you would tell one who has been your adversary for so long just what you hope to accomplish by your act."

"Yes, I will tell you. I don't want to pretend that the religions of Yahweh and Melkart can live side by side. They cannot. Their values are almost precise opposites. I am an observer of the religious scene by profession, Obadiah. If Yahweh's people accommodate themselves to Melkart, Melkart will win. Battle lines must become apparent, so that people will be forced to choose between the two religions."

Obadiah seated himself slowly. There was a touch of warmth in his eyes, and the lines in his face were softer. "Zebul, I only wish that I could relax and be confident of your purpose."

"Such confidence requires time. This particular decision, I am afraid, does not allow for that time. You may do as you wish or think about me as you will, but my decision about seating at the king's table is final."

"You speak candidly. You never have done that before. You will allow me, then, also to speak candidly. I will accept your new direction as being honest, but only to a point. I shall cooperate with you and help you so long as I can evaluate the results of your actions. You must know, however, that I shall watch you carefully, because I will not be a party to intrigue."

"There can be no other way."

Obadiah rose. More slowly now, he moved toward Zebul. He grasped the priest's arms and kissed him on both cheeks. "I hope very much that this day will mark the beginning of a common purpose."

"So be it. One thing. What news is there of Elijah?"

"There is none. He has vanished. The search has been thorough, and is continuing, but no man in Israel knows the land like Elijah. He probably is hiding in one of the thousands of caves in the wilderness."

"The search continues?"

"The search must continue until it rains. If Yahweh controls the waters of the heavens through the mouth of his prophet, Asherah will lose face. If Elijah can be found, Jezebel will force him to end the drought. Then she will credit Asherah for forcing Yahweh to give in."

"There is much talk among the people. Elijah's pronouncement has become widespread." Zebul smiled, thinking of his visit to Ahijah. "It seems that Yahweh has found a champion."

"Elijah has caught the people's fancy. This is why Jezebel is forced to place you at an equal table."

"Ah! She thinks such an act will temper the public mood."

"Yes." The lines in Obadiah's face hardened. "The queen will not like your answer, Zebul."

The fat priest chuckled. "So then Jezebel must make a move."

Obadiah did not return the smile. Solemnly, he opened the door and walked slowly to his chariot. Zebul watched as the governor turned toward Ahab's palace.

With a sharp clap of her hands Jezebel sent a messenger scurrying for Meor-baal. Obadiah, outwardly self-possessed as ever, inwardly fought for some way to fend off the disaster he knew was imminent.

"My queen . . ." He addressed her quietly, careful to keep his voice even. She whirled to face him. He noticed with surprise that her face appeared flushed, even under the olive complexion she so carefully cared for. "My queen, I speak humbly, but I am bound by my king to remind you of his command, which he repeated to me, that the prophets of Yahweh are not to be harmed, nor are Yahweh's worshipers to be kept from their worship."

"How dare you challenge the authority of your queen!" Jezebel shrieked in her fury. Then, struggling to regain control of her emotions, she spoke more calmly, pausing between sentences, cautious of her precise wording. "Obadiah, Ahab has given to my hand complete control over the religious life of Israel. His command which you repeated to me did not cover the eventuality of a revolt."

"A revolt?" Obadiah challenged.

"What else would you call the high priest's refusal to sit where he is assigned?" Jezebel raised herself to her full height and spoke haughtily. "Never have I heard of such insolence in the court of the king."

Obadiah fought back the empty feeling that rose in his stomach.

"Listen, 'Governor of the King's House.' " Jezebel stared down at him from the dais on which her throne sat. "Perhaps I should tell you something to impress on you how serious a matter your loyalty to Yahweh can be." She paused, savoring the silent tension produced by her words. Obadiah retained his dignity. Jezebel watched for the slightest evidence of nervousness—a twitch about his eyes, a slight jerk of his shoulder, the fractional break of eye contact. He remained resolute. She reseated herself. "Your King Ahab offered sacrifices to Melkart and evoked his blessing when he went to fight Ben-hadad on the northern border."

Obadiah felt the muscles in his cheeks tighten briefly, and he knew Jezebel caught his surprise. Having pierced his armor, she pressed her advantage. She continued in a mellow and confidential voice.

"Obadiah, Ahab is much more interested in Israel than in the protection of a weak tribal god. Melkart and Asherah are stronger than Yahweh. It is only logical that he seek the aid of the stronger." She paused, then measured her words. "Someday soon you will have to be disloyal either to your king and queen or to your god. On that day, you had better choose wisely."

Obadiah returned her gaze coldly. "I shall choose wisely," he said.

At that moment, the chamber door opened and Meorbaal was announced.

"Ah, my honored priest. You have come quickly."

"As you beckoned, my queen."

"Meor-baal, we are encountering some difficulty with a suddenly obstinate high priest of Yahweh."

"Zebul?"

"I know of no other high priest of Yahweh."

"Pardon my surprise, Queen Jezebel, but I did not anticipate such an act. Do you know what he plans?"

"No. Only that he refuses to sit where he is assigned."

A grave look came over Meor-baal's face. "My queen, this is not good." He spoke solemnly. "He is making a play for the people's sympathies."

"What alternative do you propose?"

"I know of none. He cannot be given the higher seat. We have struggled too hard to bring the worship of Baal to this point. Zebul has made a good tactical move."

"You will have him destroyed." Jezebel's eyes smoldered. Obadiah gasped, not expecting such a drastic move. Meor-baal waited for further direction. Jezebel continued, "His death must appear to be an accident. He is not popular with the people, so he will not be mourned for long."

Obadiah's mind raced. "My queen, you know my sympathies, so I shall not try to cover them. But should the high priest die his successor must follow. What will you have accomplished?"

Meor-baal interrupted. "My queen . . ." He paused and glanced furtively at Obadiah. "My queen, perhaps I should speak with you privately."

Jezebel stared coldly at Obadiah, who remained silent and expressionless. She maintained her gaze and answered with a hint of mystery. "No, Meor-baal. I think the Governor should know the official business of the court."

The Baal priest continued. "My queen, is not Zebul a usurper?"

The queen leaned forward, "A usurper?"

"Yes. He claims to be high priest. There is only one high priest of Baal. He resides in Byblos. Likewise there is only one real high priest of Yahweh. He resides in Jerusalem. What right has Zebul to claim to be high priest of Yahweh?"

Jezebel sat back in her throne, smiling. "I see."

Obadiah shifted his weight, trying to cover up the nervousness he was certain the queen noticed.

"Zebul can be executed as a usurper," Meor-baal continued. "He is not popular with the people, as you noted. They will accept that explanation if we make it with the pretense of purifying the religion of Yahweh."

Jezebel smiled. "Excellent. The Yahweh fanatics will be left without priestly leadership, too. See that the job is done well."

With a bow, Meor-baal strode from the chamber.

The queen turned to Obadiah. "You see, my good Governor, the strength of Melkart. You are foolish to continue to protect a weak god." With a flick of her arm she announced, "You are dismissed."

Bowing, Obadiah made his exit. He walked across the courtyard with his usual composure, but his mind raced back over the events of the day. *Why did Jezebel let me know her plans regarding Zebul? An error? No, Jezebel was too brilliant for such a mistake. Why, then? Perhaps I should warn Zebul. But for what reason? Because of his size, he cannot hide. Jezebel would have someone watching Zebul, anyway. I could not even get close enough to warn him. Perhaps that is her way to trap me?*

The thoughts plummeted end over end through his mind. *What is Jezebel's next move? What is my next move?* Gradually, as he made his way across the black pavement and through the corridors, the possibilities began to fall into order. Zebul was beyond saving. Jezebel was using this opportunity for all-out war on Yahwism. She also was trying to force the Governor of Ahab's House either to prove his disloyalty or join forces with her.

Obadiah entered his chambers and crossed the large room that served as his center of business and entered a small room that overlooked his private courtyard. He lay back in a heavily-cushioned, satin-draped lounge chair and stared out his window at the garden. Oleanders lined the walls on three sides. Gnarled olive trees, their branches interlaced curiously, filtered and softened the glare of the sun. "Oh, that the world were so peaceful," he whispered aloud.

Methodically, Obadiah began to consider the strengths and weaknesses of the Yahwists' position. Ahab, vacillating at best in matters of religion, was gone. In the end, when all of his alternatives were considered, he would agree with the conclusions that underlay Jezebel's action. The Yahweh followers had no single, strong leader other than Elijah, who was in hiding. Public opinion had been caught up in the excitement of the new ideas and moral laxity of Melkart and Asherah. The people moved with the tide created by Baal's offensive.

Ah, public opinion, he thought. *It moves with the force of the ocean, crushing everything not caught up in its sweep, an ally when it moves your direction, an archenemy when it does not. What strange and unknown force directs that sea's energies? Such strength! Does it move by itself and determine its own way, or is it moved along a current of history of which it is only a passive part? If Yahweh really is the one great God, someday the sea will change its direction.*

But until that day, Obadiah concluded, the Yahwists have no hope of winning. The logical course of action, then, is to protect as many as possible of those who are faithful to Yahweh. And to do so, he must take the greatest care not to be proven unfaithful in his responsibilities as Governor of Ahab's House.

Tongues of flame flickered from tips of shallow, elongated clay oil lamps. The dancing light emphasized in shadow-etchings on the walls the movements of nervous men. Every raised arm, every small shuffle, every twitch was exaggerated in profile on a wall. The shadows criss-crossed one another in varying shades of gray and black, broken by V's above each wall niche from which oil lamps cast their lights.

Obadiah stood in the center of the large room. His sensitive nostrils caught the pungent odor of unwashed bodies, but he forced his mind to accept the smell and ignore it. Every man there was bearded. They sat, leaned, squatted, and stood all around him. The eyes and hands of each one told their own stories: nervousness here, as though tragedy already pressed its weight; blank acceptance here, as though the news had not yet been apprehended; twitching here, as from a swordless warrior fanatically ready to dash barehanded into battle; calmness here, as though the price of war had been considered long ago and accepted as part of the game. The moods of stark terror, anticipation, excitement, worry, cowardice, bravery, fear, thrill, and shrugging acceptance were as varied as the dress of the men. Some wore wide leather waistbands over short drapes of cloth. Some wore their hair long and in tangles. Some wore sandals with leather straps wrapped around their ankles and lower legs. Some were barefoot. Some had the long, flowing, uncut hair of Nazirites, who vow never to have a razor touch their hair nor wine their lips until the vow is fulfilled.

Obadiah had heard the news only hours ago. He was outside the city walls checking the granary shafts at the time. Zebul had been hauled to a fast-erected stand in the marketplace, his head and arms bound in a wooden ox yoke. According to the report, the high priest had stood silent and erect as the charge of usurpation of his claimed office was read. At first the people reacted in stunned silence at the accusation. Then their silence gave way to low murmuring against the queen. But the newly appointed priest-in-charge skillfully read the queen's proclamation of defense for the purity of the ancient religion of Israel. The final denunciation of Zebul was scathing, and it capitalized on his lack of popularity. The people's mood changed to glee.

Zebul's death was that accorded a conquered and despised king. The yoke was removed and he was bound hand and foot. His feet were roped to the back of a chariot and he was dragged full speed through the rough streets of the city, his fat body rolling and bouncing along the hard black stones. No one knew how long he lived before the careening horses finally were brought to a stop. Except for his size, Zebul's body was not recognizable. His wife had remained stoic. Except for her station in life, she had long ago ceased to care what happened to her fat husband. By now, Obadiah knew, the dogs would have licked the blood from the streets.

As Obadiah revealed the story of Zebul's transformation to the prophets of the Samarian guild, they responded with mixed emotions, but he could sense the building of a sympathy for the once-despised priest. Along with the sympathy a sense of foreboding also grew. Soon, though, their reactions began to take more definite forms.

A young, stringy-bearded prophet shouted out his challenge. "Yahweh is stronger than Melkart and Asherah! We will stand face to face with the prophets of Baal and show them the strength of the true God. Who is with me?"

Immediately a clamor went up, some of the men shouting defiance of the gods and prophets of Baal, others crying for silence and sanity.

Finally the oldest prophet, thinly robed, small of stature, with red blotches over skin that had lost its hair, arose and with the aid of a staff made his way to stand beside Obadiah. He held his arm high. Voices died down until the room was silent. He spoke slowly and laboriously. "Let us seek the advice of Obadiah. He knows well the mind of Jezebel."

Obadiah responded immediately. "I believe Queen Jezebel will seek to destroy as many prophets of Yahweh as possible. I advise you to go into hiding."

"He calls Jezebel his queen!" An angry young man was on his feet. His back and head arched toward Obadiah, his face contorted with anger. "How can you be faithful to Yahweh and call Jezebel your queen!"

Obadiah spoke firmly but simply. "My advice stands."

Another prophet, tall, wiry, wearing a leather waistcloth and leather sandals, spoke gently but with a resonant voice that made his words sound profound. "Obadiah, I speak as chief of the coenobia of prophets. You cannot expect Yahweh's prophets to escape from danger. The very nature of our lives is danger. It is especially in the hour of danger that we are called to speak."

"Nevertheless," Obadiah responded evenly, "God hides Elijah, who surely is not afraid of danger. Perhaps Yahweh, too, feels that retreat occasionally is a virtue."

The reference to Elijah relaxed the prophets. Even those who were antagonistic to Obadiah remained quiet, though sullen.

"There are caves in the limestone of our city's hill. You know of them, but the prophets of Baal whom Jezebel brought from Tyre and Byblos do not. You must find the best hidden and least accessible ones to hide you. Some of you younger men must take on yourselves the task to search out the best choices. I will see that you are provided with food and are kept informed of events. Once in hiding, you must never come out except at my instruction. And one other thing. You must trust me without question. If you cannot do so, find your own place to hide. I have neither the time nor the stomach to tolerate your distrust."

He paused, then turned to the tall, wiry leader. "Your name?"

"Macaiah."

"You will be my contact man, Macaiah, chief of prophets. You will notify me in some way when you have located satisfactory hiding places."

Obadiah turned to go.

"Obadiah," Macaiah called. "A moment more."

The governor paused.

"What is to be the fate of the coenobias at Jericho, Bethel, and Gilgal? Are they being warned?"

"If they are to be warned, you must see to it." Obadiah bowed slightly and made his way up the stone steps to the street.

Macaiah turned to face the guild of prophets. "Someone must go to warn our brothers. Six of you, strong of limb, must go by twos to the other three coenobias. Who will go?"

A flood of hands, amid clamoring, rose to indicate volunteers. Macaiah scanned the group and made assignments quickly, aware of the personalities who could work together best. Those who were chosen gathered around their leader for last minute consultation.

The heavy sword, held double-handed by a broadchested soldier, came crashing down to cut through hair, flesh, sinew, and bone, and stopped with a thud, embedded in the thick tabletop. Ahijah's head rolled slightly beside the swordblade and stopped, open-mouthed and staring. Two soldiers released their holds and the body slumped to the floor. The two captives gasped slightly at the moment of the old prophet's death; then they remained mute. Circles of blood on the table and floor widened in the silence.

"A pity," the captain of the guard mocked after a moment, "that you did not arrive in time for the questioning. You would have enjoyed it." He moved over to the two prophets. Slowly, he wrapped a leather strap around his hand, smiling broadly. "At least, your arrival here at Bethel warns me that my work will be harder at Gilgal and Jericho." His eyes narrowed and the tightness of his mouth erased the smile from his face. "Will you spare yourselves by telling me where the prophets may hide? And will you pay allegiance to Baal?"

The two men simply stared into the captain's eyes.

Grimacing, the captain threw his weight into the blow. The leather-wrapped fist smashed into the first prophet's face. He crumpled to the floor, his jaw broken. The next blow cut the second prophet's lips against his teeth. Blood streamed from his mouth and nose, but he remained on his feet.

"These fanatics won't talk, and we have no time to

waste on them," the captain shouted to his men. "Kill them."

The captain stalked outside, barking orders to his soldiers to mount and take positions. In a moment the five who had remained in Ahijah's house to carry out their last order emerged. Two of them were returning copper swords to their sheaths. They quickly mounted their waiting horses.

The detachment moved east toward Jericho and Gilgal.

Chapter Seven

LIGHT CREPT SLOWLY into the mouth of the cave. By mid-morning its heat stirred Elijah. Half awake, he felt the grumblings of hunger in his stomach. He rose slowly to his knees, sat back, and rubbed the traces of sleep from his eyes. Then he made his way to the pool. The cool water stirred his senses and heightened his hunger.

Standing by the pool, he turned carefully and slowly to scrutinize his new surroundings. Oleanders stood as tall sentinels along both banks of the wadi. Up the wadi to the east the cane was broken and twisted from the torrents that had turned the dry wadi into a furious, narrow river during the winter rains. Thornbushes grew in patches of earth for several yards up the steep sides of the wadi. Except for the pond, which had its source from inside the porous lime-stone mountains, the older growth of the wadi was caked dull gray with mud. Above the ugly line marked by the stream at its height, spaced among the thornbushes, grew clusters of retem bushes, several long green slender twigs rising from a common base. Occasionally Elijah caught the fragrance of the small, pink blossoms that still covered each twig. From high in the rock walls came the frequent, low coo of rock pigeons.

The cave itself was shallow. The prophet could see the full depth of it from where he stood, more of a cleft than a cave. Its floor was covered with the same dried mud that dominated the wadi bed. He scanned the small area for berry bushes. There were none.

Elijah bent to the pool and drank its water from his cupped hands. He felt the coolness travel down his throat and into his stomach. Just as the hunger pangs started again, accentuated by the drink, he heard the thrashing of wings and looked up to see a large raven tear a pigeon from its nest. In a moment, frightened pigeons deserted their perches, and the loud caw of the raven mixed with the desperate sounds of the captured prey.

But the raven, trying to tear at the pigeon while in flight, loosed its hold on its bounty. It fell into Elijah's lair. He darted for the bird and retrieved it before the raven could recapture his prize. The pigeon was dead, its eyes pierced by the raven's beak. *The ravens were to feed me*, Elijah thought, *so I shall eat of God's food.*

As the raven perched nearby in an oleander and cawed his raucous protest, Elijah plucked the bird. He had no fire, so he was obliged to eat the flesh raw. Smoke would reveal his hiding place, anyway. "Thanks," he said aloud to the raven. "God didn't promise me a banquet, but I'll enjoy what he gave me." He laughed and pointed an arm toward the raven. "Through you," he added.

He pulled the insides from the pigeon and tossed the refuse some distance from him and in full view of the raven. "But you shall not go hungry, my benefactor," he said.

The large bird cautiously left his perch and flew to a rock near the promising meal. Still cawing loudly, he watched Elijah carefully, his coal black feathers glistening almost purple in the sun. Gaining courage, he moved to the ground and, ever slowly, walked toward the food. Elijah spoke softly, "Come now, my new friend. I saved you the trouble of preparing your meal. Eat well." Finally the raven tore into the food, keeping a wary eye all the while on the prophet. As he held the mass with his feet, he pulled bits loose with his beak. With each mouthful, he tilted his head back to swallow the morsel.

Elijah had seen a raven feeding many times before. The sight always fascinated him. This king of birds surely was one of God's most intelligent creatures.

The raven finished his meal before Elijah. He flew to a high branch, cawed loudly, then flew to a hole in the steep wall not far above Elijah's cleft. He flipped himself nervously to face one direction, then the other, but did not turn toward the hole. He cawed again, then flew away.

Elijah watched the black wings lift the raven quickly up the valley toward the plateau high above and disappear over the rim. He looked toward the hole the raven had called to his attention. Had the bird wanted him to know about something? Or had he become aware again of a man's presence and decided at the last moment not to reveal a treasure?

Ravens cache food away in case of famine, Elijah recalled. Perhaps the hole was this raven's storehouse. Clutching bushes and small outcroppings, the prophet worked himself up to the hole and looked inside. Something was there. He reached in and pulled out a handful of the raven's cache. "The little thief!" Elijah laughed. He looked at the round breadcakes he had known in his boyhood. They were flat cakes of bread made by tent people as they followed their flocks during warm weather. The raven, whose diet knows few restrictions, evidently found a way to snatch one occasionally from the Bedouins, or discovered discards after a tribe broke camp. Elijah picked out the two freshest cakes and ate them on the spot.

Filled, he drank again from the pool, then sat beside it and put his feet into the cool water. After a while Elijah broke a limb from an oleander and used the leafy branch to sweep the dried mud from the cave floor. He spent the afternoon cleaning debris and weeds from a small area between the cave and the pool.

As the shadows closed in on the canyon, the raven returned. He gripped a breadcake in his beak, which he efficiently deposited in his cache. Then he attacked another rock pigeon to repeat the performance of the morning.

The next day, two ravens appeared, and as one rainless day passed into another, other ravens joined the pair until several of them kept Elijah busier than he wanted to be. But he prepared their food, thankful that his own needs were met. Occasionally the ravens brought pieces of meat from the carcass of a kill too large to be carried. Elijah looked the meat over carefully each time to be sure it was fresh—and sometimes it was not—for ravens would not turn down a meal of carrion.

He was bored much of the time until he settled down into a routine, but he was determined to remain in his hiding place until he felt God's urge to leave. Ahab's search surely continued even though the king would not become critically concerned until the end of the normal dry season.

Soon the days settled into a pattern. Elijah rose to eat with the ravens, who continued most days to stock the cache with stolen breadcakes. The birds were large, some two feet from tip of beak to tail, and their antics in flight sent chills of admiration down Elijah's spine. Gradually they became his friends. He talked with them gently and named each one. The leader, the first one to appear, was *El'echol*, "food from God."

After the ravens left he sat by the pool and prayed to Yahweh. He prayed for faith. He softly sang the songs he had learned as a boy on the high plains of Gilead, holy songs, many of them written by David, Israel's greatest king. He recalled the laws of God and recited from memory all he could remember of the sacred words.

His boyhood years and his youth had been happy, and he mused on them often during his wait. His parents were semi-nomadic. They lived the Bedouin life during the warm season and settled down during the winters in the little village of Tishbe. He smiled as he recalled Jonadab, his dearest friend, whom he first met at a wateringplace. As they met on other occasions, his friend had convinced him to join the new movement, the Rechabites, named after Jonadab's father, Rechab. Rechab taught that Yahweh's laws could be obeyed only in the nomadic life. City walls brought temptations and tied down the spirit of a man. He would not even allow wine, not because it was intoxicating but for fear that his people would learn to like it so well they would plant vineyards, the first step toward a walled town.

After three years with the Rechabites Elijah had decided that they were wrong. His own parents were no less faithful to Yahweh during the winter months than the summer, and Rejab, among others, was faithful even in Bethshean, hardly a loyal Yahwist city.

The night of parting with Jonadab had been painful. They sat around a campfire, Jonadab driving home the arguments that once had convinced Elijah to join the group.

"There is danger in leaving the life of a nomad, Elijah," Jonadab had argued. "Here you are free."

The young Elijah picked up a clod and silently rolled it in his hand. Jonadab's voice droned on. "Walls build a prison around the spirit." Jonadab gestured expansively. "Here you can think as you want and talk with Yahweh beneath the stars and the sun."

Elijah sighed wearily. "Jonadab, you repeat words you have heard from others."

"That does not make them less wise." Jonadab's bony chin jutted out to emphasize his conviction. "My father told me of the intoxication of the city. Like sweet wine, your mind becomes inflamed and you think of reasons for doing what you know is wrong."

"Rechab was a fine man," Elijah retorted. He said no more.

Jonadab pulled his legs to his chest and rested his head on his knees. A jackal howled its long wail. The tall, wiry nomad rose to his feet and, with his thumbs tucked into his wide belt, stared at the low, steady flame. Finally he turned toward his friend. "You cannot be successful in what you plan, Elijah. Either you will become the worst of ruffians or you will die a disillusioned and broken man."

Elijah looked up at the tall nomad, and he spoke in a tone both agitated and intimate. "And you expect Israel to be saved from Baal because you herd sheep and chant the *Shema* in these hills?" Elijah chuckled. "Or would you have me stand on Mount Nebo and shout curses to Melkart?" He threw a clod into the fire, and sparks flew in protest.

"Do you not believe in the strength of example, Elijah? Can't you see that those who really believe in Yahweh will join us? Better that a few protect the laws of Yahweh than that all men bow the knee to Baal. It is the will of God that we multiply and raise our children to obey the laws of Yahweh. The faithful of Israel will know of us and will join our tribe."

"You pull a veil over your eyes, Jonadab. The cities of the plain and hills do not even know we exist. They know only our wool. We could live and die protecting God's laws. What difference would that make to the rest of the world? No, my friend. You stay if you must. I cannot watch in peace while our people pray to their little baals and listen to the wind for answers."

Jonadab grunted. "The choice is their affair."

"No, Jonadab. It is my affair, too. Israel is my affair." Elijah picked up his mantle and stood to face his friend. He stared imploringly at the tribal leader for a moment, then said softly, "Good-bye, Jonadab."

"Wait, Elijah." He spoke softly, pleading. "Elijah, you can teach us the ways of Yahweh. When you joined our camp my father was convinced that Yahweh sent you. He taught you to read the Law and to think the ways of Yahweh in a manner I never could learn. You have insights. Yahweh speaks to you. We need you." Jonadab placed a hand lightly on Elijah's shoulder. "Stay with us, my friend."

Elijah's muscles grew tense under the feel of Jonadab's hand. He spoke nervously, as though the words brought pain. "You truly have been a friend, Jonadab, and your father more than a teacher." He paused. "I have learned much from Rechab, but Yahweh has spoken to me also. My heart has stirred for a long time for a duty I should someday perform. Who can say what the outcome of my life will be? All I know is that I must go."

Elijah tenderly grasped the arms of his friend, squeezed them tightly, and without another word walked away.

At the top of the crest overlooking the circle of tents, Elijah looked back. Jonadab had gone to his tent. The dawn was new and a mist rose from the sparse pastureland to meet it. Through the haze Elijah watched the animals. Camels, sheep, and cattle mingled together around the mass of black, square-rigged tents. Black sheep and dirty white ones, all with huge, fat tails, grazed contentedly in small groups. He hated to leave the traveling sanctuary. The Rechabites lived austere but happy lives, hidden from the world halfway between the Dead Sea on the west and the Great Desert on the east—the first hidden from their camp by a high rocky mountain ridge that once had known the trudging footsteps of the great Exodus, the latter by low, rolling plains.

The procession wound through the narrow streets of Aphek. Hundreds of villagers filed past Obadiah, following the woman. She carried a dummy dressed in women's clothes and ornamented heavily with jewelry. Her chant told Obadiah what he had come to find out. The villagers did not know where Elijah was in hiding. The people chanted with the woman leader in monotonous tones:

> O Mother of the Rain, O Immortal, moisten our
>   sleeping seeds.
> Moisten the sleeping seeds of Asherah, who is ever
>   generous.
> She is gone, the Mother of the Rain, to bring the
>   storm.
>   When she comes back, the crops are as high as
>   the walls.
> She is gone, the Mother of the Rain, to bring the
>   winds.
>   When she comes back, the vines have attained
>   the height of houses.

She is gone, the Mother of the Rain, to bring the
      thunders.
When she comes back, the crops are as high as
      camels.

Obadiah watched the procession without dismounting.
When the last of the throng passed by he remained unmoving until the chants could be heard only dimly from
other streets out of sight.

He had seen the people resort to superstition often since
Elijah pronounced Yahweh's curse. In the drought people
grasped at every childhood story and every dim belief that
promised relief. The people of Aphek were desperate.
Their River Kanah was only a trickling stream now, and one
day soon it would be dry.

He had seen other villagers try to placate Asherah and
beg her mercy. In their desperation they combined their
old and tenacious beliefs in local baals with their new
awareness of the Great Baals, Melkart and Asherah.

In Socoh, near Samaria and toward the Great Sea, naked
women pulled plows in the parched earth, believing their
nakedness would entice the Goddess of Fertility to send
rain. The villagers of Jokmeam, toward the Jordan, had
sent all the virgins of the village into the seeded fields at
dawn for the ritual of water pouring. The virgins poured
water over their naked, fertile bodies in hope that the
water would carry their fertility to the soil, to prime the
soil to bring forth its yield again—in hopes, too, that Asherah would understand their need for rain. The people of
Hazor recalled an old belief that if the bodies of lepers were
not burned the rain god would be angry, so they dug up
the bones from every leper's grave they knew of and
burned the remains, amid screams and chants for Asherah's
mercy.

Throughout the farmlands of Israel, Obadiah had seen
bits of dried dung hanging from the branches of carob trees,
in the belief that any slight breeze would move the dung to
call their needs to the attention of the gods of the wind and
rain. Occasionally he had seen a frog or large black beetle

hanging from a limb, put there by farmers in the belief that the struggles of the animal or insect would create a tiny stir of breeze to remind Asherah that she forgot to send the rain by the wings of the wind.

In a low, tired voice the governor told the captain to turn the contingent of troops and begin their return journey.

They left the village gates and started moving up the sloping hills toward the east. Obadiah rode at the head of the column with the captain, but the captain left him to his thoughts.

The captain was a Melkart man, but he was puzzled that Elijah, in the name of a god so much weaker than Baal, could control the rain this long. Why had not Jezebel's priests and prophets been able to bring rain? There were so many of them to counteract the curse of the prophet. But the captain's nagging doubts would not divert him from Melkart. Had not Melkart conquered more nations than Yahweh? Had not even the king of Syria acknowledged Melkart as his God?

Obadiah was troubled at the superstitions of the people, but he was even more concerned about how the famine attacked their morality. Many of them openly engaged in orgies in their fields and in sacred groves of trees, hoping to bring fertility back to the land by paying such homage to Asherah, hoping that the act of procreation in their own fields would entice new growth from the barren land. He could not but believe that the religious significance became an excuse for further indulgence, desperation forgotten momentarily in passion.

Upon his arrival in Samaria Obadiah informed Ahab of the village scene.

"And you deduce from the procession that the villagers do not know where Elijah hides?"

"If they were faithful enough to Elijah to hide or protect him, they would not perform an ancient rain goddess ritual. Indeed, they would be your ally in seeking Elijah."

"Yes, of course." Ahab sat thoughtfully, his hands clasped in his lap. He did not beckon Obadiah to sit, and the governor stood patiently. Finally, the king spoke. "According to your reports, Obadiah, you have had Israel searched thoroughly for the hairy one. Where have you not looked?"

"Searchers have been in every village, town, and city in Israel, and the countryside has been searched. I have sent cadres into the Bedouin areas across the Jordan, but there are wildernesses that are impossible to search, though reports satisfy me that the captains made extensive effort. Tribesmen and villagers alike know of the search and they, too, pray for an end to the drought, but no information has come from any of them."

"Perhaps he is not in Israel."

"That is possible."

"Draw up papers to be sent to the kings of Sidon, Moab, Syria, Edom, Midian, Ammon, Judah, and the leaders of the Philistines. Solicit the aid of each king to find Elijah. They know the drought, too, and will be anxious to help. Elijah especially must have many friends in Judah. Give special attention to the draft to King Jehoshaphat. Send the papers by teams of runners. Tend to the matter immediately."

"Yes, King Ahab. I shall do it promptly."

As Obadiah left the throne room for his own quarters he had the feeling that he was only going through motions, his body functioning apart from his mind. The search effort was wasted, he was certain, on a prophet so obviously protected by Yahweh, but Ahab must not develop doubts about his governor. The prophets hidden in the limestone caves below the city had not been found, and they must be kept safe against that day when Elijah might be successful, and Yahweh again becomes the God of his people.

Miriam heard the door and watched Rejab enter. Neither greeted the other. Rejab sank his heavy weight onto a stool and leaned tiredly against the wall. She walked to him and placed a hand on his shoulder, looking down at him with eyes that wanted to ask but feared the answer. Slowly, he raised an arm across his chest and covered her hand in his. Still he did not look up.

"Rejab."

His eyes grew red at the edges, eyes she could not see as his head drooped, but she saw the slight hollow form beneath the flesh of his cheek and the gristle of his jaw tighten hard as he clenched his teeth.

"Rejab, I'm your wife." She spoke evenly, without tremor. As he was strong beyond the walls of his home, she must be strong within them now, in his despair.

"Elijah . . ." Rejab felt his voice try to break, and he paused. When he continued, he threw out the words all together, impulsively. "Elijah is pretty effective, isn't he?" His laugh caught in his throat and broke. The tears came from deep inside him, below his lungs, as the spasm of grief shook his shoulders. Miriam grasped his head and pulled him to her bosom. She ran one hand through his hair, above the ear, saying nothing. He pulled her to him and pressed his head into her stout body.

The spasm lasted but a moment. Slowly, he pulled her hands into his and stood. He was only a bit taller than she, and she tilted her head slightly to meet his eyes. She studied them quickly, expertly, measuring the depth and duration of his despair, to plumb before the moment of honesty passed the strength still left in this man who had protected and provided for her for so long. She caught a glimpse of the fight still left in him, but she caught, too, a fleeting shadow deep in his eyes she never had seen before. Then the moment of openness passed, and the mask slipped back into place.

Miriam pushed her face into Rejab's breast, trying to quiet the fear that was throwing off its bedclothes deep inside her.

Rejab placed his arm around her and silently walked her to the two wide, well-cushioned stools they had sat in together through years of evenings. He propped other cushions against the wall, and they both sank into their places. They looked at each other. Their lips met, as though a thousand signals built over the years announced the time to kiss. The kiss was not passionate or lingering, but the brief moment of touching released forces from one to the other, as though courage and hope were physical.

Miriam looked at him and touched his smooth cheek. "Rejab," she said softly, "I want to know."

Rejab clasped his hands across his large belly. He watched his hands as though he had not studied them for a long time, and turned them up to stare at his flesh-puffed knuckles, then over to gaze at his soft palms.

"Rejab."

"Yes, Miriam, all right." He stared at her a moment. "Miriam, the elders ruled against me."

The woman heard the words, but her mind would not accept them. For generations the venerated elders of Beth-shean, as at villages and towns and cities all over Israel, had sat in their special places at the main gate to the city to judge cases of dispute. Wise men they were, and honored among all the people. "And the reprover," she asked slowly, "did you appeal to him?"

"Yes. He heard the evidence and sided with me. He called for an investigation. But the elders did not so much as look at him. I saw him shake his head in despair."

"Rejab," she asked carefully, "what does it mean?"

He glanced at her, then fixed his eyes on his hands again. How could he explain to his wife the world he occupied outside their home? The competition, the buying and selling of foodstuffs, the weights and measures, the tricks of bargaining she knew. But the aggressive viciousness of recent months, how to explain that?

"Miriam," he began, fumbling for an explanation he never had put into words before, "Miriam, there is a new spirit among the wealthy. You remember Jaala?"

She nodded, and Rejab saw a muscle twitch in her eye.

"Jaala has given himself and his family to Akkub." He spoke with somber finality.

"But they will be slaves only a few months," Miriam responded. "Then comes the fiftieth year, the Jubilee Year. Then they will be free again, and free of debt. Is that so bad?"

Rejab did not look at her.

"Rejab," Miriam pressed, "why does Jaala's bad luck concern you so? The law is clear. His decision may prove to be wise in the long run."

"Akkub and his merchant friends do not observe the spirit of the old laws of our fathers very well. There are ways around the laws of freeing slaves."

"But the elders . . ." She stared at Rejab, her mouth still open, her eyes wide, and she remembered the unfamiliar shadow she had seen earlier in his eyes.

"Yes," Rejab said bitterly, "the elders." But he could not let the conversation end there, to leave his wife with the horror of her shocked imagination. He took her hand. "Miriam, the drought is making people more vicious. They are fighting for their lives, the wealthy and the poor alike. But Elijah is right. The new spirit that has swept the merchants is the work of Baal." He shook his head, arguing with himself. "Who can explain why men act as they do? Is it because they follow another god or because they simply forget Yahweh? Who can know? Perhaps both. Perhaps men are born to evil. Perhaps they are cruel by nature, or perhaps they simply do not see the hurt they cause. Perhaps Akkub and his friends do not know that their reasonings are the reasonings of Melkart, that God of Power."

Miriam spoke flatly. "Does it matter? That they know or don't know the source of their evil, does it matter?"

"It matters that Elijah knows. Miriam, there had to be an empty place for Baal to enter to make his home. Who knows when the emptiness started? Perhaps fathers taught our rituals but not their meanings. Perhaps grandfathers taught evil without knowing it." He paused and looked at Miriam. "Sometimes I think there should be no rituals. Men should know when their faith is dead. They should know. Sometimes I think there should be no motions that make men think they have faith. Perhaps that would be better."

Miriam answered evenly. "But the rituals teach faith. They teach of Yahweh."

Rejab looked away and shook his head.

"I'm sorry, Rejab. That is another subject. I want to know about the elders' ruling."

"They say I have no proof. It is my word against Akkub's."

"But you are not the first one to complain that Akkub uses heavy shekels to weigh his purchases."

"No, others have complained, but the elders say that every case must be considered on its own."

"Rejab." The tone of Miriam's voice made Rejab turn to his wife. "The wives have said things, Rejab. I don't know if they are true."

"Things?"

"Leah works in Pashur's house. She overheard Pashur tell his wife that he gives gifts to the elders."

"Yes, I suppose many of us have suspected it. Pashur and Akkub are only two of those who do such things." Rejab stood and walked to the center of the room, his hands clasped behind his back. He stood erect, his eyes straight ahead. "Miriam, I should have been more careful. A merchant, even a small one, should know of such practices. I had heard of it in Damascus and other places, but in Israel? I did not expect it in Israel."

"You should be able to trust your countrymen." Miriam spoke in the tone of confidence, naively, edged with a touch of a wife's bitterness at her husband's misfortune.

"A man is a fool to trust and a coward not to," Rejab answered softly. He laughed, a grating, short laugh from the top of his throat. "Some choice, Miriam. To be a fool or a coward."

For a moment, silence enveloped both of them. It momentarily built a cage around them, and neither husband nor wife spoke. Rejab stood still, his eyes straight ahead, studying the swirls and lines in the plaster that covered the rock wall of their home. Miriam sat where she was, her hands playing with the folds in her dress. She studied the threads, some of them coarse, others fine. She made creases with her fingers. Finally, when she spoke, her words broke the cage and it shriveled away. "Rejab, what now?"

Rejab looked harder at the wall, trying to avoid saying what he must say. He did not look at her, and he did not answer immediately. Miriam was about to repeat her question when he said, simply and without emotion, "Now I have a decision to make about how to conduct my business."

"What do you mean? What decision?"

He looked at Miriam now, and a chill ran down the wife's spine when she saw again the shadow behind his eyes. "Miriam, the loss hurt badly. I have little left with which to buy produce from the farmers. I must borrow money."

"You have borrowed before, many times."

"But now I'm afraid. I never was afraid before." Rejab returned to the stool and slumped onto it. Miriam reached to place a hand on his arm.

"Why are you afraid? The interest rates?"

"The interest rates are usurious. They make it hard to make a profit. But that I can cope with. It is impersonal, a fact to deal with. No, I'm angry because of the interest rates, but I don't fear them. It is the future I fear. I fear the direction business practice is going. I fear what I am too little to change."

Miriam squeezed Rejab's arm more tightly, but remained silent.

Rejab continued. "I cannot sell at a profit for the price Akkub and Pashur and others like them will offer for my produce. Either I must cheat the farmers by weighing with heavy shekels, as Akkub did to me, or by mixing bad barley with good to sell—and then I run the danger of being caught."

Miriam spoke sharply. "Rejab, you wouldn't do business like that!"

"That is the decision I must make."

"Then there is no decision. Would you follow Melkart or Yahweh? Right is right, and wrong is wrong."

He answered her indignation bitterly. "And bankruptcy is unpleasant."

"God will provide." The shadow behind Rejab's eyes moved again. Miriam gripped his forearm with both hands. "Rejab, we must have faith. Yahweh will provide."

He sighed. "Miriam. My dear Miriam." He shook his head. "Miriam, there are times when God will provide. We have known those times. But there are times when Yahweh's people must suffer like all men. This is one of those times. If we obey the laws of God, we must obey them even though we know the results will mean disaster. There are times we must suffer in doing right. Miriam . . ." He placed his hand over her two and turned to face her. "I am telling you that I cannot survive in my business and observe God's laws. In a short time my funds will run out. If I borrow, the creditors will take my business and it eventually will be absorbed by Akkub or someone like him."

"But you have a reputation for honesty. Won't merchants buy from you because of that? Won't they stay with you?"

"No." His tone was more resigned than ever. "No, Miriam, farmers are selling to me from the last of their harvest. They should be planting now, but the drought has made many of them hold their seed. They fear Elijah's curse and fear there will be no harvest this season. Fear is everywhere. Even Akkub and Pasher are afraid of the drought. My friends are afraid. I am afraid. No, Miriam. Everyone in Bethshean, everyone in Israel, fights for survival. They will buy from the one who gives them the best price."

"But won't they be cheated?"

"Every man believes he can deal with such practices."

Miriam looked at her husband, her eyes wide. "Rejab, what will you do?"

Rejab stroked her hand, then pressed it firmly under his palm. "I don't know, Miriam. I don't know."

Chapter Eight

ELIJAH BRUSHED the red dirt from his leg, then looked back up toward the tangled debris. It had been a good home all through the dry summer and into the time when normally the winter rains come.

He sat down in the mouth of the little wadi and looked out through the mimosa-like branches of a shittah tree at the Jordan. The broad ribbon of green jungle across the narrow plain hid the river from view. The rough road that ran along the plain between his hiding place and the Pride of Jordan was deserted, so far as he could tell. The plain, which should be plowed after the early rains of winter, was dry and hard, the grass sparse and brown.

He felt a tinge of sorrow for his people. The grain had been gathered months ago, in the spring. The drought began before the time of the late ripening rains, so the crop was minimal. Perhaps, with cautious use, the grain would last them through the year.

The grape harvest would have been a bright spot, Elijah surmised, for the roots of the vine reach deep into the hill-side to find water. He recalled the comradeship that develops between a father and his sons as they live in tents and little huts set up in the vineyards so they can protect the grapes from wild animals. Once the crop is gathered, the Feast of Tabernacles begins. Special prayers are offered during the event to petition Yahweh to send the winter rains early. Elijah frowned as he recalled the scene in the Jerusalem Temple, when water drawn from the Pool of Siloam is poured onto the altar to symbolize the need for rain. The Day of Atonement, ten days later, surely came this year under a cloud of fear.

Elijah was lost in his musings, oblivious to the occasional caw of ravens and the chirping of locusts. He watched without really noticing the rare flock of stork or cormorant flying low over the Pride of Jordan on their migration to Africa.

He shook his head. Even now, he knew, with the rains two months late, his people would pray to Yahweh in their homes, then turn to their baals in the fields. They would recite the Yahweh rituals over their meals, then the men would visit Asherah's groves and have intercourse with her holy prostitutes. In their scramble to influence the heavens for rain the people would placate every god they knew of in every way they could.

"Then how, Yahweh, will you show the people that you control the rain?" The prophet looked up into the cloudless sky, as though an answer might be written there. But the dull blue expanse was empty. The afternoon sun, ringed with ever-widening halos of heat, drew shimmering waves from the little plain in front of him.

"And now I must go to Zarephath," he sighed, "to hide in the home of a widow." The word from Yahweh had been vivid, but he still was not sure whether God had spoken to him in a dream or out loud while he was awake. Zarephath was a long way from his wadi, above Tyre on the coast of the Great Sea, in the nation of Jezebel's birth. "Well," he chuckled, "Ahab will never think to look for me there."

The ravens had not come this morning nor the day before, and the pool was becoming stagnant as it dried up.

He looked again at the Pride of Jordan. To journey north for thirty miles or so to the Sea of Chinnereth through that jungle was too dangerous, with its snakes and wild beasts. But if he traveled by the road that ran along the plain he surely would be seen by someone desperate enough for the drought to end to report his presence to Ahab's searchers. The ancient King's Highway, high above and behind him on the tableland of Gilead, was the most dangerous of all.

He decided to travel the first distance at night. Once at the Sea of Chinnereth he could move up its east side, which was in the country of Aram-Damascus. Then he would have to skirt wide around Dan, a journey that would take him along the base of Mount Hermon and up into Coele-Syria, the valley between the Lebanons.

As Elijah began his journey he noted that the ground was very hard, unsoftened by the October rains. The plain had not been planted. He crossed the familiar wadi beds each in turn, each usually swelled in the fall by several small springs, but now only their main channels held a trickle of water. Narrow strips and patches along their banks were broken up and planted in wheat, the farmers hoping to irrigate tiny crops should the drought continue.

Normally, wheat fields stood on several levels of the wadi's chasm. The farmers planted them a few days apart so they would not ripen all at once. Now, he knew, the little fields were hard and barren. *What goes on in the homes of the farmers during a drought?* he wondered. *Do the men reassure their wives? Do they pray for rain? Do they talk of how they will stretch their food? Can they make love while they fear what harvest time will bring?* Elijah was not a farmer, though his people, as sheepherders, were close to the land. They moved their flocks to wherever the grass was best. A year of drought was hard on them, and the tribes would fight over water holes, but they were mobile and better able to survive a famine, even with the hardness of it.

He made his bed before daybreak, expertly criss-crossing

branches in a sidr tree to form an arbor as protection from the sun. He slept fitfully under it as his mind refused to rest. When he awoke to stare at the cane arbor, he wondered what was most important, that men and women and children live without hunger or that Israel throw off the Baal worship. But Yahweh had spoken, and he would not waver from his commission.

Elijah had traveled most of the next night by the time he approached the sea. The prophet could make out only a glow, but he knew instinctively that the light was from a ring of torches that surrounded the ancient pagan site of Beth-yerah where the Jordan emerges from the sea.

He gritted his teeth, the rage against Melkart and Asherah burning away the tinge of doubt he felt in his dreams. The passions the Israelites aroused at the altar of Beth-yerah would not be satisfied either with a night of orgy or the return of rain. Once the people became committed to power, they themselves would produce a greater famine for the poor than the drought ever could. "Yes," he whispered between clenched teeth, "better a short famine of rain than a lifelong famine of bare existence while the poor watch the powerful increase their luxury."

He crossed into Aram-Damascus soon and was in less danger from Ahab, since King Ben-hadad was the Israelite king's archenemy. Nevertheless, Yahweh's curse by the mouth of his prophet would be well known here and the people as anxious as Israel for the drought to end. But he was not known by sight, so careful travel during the day still was possible.

Elijah stood on the beach for a moment, then gave himself over to the invitation. He stepped into the water, bent over, and splashed some of it onto his face. Then he waded farther out and broke into a swim. The water was not cold once he adjusted to it. Turning back toward the shore, he made the distance in a few strokes. Revived, the dust rinsed from his clothes and body, he strode back onto the red lava soil and sat on a black rock.

The morning sun shoved the shadows downward from the hills that rose to the west. A single lark began to sing, then was joined by another and another until the new morning was filled with their silvery joy. The reflection of Mount Hermon took shape in the clear water, and Elijah noticed fishermen at work some distance from shore. Their trade would become increasingly important as the drought continued.

The prophet found a secluded spot in one of the several wadis that ran east from the sea. He slept only three hours, then resumed his journey. He moved faster in the day, skirting the impassable Jordan above the sea by climbing to the high tableland to the east.

The dark red soil of Bashan stretched as far as he could see. Below him, hid in the twelve-hundred-foot-deep chasm, the black rocks beat the Jordan's wild torrent into foam. The vast twin ranges of the Lebanon mountains rose awesomely directly north. The peaks of Mount Hermon filled the sky. Across the valley of Coele-Syria to the west was Mount Lebanon. Through the wild gorges, steep cliffs, and torturous rivers and wadis he must travel to Zarephath. He forced the trip from his mind. One day at a time. One foot in front of the other until the journey's end.

The sun shining directly from the west was hard, and as he turned east his shadow fell long before him. He could see a long distance across the treeless plain. Sheep grazed in distant clumps on the brown grass. Beyond them was a cluster of black goathair tents. He headed toward them to claim the hospitality that traditionally was extended to the traveler.

Barking dogs announced Elijah's approach to the tents soon enough for the ruling sheik to meet him on the plain. By the time they arrived at the door of the largest tent, wine was ready and poured. Happily and gratefully, Elijah drank his first taste of wine since he spent the night with Rejab many months before.

The sheik was not fond of Israelites, but, as custom required, he made Elijah a welcome guest, the more because he was a prophet. Discourtesy to a prophet was not at all wise, even if the prophet served another god.

When Elijah revealed who he was, the sheik looked at him in stunned horror, but he quickly regained control of himself, then avoided any reference to Yahweh or to the drought. There was no point in antagonizing a prophet who, just possibly, really was in control of the weather. But on the next day, after Elijah left, the leaders of the clan would talk long about the battle of the heavens.

The evening meal, though quickly prepared, was sumptuous. Elijah slept well that night, though the strangeness of sleeping on a mat under cover of a tent caused him some difficulties at first. The next morning, after a breakfast of breadcakes and goat's milk, the sheik provided the prophet with a pouch of nuts and bread, and a skin of water. "Your journey will be dry today," he insisted, "and the food will last you for two days." Then, just as Elijah was departing, the sheik asked—half begging, half demanding—for a blessing.

"You have been kind to Yahweh's prophet," Elijah answered, "and though the drought will continue, may Yahweh guide you to good pastures and running water, and may you come through the drought without the loss of a single sheep or goat." Elijah's voice grew stern then. "But I adjure you in the name of Yahweh that you tell no one that you have seen me. If you do, all that I have blessed you with will be removed and the drought will render you poor."

The sheik nodded his thanks and understanding of the condition.

Elijah hoped to reach the Beth-gad road and spend the night somewhere below the summit of Mount Hermon. The cool daytime weather of the early winter made for comfortable walking, but he was glad he would not have to sleep in the open here on the plain, for the winds that blow in from the desert at night are quite cold.

Three hours later the prophet neared the border of Israel again. Beth-gad was only four miles to the west, down the steep hill that starts just beyond the strange Lake Phiala. It was an ancient city of gods, and though now part of Israel, Baal was the god most fervently worshiped. Elijah felt the rage build up again inside his chest. He could guess what was taking place that moment at the shrines around the headwaters of the Banias, one of the sources of the Jordan.

An extensive social scheme had developed to accommodate the tragedies that occurred around such shrines. The offspring that came from the sexual unions were set apart as holy, partly revered, partly disdained, to spend their lives wandering from shrine to shrine or, if they were more fortunate, to serve as priest to a wealthy family or even perhaps in a temple. But the real tragedy was the child who, perhaps stoic, perhaps screaming, certainly terrified, was sacrificed to appease Melkart or Asherah in hopes that Baal would reverse the family's bad fortune.

There would be more of that, Elijah knew, as the drought continued. Desperately religious parents, groping for some way to call Baal's attention to their plight, would make the supreme sacrifice to prove their allegiance to their god. At times an entire city would organize a mass ritual of child sacrifice. At the end of such a day the streams that ran below the altars would be red with blood, and the smell of burned flesh would fill the air. Parents would watch in stunned silence until grief tore shrieks of despair from the mother's throats and fathers would clench their teeth to remain strong while tears welled from their eyes to flow down cheeks of faith.

Elijah turned his face upward. "Is this the only way, my Lord?" he asked. "Must children die because of the drought?" But he knew God's answer even as he talked, for Yahweh had spent long years coping with the problem. The prophet looked northeast toward Damascus. Child sacrifice was a way of life there—at the beginning or end of a military campaign, at the start of the planting season, whenever the spring or winter rains were a little late in coming. And child sacrifice had seared the consciences of the people so long that they became cruel, like Nahash who demanded of every man of Jabesh-gilead that he yield to having one of his eyes put out.

Baal had the great advantage of building on superstitions. There below him, at Beth-gad, the headwaters of the river came gushing from a cave at the foot of a great iron-red sheer limestone cliff. Only the gods can provide water, the ancient Canaanites had believed, so this spot where water suddenly is plentiful must be holy to the gods. And is that not Mount Hermon that towers above, the very citadel of the gods? Does not mist come from its summits? Do not its slopes hold snow all the year around?

Yahweh would not claim such a home, and since he does not, it must be because the god at Beth-gad is stronger, at least here, than Yahweh. And now the Baal priests claimed the spot for Melkart and Asherah, so Baal must be the strongest of all.

Yahweh, then, must be weak, with his demands that the widow and orphan be cared for, that the foreigner be treated with compassion, that every man be given a piece of land to be his own, that a man and wife dedicate their entire lives to each other, that in business dealings men be fair and honorable.

The prophet resumed his journey, tired more from his thoughts than from his walk. Shortly, he would be climbing upward, into the evergreen oaks of Hermon's lower ridge, to pass shrine after shrine—or rather, small temples, some thirty to fifty feet long—strewn all along the base of the great mountain. At every one of them, pilgrims or nearby farmers prayed and sacrificed animals to entice Baal to send rain.

Ten miles later, toward evening, Elijah gained the road from Beth-gad to Hermon's summit. The night would not be pleasant, though the small trees and bushes that lined each semblance of a wadi would divert the chill winds. But his mantle was warm and he would sleep well enough.

The sun reached the slopes of Mount Hermon early. Its rays filtered through the branches to wake Elijah up just at sunrise. Sitting up, he pulled his mantle up and shoved his arms through the holes at each corner, then tied the band at the neck.

When he emerged from the clump of trees, he noticed a sparse but long trail of people ascending the road toward Hermon. He looked toward the summit. The slopes hid the peak from view, but a cloud of smoke filled the sky above, climbing high into the clear blue of the new morning.

Four roads ran to the temple at the top of Mount Hermon. One, far around on the eastern side, provided a fairly easy ascent for worshipers from the region of Damascus. Two difficult roads wound upward from the west for the Baal worshipers of the great valley between Mount Hermon and Mount Lebanon. One of them, on which the prophet watched the thin trail of climbers, would bring a few Canaanites and many Israelites from Beth-gad, Dan, and all the region of the headwaters of the Jordan.

Caution drew Elijah back into the trees, but as he watched the pilgrims laboriously force themselves up the mountain he knew he must find a way to witness the ceremony which could only be attended by the hardy. Older people would observe in lower temples what obviously was a public call to worship and sacrifice.

As he watched, he heard the unmistakable cries and chants of a group of prophets. Looking down the road, he saw them dancing and twirling in the strange manner they had of jumping and twisting around in the air. Quickly, he made his way to the road to join them as they passed. Soon, he knew, their physical antics would diminish from fatigue, though he would have to chant and wail himself often enough to appear as one of them.

The climb to the summit became more torturous as it steepened and the air became thinner. The thin covering of evergreen oaks dissipated. The prophets, now wheezing and light-headed, forced themselves over bald gray limestone for the last two thousand feet. The mountaintop, over 9200 feet high, was almost level.

A rock wall was arranged in a circle like a pinwheel to surround the summit. From its center rose the huge column of smoke that formed the cloud Elijah had seen from below. He left the band of prophets to avoid the inevitable conversation that would expose him, and tried to appear in a prophet's trance as he walked around the wall to the opening in the pinwheel. There at the entrance stood a nearly square temple which he guessed to be over thirty feet each way. Throngs of worshipers waited in line to enter, some of them quiet, some talking as though on an outing, some with hands raised ecstatically toward the smoke-filled heavens.

Elijah passed through the wide entrance beside the temple and into the walled enclosure of the pinwheel. An earthen cone rose three times a man's height in the center. Flames leaped from a large and deep hole at its top. Wide billowing clouds of smoke and occasional tongues of fire rose to the chants of a ring of Baal priests who stood nearly shoulder to shoulder around the base of the cone. Worshipers thronged every available space between the priests and walls, chanting in rhythm with the priests, raising and lowering their arms in accord.

The sun already was high, hazy but still blinding through the smoke. Elijah knew he must leave. He would not keep silent when the orgy started, certainly not when the chosen beauty and her male companion were thrown into the open fiery pit and the ear-piercing, horrendous, screaming wail of the crowd joined the burning flesh of the sacrifice to Baal. *See,* the people would reason, *we give you the best of our lives; can you but give us now the means to life?* The prophet made his way out of the enclosure.

Directly east of him lay Phoenicia. The coast stretched long, etched against the sea in varying colors. Its narrow plain sometimes disappeared completely as the Lebanon Mountains forced their way to the sea. There was Tyre, the home of infamous Jezebel, and Sidon, and the vast stretch of sea beyond. Between the two harbors, hidden by the mountains, was Zarephath, his destination.

He shook his head. Perhaps he should not have come here. Looking over the land, the task of proclaiming Yahweh seemed too formidable. There was Samaria, disdaining the conservatism of its southern brothers to lose itself in a mirage of power and wealth at the cost of truth, closing its eyes to the evils of its pragmatic and open-minded acceptance of patently false ideas that it would not examine. And there, beyond his range of vision to the south, stretched the conservative Judah, whose people carved life out of the hardness of the desert, but whose stern religion and fiercely independent politics sometimes perverted Yahweh worship into a parody of truth. Even so, Judah worshiped Yahweh passionately. Their King Jehoshaphat established a reign of justice based on the Law.

How could Yahweh break through Samaria's shell? How could he win at all without some spectacular display of power? An emptiness, quite apart from his hunger, gnawed at Elijah's stomach. *How many people are down there under the sweep of my eyes?* he thought. *Ten times ten thousand? Or double that? Or more? And every single one of them with a separate shell.*

Elijah turned to the Hasbeiya road that moved down Hermon's west slope, wishing he had not come to this peak. Far below and to the north, Baal-bek stood out prominently. It was the home of the most magnificent temples ever erected to the Baals. The city's reputation was widespread. He had heard even of Israelites who went there to worship, and Jezebel made annual pilgrimages to the temple city.

The western slopes of Mount Hermon received more rain than the eastern slopes, and so was greener by far. The change of scenery quickened Elijah's flagging spirit.

It was dusk when he neared the city of Hasbeiya. The houses were almost concealed among the terraces and trees. Some late workers still plodded up the hill below the city toward the large double gates. Elijah made his way around the walls to the wadi in hopes of refilling his empty waterpouch. The wadi was dry, though, and he had no vessel to draw water from the well that stood nearby. He shrugged and turned to descend the slope down to the Hasbany River.

He slept on a patch of grass and awoke the next morning to the sound of voices. The prophet opened his eyes to the stares of women, each of whom balanced a waterjar on her head. They looked at him only a moment, then went about their business of filling the pots. *The well by the wadi must be dry,* Elijah thought.

He walked to the women, who watched him quizzically but unafraid as he approached. "I want to cross the mountain," he said. "What is the best way to go?"

The women looked at one another, recognizing by his accent that he was an Israelite and by his clothing that he was a prophet. "Why do you not go down through Ijon and around the mountain?" one asked.

"I must cross the mountain," Elijah answered evenly, cautious not to reveal that he must not cross into Samaria.

The women stared at him and jabbered. Two turned and walked away. Three remained, impatiently, and at last the more responsive one said, "The mountain is cold now."

"Yes, I know," Elijah responded.

The woman shrugged. "Very well. Cross the river here and go toward the sea. In about two hours, perhaps less, you climb a ridge to a little village. Down from the village you will go along a trail, very treacherous I am told, to the Kuweh. The Kuweh is a natural bridge that will take you across the Leontes River. From there travel will be difficult, and I do not know the way. Ask someone at the village how to get to Mashgharah, where mulberries grow. There is a road from there to Jazzin and on to Sidon."

Elijah smiled broadly. "Thank you," he said. The woman turned back to her work. He refilled his waterpouch, then waded across the Hasbany, clenching his teeth at its cold waters, and started up the rock-strewn hill that enclosed the river.

The day's journey took him upward into the majestic Lebanons until he made his way along ever-deepening chasms. He gathered nuts and olives when he could, daring the precipitous cliffs to reach fruit the villagers had not harvested because of the danger. He crossed the roaring

Leontes River over the natural bridge called the Kuweh, and made his way to the mulberry village of Mashghareh. So far, all was as the woman had predicted.

Jezzin, he learned from Mashgharah's villagers, was his next destination. It was only five miles away, if he could fly like the raven, but the city lay sheltered among high, rocky cliffs, and so the prophet's journey would be double the distance.

He would have to hurry to reach Jezzin before the gates closed for the evening. The air already was cold, and the night would be freezing. He broke into a trot, which he maintained until he reached the steep climb up into Jezzin's protected valley.

Chapter Nine

ELIJAH PASSED THROUGH the city gates under the scrutiny of gatekeepers. He addressed them, "Are there Israelites in Jezzin?"

"Yes," came the answer. "Go down this street to the marketplace and ask for Eliham."

He nodded and made his way through the late afternoon bustle. Coming to the marketplace, he interrupted a small man who barked out his wares while stacking foodstuff in front of him. "I am looking for Eliham."

The man did not pause in his chantlike announcements, but pointed to his left with two fingers. Elijah assumed he meant two booths, so he passed one and stopped at the next. "Eliham," he called. A head raised. "Eliham?"

"I am Eliham."

"I am Elijah, a prophet of Yahweh. Would you give me lodging for the night?"

A look of surprise swept over the man's face, and a smile spread quickly. He rose to his full height, arms outstretched. "Come, come." He spoke loudly and caught Elijah in his arms. Pulling the prophet into an embrace, he clapped him on the back and kissed both cheeks.

Elijah, surprised at the exuberant greeting, looked up at the man's face. Eliham was a head taller than the prophet, with a broad chest and square shoulders. His hair, capped with a headcloth tied by a bluish-purple band, fell below his shoulders.

"You know of me, here at Jezzin?" Elijah asked.

"Yes, I know of you, and you have a great surprise in store. Come, help me close the booth, and we will go home."

Together, the two men packed the wheat, olives, and nuts into large woven baskets and loaded them onto two donkeys. Only when they were finished and leading the donkeys out of the din of the marketplace did Elijah ask, "What surprise did you speak of?"

Eliham chuckled. "You will see."

As they wound through streets that followed the contours of the valley, Elijah learned that Eliham's house sheltered the only Israelites in Jezzin.

"This is a pagan place," he told the prophet, and pointed to the mountain that rose high above the eastern side of the city. "Up that mountain are groves of very old oak trees. In the largest grove is a shrine. In years past, I am told, it was where the people of Jezzin worshiped their own baal. But now it is the home of the Great Baal worshiped by Jezebel.

"Through Jezzin," he continued, "passes a fair road from Sidon to Damascus. The people here learned of the power of Melkart and Asherah from the merchants who passed through. They came to believe that everyone really worships the same god, so they transferred their allegiance from their little baal to the Baal of great nations."

Eliham shook his head. "Isn't that the way of men, Elijah? To throw off a foolish superstition for a more respected one and believe in so doing that they discover truth?"

Elijah did not smile.

Eliham continued. "There are villages all over these mountains and in the valleys. Every one of them has at least one shrine to some baal. Some of the people, especially the old ones, still believe in their little baals, but . . ." He paused and looked at Elijah. "Now they are all turning to the big Baal." He stopped the donkeys and gripped Elijah by the arm. "Melkart and Asherah are winning, prophet of Yahweh."

The sense of despondency that swept over Elijah as he viewed the panorama from Mount Hermon rose again in his throat. He answered firmly, hiding his concern. "No. Baal will not win." He looked hard into Eliham's eyes. "Baal will not win," he repeated softly.

Eliham looked away and pulled the donkeys into a walk. In a few minutes they arrived at a square rock house. An open, arched portico was set in the center of the front wall, with two windows fixed on each side. A second-story room was built on one third of the flat roof, and a staircase ran up the opposite side wall from the room.

The host led the way behind the house to a rock enclosure, where the two men stored the produce in a well-built shed. Eliham locked the gate from inside the enclosure and they went into the house through a back entrance.

Three faces looked up at the men as they entered. Ruth, Eliham's wife, greeted her husband, "You are home early, Eliham." Then she noticed the guest and rose to meet him.

But Elijah was staring at the other two faces in shocked surprise. The two faces, wide-eyed and open-mouthed, broke into excited smiles. The man and woman struggled simultaneously to rise from the table.

Rejab reached Elijah first and the two men embraced. Miriam was at his side, pulling the prophet's head down to kiss his cheek. Eliham stood to one side with his wife, smiling into her questioning eyes. When the first excitement of the greeting began to abate, he caught Elijah's arm.

"Elijah, meet my wife, Ruth."

Ruth reached out both her hands to his. "You are Elijah, the prophet of Yahweh?"

He nodded.

She squeezed his hands tightly. "You are welcome in our house, Elijah." She beckoned toward the table. Eliham quickly drew up another stool for the prophet, while Ruth poured wine for them all.

Seated, Elijah grasped Rejab's fat arm. "How do you come to be here, my friend?"

Rejab looked at Miriam, then back at the prophet. "Elijah," he began, "matters became very hard in Israel. I had to choose. Either I had to cheat in order to compete and keep my business or I had to lose my business and starve." As he related the incidents of false weights and foreclosures, Elijah sat without speaking, but Miriam noted the gradual tightening of muscles in the prophet's arms and neck. She noted, too, that he ate the food slowly that Ruth set before him.

"And so," Rejab concluded, "Miriam and I decided to come here to her cousin's house at Jezzin."

Eliham interrupted. "Rejab is a good merchant. We have combined our efforts. He spends his time buying, while I spend my time selling. My market—*our* market—is open more now than when I either had to wait for farmers to bring in their produce or close shop and go into the fields to buy."

Rejab smiled excitedly. "I travel even beyond the farmlands of Jezzin now, into Coele-Syria, or the plain of Ijon. When no more grain is available, I will go to Sidon for fish."

"We are getting along well, Elijah, the four of us working together," Ruth added. "Not as well as before the drought, but better than most."

"I am glad," Elijah said softly. Then he asked, "But do you not have the same problems of weights and measures here that you had in Bethshean?"

Eliham laughed. "No, Elijah. Here I am one of the largest merchants. Since Rejab came, the two of us handle more produce than anyone. We are big fish in a small pool, rather than the other way around. We are honest, and the others must follow our lead or lose their customers." Eliham's voice deepened and grew more cautious. "Elijah, when will the drought end?"

"You said Melkart and Asherah are winning?"

"Yes, I said that."

"The famine will not end until the people know beyond a doubt that it is Yahweh who controls the rain."

Eliham poured wine into his cup. "And suppose that day never comes?"

"The day will come," Elijah insisted, "and when it comes, even you, Eliham, will know that Yahweh is God."

"I know it now," he responded sternly.

"You know Yahweh is God, but you really do not believe he is stronger than these forces of evil."

The host set his cup down and stared at the prophet.

"You don't believe Yahweh can defeat his adversary, do you, Eliham?" Elijah repeated.

"And do you never have doubts about the outcome, Elijah?"

The prophet looked from one inquiring face to another. "Yes," he answered finally. "I have moments of doubt."

"Then why do you judge us?" Ruth interjected.

"I do not judge you. I simply state that Yahweh has said he will win. What he says, he will do. Baal is very strong even in Israel. How Yahweh will win I cannot say. But he will win. My certainty is greater than my doubt."

Eliham rose from the table. "It is time for sleep."

Ruth handed Elijah an oil lamp. "You will sleep in the guest chamber upstairs," she said, and smiled tenderly at this prophet she wished she could believe. "Sleep well, and come down only when you are ready."

"Thank you, Ruth. Good night, my friends." He turned to go outside and up the side stairway, then stopped at the door. "Yahweh *will* win," he said.

He awoke early and lay for a while thinking of the conversation of the night before. *Even Yahweh's faithful do not believe he will win,* he thought. *What must Yahweh do then to convince those who do not believe?* Three years of drought. Elijah began to see why Yahweh had to make the famine so long. The victory over Baal must be a resounding one.

Breakfast was not strained as Elijah had feared it would be. Eliham assured the prophet that he would pray hard for Yahweh to give him faith. Rejab and Miriam, always stalwart supporters, told him of the widespread knowledge throughout Israel of his pronouncement.

"But they still pray to Baal, just in case he is stronger than Yahweh," Elijah countered, recalling the scenes he witnessed on his journey.

"Yes," Rejab answered. "But they know that Yahweh has spoken. That's the first step to victory."

Elijah left as early as possible. His pouch was full of breadcakes and his head was full of directions. He must travel west for a short distance to a difficult road that cuts south. The next day he would stand by the Great Sea.

The sun stood high at noon when the prophet caught sight of the dark soil of the sea coast, a muted contrast against the blue waters. He turned south to follow the ancient dirt road down the coast. Occasionally, he slowed his walk to watch the sails of a ship glide effortlessly along the surface, an intriguing wonder for the prophet from Gilead.

The mountains edged in closer toward the sea as he continued, soon closing the plain almost completely. There, on the point, was his journey's end. Zarephath stood gleaming in the sun. In her harbor, low-slung ships with sails down sat at peace.

Ahead, he saw a woman come out of the city's gates and approach a small cluster of trees that grew near the edge of the harbor. She bent to pick up some dry twigs from under the trees, added them to the small bundle in her left hand, then stood upright, her eyes searching the trunk of the tamarisk. Grimacing each time as the twig snapped, she broke several dead twigs that jutted lifeless from the trunk.

Engrossed in her task, she did not notice Elijah's approach. "I could use a drink of water," he said softly.

The woman jerked around, startled, and dropped the sticks she had so painstakingly collected. As Elijah bent to pick them up, she looked at him carefully. His rough, sturdy mantle and stiff leather girdle marked him as a prophet, while his unruly, abundant hair and beard frightened her. He obviously had tried to wash off the dust and dirt from some journey, for she could detect streaks on the backs of his legs. His clothes were filthy.

He stood and handed her the sticks. She was a stout woman, but the loose skin at her cheeks and neck revealed the famine's effects. Her head was covered with a shawl, and a wide, loose tunic hung from her shoulders to the ground. She was almost as tall as he was, and he looked straight into her eyes, which were lined with strong but thin eyebrows.

"Please," he said, "I am very thirsty. Please bring me a vessel of water to drink."

She could hardly refuse. Custom demanded that she not turn a stranger away without water.

"Very well," she answered. "I will return in a few minutes." She moved toward the city gate, clutching her bundle of twigs.

Perhaps this is the widow God had in mind, Elijah thought. He called after her. "Bring me a bit of bread, if you will, just a small piece."

She stopped and faced him, her eyes unblinking, a look of placid resignation on her face. The two looked at each other a moment before she spoke. "I'm sorry. I have no food to give you."

Elijah felt a stirring in his chest, a sign, he felt, that this must be the right woman. He pressed his request. "None at all?"

The woman did not move. She stared at him, her jaws tightening, and Elijah saw tears form in her eyes. "No," she said. A tear slid down her cheek, but she made no effort to brush it away. The prophet did not speak, and she mistook the look in his eyes for disbelief. "I am telling you the truth." Still Elijah only looked at her. She gripped the bundle of twigs tightly and shook her head.

Anger at his unfeeling attitude rose to her throat. "As the Lord Yahweh your God lives," she swore, "I do not have a cake of bread in the house. All I have is a handful of meal left in my barrel, and a tiny bit of oil in my cruse." She thrust her handful of twigs toward him. "I just gathered a few sticks to return home and cook a last meal for myself and my son." The tears flowed freely now, but she still looked straight into his eyes. She shook the sticks at him. "Then we will just wait to starve to death." Her words were more resigned than bitter.

Elijah spoke softly. "Don't be afraid. Trust in my God. Go prepare that last meal for you and your son. But first, prepare a small cake for me. Yahweh makes a promise to you, and I stand as witness to it, that your barrel will not run out of meal and your cruse of oil will not become empty. Your provisions will last until my God sends rain to end the famine."

The woman stood immobile for a moment, then raised her free hand to her face. Finally, she lowered her hand and looked at him again. Elijah did not rush her response, but allowed her time to think and consider. "Yahweh will do that," she asked, "just for giving you a small breadcake?"

He smiled. "Ahab is searching all of Israel for me, for it is at my mouth that Yahweh will bring the rain. I came to Zarephath to hide. I shall stay with you and your son."

"If your mouth controls the rain, why don't you call on it to come and save us all a lot of grief?"

"Yahweh will not send rain until my people are ready to turn away from Baal."

"You are asking me to choose Yahweh now over Baal?"

Elijah did not speak.

The woman pulled her shawl across her face. "Very well," she said, "I have nothing to lose. I have prayed enough to Asherah. She is of no help." She turned toward the gate. "Come with me, prophet of Yahweh."

Elijah followed her, a few steps behind as she led the way through the gate and up the streets of Zarephath. A short walk brought them to a small stone house. Mortar had fallen out from between some of the stones. Its second-story guest chamber was little more than a lean-to, built of rough, undressed wood and roofed temporarily with branches to form an enclosed arbor. A rope, hung with clothes, stretched from the front corner of the lean-to to a rock pillar at the stairway end of the roof.

"Why did you bother to wash if you were about to die?" Elijah asked.

"Water is free and the well is not dry. If my son and I must die, we will die as honorably as possible." She entered the lower door and signaled Elijah to follow.

A half-grown boy sat listlessly on a low stool. He raised his head and looked at Elijah, then at his mother. The woman did not smile, but moved to the back wall of the house. She took two large jars from a shelf and tucked them into the arm that held the twigs, then she went out the back door to the oven in the enclosure behind the house. She nodded as she passed her son. "Give the prophet a drink of water."

The boy stared, immobile, at Elijah.

"My name is Elijah. What is yours?"

The boy did not answer, and the prophet could read no emotion on his face. "I am a prophet of Yahweh," Elijah persisted. "What is your name?"

"I am Bosheth." The boy's lips hardly parted as he spoke.

"My throat is dry. Will you get me a drink of water?"

Bosheth moved then, slowly. He took a small bowl from a shelf, removed a cover from a large earthen jar, and dipped the bowl. Elijah looked at the boy's thin arms. When Bosheth turned toward him with the bowl of water the prophet caught the drawn look on his face. He took the bowl from the boy's hands. "Trust me," he said quietly. "My God Yahweh is going to feed the three of us."

Bosheth raised his eyes. He had his mother's features, and Elijah guessed that if it were not for the famine the boy would be stocky. His shoulders were broad for a nine-year-old, but bony. "Are you going to stay here?" the boy asked.

"Yes," Elijah responded. "I shall stay in the guest room upstairs."

The boy turned and walked outside to join his mother. Elijah could hear them arguing, until the mother's voice rose angrily to order the boy quiet. The voices died down, but Bosheth did not return.

Elijah found a stool and sat down. The house was small, with only one room. A table was set to one side, and four wooden stools were placed against two walls. Shelves were attached to the back wall, near the door, with utensils and vessels of various sizes stacked neatly on them. The waterpot was on the floor beside the shelves, with two smaller pots beside it for bringing water from the town well. The other side of the room was bare except for a stack of neatly folded covers.

The woman returned after awhile with a medium-sized individual cake. She held the still-steaming bread in her hand with a cloth. She set it on the table without saying a word, then went to Elijah, took the bowl from his hands, refilled it, and set it beside the cake. "Now, prophet of Yahweh," she said with slight belligerence, "you have your food. Eat."

Elijah pulled the stool to the table. He broke off a piece of the round, flat breadcake and stuffed it into his mouth, then drank from the waterbowl. Not until he had eaten half of the cake did he look up. The woman stood beside her son, one arm around his shoulders, the other arm hard at her side. Her fist was tightly clenched. The boy's eyes darted from the prophet to his mother and back to the prophet.

Elijah took another bite. "You cook a good cake," he taunted, testing her decision. Tears welled into her eyes and she held her son more tightly.

The boy could stand it no longer. He wrenched himself from his mother's hold and ran to Elijah. The prophet raised his arm just in time to deflect the small fist that came hard toward his face. Bosheth's thin arms flailed at Elijah, but the prophet caught every blow on his arm. The boy screamed, "You thief!" and in exasperation ran to the sleeping pads on the other side of the room and buried his face in them.

Elijah looked at the woman. Her face was buried in her hands. He took the last bite of the cake and turned the waterbowl up to drink the rest of it.

He set the bowl down, then rose and went around the table to the woman. He pulled her hands into his and held them until she looked up. Her face was wet, the flesh puffed from her silent crying. "Now," he said, "go and fix that meal for yourself and your son."

She stared into his eyes.

"You proved your confidence in Yahweh," he said, "even in spite of your fear and anger, as you watched me eat the last of your food. You would have stopped me if your doubt had been stronger than your faith. Go and cook the meal."

Slowly, she pulled her hands away from Elijah's, still staring with wonder at him. She backed away, then turned at the door and walked to the oven. She bent down to the two small jars and looked into each one. Her eyes widened. She picked up one of them and reached into it with her fingers to confirm what her eyes saw. A powdered grain met her touch. She reached into the other jar, then pulled back her fingers. She held them up in the sunlight. Clear oil glistened on their tips. She looked back toward the house, then up toward the sky. With stiff, uncertain steps she walked toward the open door. Elijah stood just inside. She collapsed to her knees and threw her arms around his ankles. Oblivious to the soil that covered them, she began to kiss his feet. The boy watched in amazement from the pads.

Elijah reached down to pull her up. Holding her shoulders, he spoke softly but firmly. "I did not give you the oil and meal. Yahweh did. Do not kneel before me." He pulled her to him and held her until her weeping subsided. Then he pushed her away gently. "The boy is hungry," he said. "Go and prepare his food."

Chapter Ten

THE SHARP POINT of the awl touched Baana's ear. The
priest jabbed the tool quickly through the flesh until its
point pressed into the piece of thick leather he held behind
the lobe. Baana did not flinch. He stared ahead, at nothing. The villagers clustered in the street around the door
of the sanctuary to watch the ceremony. Abinadab stood
opposite the priest, smiling, dressed resplendently in wine-
colored robes. He was a tall man, broad-shouldered, and
carried himself as a prince might who had earned rather
than inherited his royalty.

Baana's friends watched in silence. Their faces were as
expressionless as the stones of the coastline beyond the
city's gates. The priest reached to take the earring from
Abinadab. As he fitted the mark of ownership into the
newly-pierced ear, the skin of each watching face tightened a bit. Baana was one of their own. Now he was a
slave for life.

The winter wind from the Great Sea brought a chill, and
most of the people stayed no longer than was necessary to
see the ceremony through. They drifted away then, almost

silently, one or two at a time. Baana should have been the first to leave, but he remained at the door. Abinadab reached to take his arm, but the priest signaled the master to leave his new slave alone for a while.

The master walked away. The priest stood beside Baana, watching the crowd disperse. There was no speaking, either from Baana and the priest or from the crowd. Only Baana's slow, labored breathing and the shuffle of sandals on the stone street broke the silence. Closer friends stayed moments longer than the rest, but soon they left, too, until only Baana and the priest remained. The holy man did not speak. He waited for Baana to give some sign of his need. Finally, when the new slave remained silent, the priest clapped him encouragingly on the shoulder, then turned to enter the sanctuary.

Baana still did not move. He stared at but did not see the street or the shops and stalls that lined it. His glazed eyes saw a wheatfield and rows of grapevines, with a watchtower rising from its center. Once it had been his. And his father's. And his father's father's. For centuries. Now it was Abinadab's.

That was before Meor-baal and the prophet companion came to Dor. He had listened to the prophet, and even now with the throb of his ear and the weight of the slave ring he could feel the excitement that grew that night in his loins. With his friend Shammah and several other young men he had run wildly, laughing, up the hill to the sacred grove. He remembered the hot embrace of the zonah under the entwined branches of the oak trees, and on his nakedness the cool breeze from the Great Sea. It had been the most ecstatic night of his life.

When he returned home late in the night his wife had listened well to his recounting of the prophet's talk of fertility. She accepted his visit to the sacred zonah as an act of necessity and worship, and his sexual prowess in their own marriage bed that night certified that the goddess indeed had granted greater fertility to the house of Baana.

She became pregnant that night, another sign of the power of Asherah. The women who talked with her at the well in the chill of the mornings and evenings did not try to conceal their amazement that at last their friend was with child, and because of the intervention of Asherah. She became honored among her friends.

Then they visited the priest of Baal, the holy man Meorbaal sent to dwell at Dor. They told him of their good fortune. Indeed, he told them, it was a clear sign that Asherah had heard their prayers. The spirit of Baal must truly have dwelt in the zonah. But the pregnancy was a test. Surely a child conceived of such a union on such a night was holy to the goddess.

"You must give the child to Asherah," the priest advised. "When it is but a week old, while the redness of the womb still clings to its flesh and yet after it has taken milk at the breast of its mother."

Baana had placed his hand on his wife's stomach that night, and at that moment the baby moved for the first time. It must be another sign. Yes, the priest agreed that it must be another sign. The baby is holy to Asherah.

His wife wept. She wept more as the time of her delivery approached, and Baana tried to understand. But it was the word of the god. Not to give the child to Baal would be to court disaster; to give it would ensure more children, healthy children, boy children, later on. And Baal would bless the grain and the vines with greater heads and larger clusters.

The baby was a boy, another good sign. Shammah had two daughters, almost grown. Until now, they had none. Baana felt regret then, for his joy was great when he saw the boy that had come from his own loins. But he choked back the grief, and he and his wife took the child to the priest on the eighth day.

Together, the three of them mounted the sloping hill to the shrine. Inside, the priest laid the infant on the altar. The baby cried when he was taken from his mother's arms, and louder when he was placed naked on the cold stone of the altar. The zonahs stood outside, their hands joined together to encircle the shrine. They chanted in unison, a monotonous, haunting chant that repeated Asherah's name again and again until the oaks themselves took up the chant, and the leaves and branches spoke her name.

The priest drew a thin-bladed, very sharp knife from a hole bored into the stone of the altar. He turned the infant to its side, and in one swift movement the baby's crying was interrupted by a choking gurgle. Then he was silent. His blood, tapped by expert strokes, ran quickly down the altar's drainhole.

The wife shrieked and collapsed at the first stroke of the knife. Baana caught her and knelt to cradle her in his arms.

"Now," the priest was saying to him, "you must lie quickly with a zonah." He was at Baana's side, pulling at his arm. "Quickly, now, you must select a zonah." He ushered Baana to the entrance. "They are there. Choose one and lie with her beneath the sacred trees."

The priest went to the wife. He held her face in his hands, then with her veil he wiped the tears from her eyes and cheeks. She watched him, dazed, and he removed the veil. She felt his hands take the veil from her head, and as deftly as he handled the knife to draw the blood from her child, she felt his hands pull away her robes. His hands moved to her breasts and his lips to her mouth as he pressed her down onto her strewn robes.

She did not resist, nor did she move as he consummated his act amid the pain and blood of her recent delivery. Her thoughts were on the dead body of the boy child on the altar above them.

Baana carried his wife in his arms back to their home. Neither of them spoke. The priest remained at the shrine. She wept all that night, but when she arose the next morning her face shined with a new radiance. She talked of lying with the gods, both of them, she and Baana. As the days passed and she resumed her place at the well and with the women, she talked more and more about the promises of Asherah. She would have more children. Baana's field would yield more than ever before.

She encouraged Baana to borrow from Abinadab for new tools, and for a new storehouse to store the goods Asherah would give them at the next harvest, and for a new ox to replace the old, tired one that had belonged to his father.

Baana listened to her, excited by the obvious favor Asherah had bestowed on them. He went to Abinadab.

He could not repay the loan. The crops that year were average, but he had planned for abundance. Never in the years before Meor-baal and the prophet came to Dor had Abinadab been so unyielding. The moneylender would not grant an extension. Abinadab took away his field. He could live in his house only if he became a slave.

Through the winter he searched for work, while his wife stayed with Shammah and Shammah's daughters. To repay his friend he helped him break up the field after the early rains loosened the soil. They planted, and then Baana left. There was no work in Dor, and none in Dothan, and none in Samaria. The slaves brought back from Ahab's victories worked the fields of their new masters. An Israelite laborer could not compete. In the end, he returned to Abinadab and gave himself as a slave. The Sabbatic Year was but a year away; then all Israelites who had sold themselves into slavery would be freed. He moved back into the home he had been born in, on the land of his fathers, and worked the land of his fathers for Abinadab.

Before the year was gone, the drought came. Baana could claim his freedom only to see himself and his wife starve. He had no choice.

But he went to talk with Abinadab, to beg him to let him serve until the drought ended, and then to claim his freedom. Abinadab received him well, and even called for wine to be served, but he would not yield.

"Baana," the master said, "Baal's ways are different from Yahweh's. Melkart is the God of Power, and he will make Dor a powerful city. But the old ways must go. A new class of landowners must spring up to make best use of the land, powerful enough to make trade agreements, rich enough to finance great undertakings."

Baana told his master of his experience with Asherah. He told him all of it, and tried to persuade Abinadab that Baal wanted to bless him, too.

Abinadab's answer surprised Baana, but it made sense in a way that never had occurred to him.

"You are a good man, Baana," the master said. "Now that I know of the blessing Asherah has promised you, I consider myself doubly fortunate to have you in my service. Could it be that your blessings will come through me?"

The master talked of his dreams, and his need for men who knew the land and the people, men who could supervise. "You will live better in my service, Baana, than you ever could on your small field. If you serve me well, I will set you over other men. Perhaps one day I may even set you over all my fields." Abinadab embraced him then, and Baana recalled a curious pride at being treated so intimately by such a wealthy and powerful man. He agreed to become a slave for life.

Shammah had been angry. His good friend did not understand. They had argued, and Shammah accused him of giving up his birthright. But what is freedom? He was free only to starve, to be cast about by the gods of nature who were angry one year and bountiful the next, to borrow money in bad years and repay in good ones. And soon, friend Shammah himself must face the decision. To know that the land he worked was his own, and that it was a legacy to pass to his children, was that sense of freedom worth the suffering required to hold it? Would Shammah choose to be free when faced with the cost of freedom? Baana thought not.

Now, standing alone at the door to the sanctuary, staring up and down the empty street, feeling the painful weight of the slave ring in his earlobe, the decision did not feel as he had thought it would. It was too final. He would work the land of his fathers, but the land would not be his. The grain and wine were Abinadab's. He was Abinadab's. His children would be Abinadab's.

But no matter. The choice had been made. It was done now, and it must be the way of Baal. Perhaps Asherah and Melkart blessed Abinadab more because he worshiped more. Perhaps so.

Baana pulled himself out of his trance and descended the

stairs. "Yes," he whispered aloud, "I shall worship more."
Perhaps one day Asherah would give her reward.

Shammah had been the last witness to leave. He could
hardly keep his knees from melting under him as he
watched the slave ring slip through his friend's earlobe.
What was he to say now, after the argument of last night?

Their eyes met several times, twice since all had left
save the two of them and the priest. In the end, he decided not to speak. Baana's eyes were far away, seeing visions known only to him. There would be time later to talk.

Shammah left through the city gates and turned to walk
around the walls toward his home, one of a cluster of houses
located beyond Dor's walls, on the fertile plain that rose
slowly into the hills of Sharon.

His mind could not grasp the unnatural change occurring
at Dor. Should one man own so much, and so many own so
little? Had not Yahweh given laws through Moses that provided every family with its own land forever? Did not the
land itself belong to Yahweh, to be held in solemn trust by
his people? Were not the wealthy ordered by divine law to
lend money compassionately?

Where was Yahweh? Was he now the god of the
drought? Was Baal indeed the stronger god, as Meor-baal
and the prophet had claimed? And should poor men serve
the stronger?

Shammah walked along the roadway by the field that he
soon would lose. The wind played among the now-dead
leaves and vines, its whispering sound speaking a language
of the earth. The language had been learned by his ances-
tors during the days of Joshua, and the language was taught
from generation to generation. The whispering wind said
the field was Yahweh's and should not leave the family to
whom God lent it. It said no man should have more than
he needed at the cost of his brother man's insufficiency.
But what could he do? He will lose the field. Already he

had protested to the elders, but they said nothing could be done. He had agreed to pay the money from the harvest, and he could not. No matter that he would have paid if he could. He did not pay. That was all that mattered.

He entered the house and closed the door behind him, already determined to do what he had sworn he would not do. He would not fight Baal. The God of Power was too strong, perhaps even too strong for Yahweh. But his daughters would not become slaves. No, he could do something about that.

The daughters rose to greet him, but stopped when they saw the unfamiliar look on his face.

"Father?" Maachah, the older one, called. "What's wrong?"

Shammah pulled a stool to the table and beckoned to the girls. "Sit down, my daughters, I must talk with you."

The daughters were only a year apart. The oldest one was seventeen now and already would have been married, probably, if it were not for the drought. Both of them had the attractiveness of youth, though they tended toward the plumpness of their mother. It was good that she was three years dead. It was good that she could not see what the family had come to. What Dor had come to.

Maachah and Zelophed took their accustomed places at the table, across from each other. Shammah looked at both of them. They were more inquisitive than frightened, though their knowledge of Baana's ceremony raised their concern about the coming discussion.

"Baana and his wife will be slaves for the rest of their lives," he began, "and their children will be slaves, too, if they have any more."

"But the Year of Jubilee," Maachah interrupted. "Won't they be freed then and their field returned to their family?"

Shammah answered quickly. "I know of no Israelite who has been freed this year, and this is the Year of Jubilee. Why should any slave hope for better fifty years from now?"

The girls were silent.

"I am about to lose our field to Abinadab. You both are

aware of that. Baana gave himself to Abinadab because he couldn't make a living even for himself, much less sufficient to repurchase his field."

"And so you will sell us into slavery," Zelophed stated simply. "What you say we will do. Other girls have gone." She reached across the table to catch her sister's hand.

"No," the father said. "I will not sell you into slavery."

"Then what?" Maachah asked.

"I will take you to the sacred grove of Asherah."

The girls gripped each other's hands more tightly. Both of them looked at this man who spoke so firmly yet with trembling chin.

"Father, you don't mean that," Maachah protested.

"I do."

"Israel's laws forbid a father to give his daughters to zonahs."

"Baal is stronger than Yahweh. He has shown that."

"But . . ."

Shammah interrupted his daughter. "Better a free zonah than a slavegirl."

"A zonah is not free," Zelophed protested.

"Freer than a slave," Shammah answered, "and you will have a future, perhaps even in a temple. You will be comfortable and perhaps live in a degree of luxury. You may even bear a king."

"That's a dream, father," Maachah argued. "The temple zonahs are raised from young girls."

"You are young, and both of you are intelligent. There is no other alternative. At least you will have hope. Life is worth little without hope. Gather what you will and we will go."

"Now?" Zelophed asked.

"Now. Before I weaken. By nightfall your futures will be secure."

"And what of you, father?" the older one asked.

Shammah shook his head. "By nightfall I shall be a slave to Abinadab. Perhaps by the next Sabbatic Year I shall be free, if I'm still alive, perhaps not."

"Father," Maachah asked, "is there nowhere we can go and stay together? To Samaria, or to Jerusalem?"

"No. There is nowhere to go."

"Why? Why don't we try?"

"Because I have watched others try and fail. Baana failed, and he is a good man. The spirit in Israel has changed. There is no hope any more for the poor. The city holds a worse slavery for us than Abinadab does. Now go. Gather your things."

The girls rose slowly and walked from the table. They slipped their arms around each other, then turned and embraced. Zelophed began to cry. Shammah turned his back and fought his own tears. The girls would not resist. They were obedient, as daughters should be.

The sacred grove was not far, only two miles east up the gradually rising hills. They ate their last lunch together in silence under a lone tamarisk tree by the roadside. Then they walked slowly, still without speaking, to the sacred grove.

Abinadab, seated in his carriage chair, watched the crowd disperse. He never had seen Baana so silent, so passive. The man was known in Dor for his liveliness, his cheerfulness at the festivals and feast days. The master shook away the nagging thought that his new slave would run away. There was no need for that. After all, he had chosen slavery on his own.

He snapped his fingers, then pulled the heavy woven curtains across the openings on each side. Four large, finely-muscled men lifted the carriage chair and broke into a trot, their legs moving in synchronized rhythm. Abinadab relaxed into the soft pillowed back of his seat. He sighed happily. In two years he had become the wealthiest man in Dor, one of the wealthiest in Israel in holdings. *And when the drought is over*, he thought, *those holdings will mean coins and treasure.*

The drought was unexpected. The prophet Elijah claimed credit, and perhaps even proclaimed it, but he was not the one who sent it. No, Asherah sent it, to hasten the acquisitions of those few men such as he who with determination left Yahweh and his weak teachings for Melkart and power.

Abinadab's carriage chair arrived at his home, the home he had acquired but a year ago. It was the largest in Dor, with every room of white limestone, the floors and walls covered and draped with Persian rugs.

The strong men lowered the chair and Abinadab climbed out. His wife greeted him at the door. "It is done," he said.

She clasped her hands to her bosom. "Baana is a good man to own," she answered. "He will do well in the fields."

"And I will do him well, too. He will live better as my slave than he ever did as a free farmer carving a precarious existence out of the soil."

"Asherah is good to all, isn't she?" the wife cooed.

Baana arrived at his master's house in due time and was greeted by his new master with apparent joy. The conversation that followed challenged Baana to his best effort, yet left no room for doubt that he was a slave now. Even though his master would not be cruel, he would require unquestioning obedience. Then Abinadab told Baana to spend the remainder of the day with his wife.

That night, the guests hardly had arrived for Abinadab's banquet when the host was beckoned by his chief steward. The master listened to the message, then gave instructions to keep his guests well supplied with wine.

An hour later two bare-chested, burly servants pulled open the huge cyprus doors that opened from a smaller meeting room and Abinadab entered, smiling widely. The guests turned to greet the return of their host. He mingled with them quickly and easily.

"What took you away from your own party?" one asked. It was Dekar who spoke, the chief of the elders who sat at the entrance to the city.

Abinadab smiled. "I just gained another field and another slave."

"Who was it?"

"Shammah, Baana's good friend. I loaned him money on his field sometime ago, when so many small farmers were convinced that Asherah would increase their crops."

"Shammah? Doesn't he have two marriageable daughters?"

"Yes, but they will not be my slaves. Shammah said he has made other arrangements for them. He probably made zonahs of them. It's not a rare solution these days to avoid slavery."

Dekar grasped and squeezed his friend's arm. "Then we must visit the shrine soon," he laughed. "Abinadab, Asherah has been good to you. Or is it Yahweh?"

"Who knows?" Abinadab laughed. "I try to keep all the gods happy."

"Ah, here comes Beriah to get us," Dekar interrupted. "Machir has a matter to discuss with all of us."

Beriah greeted the wealthy host and the judge. "It is a fine party, Abinadab. Who would know we are in the midst of a drought? Machir says that in such a time the wise man will build for the future."

"I believe he heard that from me." Abinadab laughed again, an easy, comfortable laugh that put people at ease. "And I must admit that it sounds pretty good."

"At any rate," Beriah continued, "Machir has an idea. Will it be an imposition on your party if several of us meet together for a few moments? We are here, and the time is convenient."

"What are parties for, if not to make life better? If Machir has such an idea, I want to hear it speedily. We will meet in the next room, over there." Abinadab gestured toward the cyprus doors through which he had come.

The group gathered quickly. Nine couches of highly polished dark red cedar, trimmed simply but tastefully in ivory, lined the room in a semi-circle, their upcurved heads toward the center. Abinadab, as host, lay on the center couch. An apparently casual but quite aggressive maneuvering began for the couches nearest the center, for proximity to the host indicated relative honor.

1 5 0

The wiry Dekar managed to gain the right-hand seat next to the host. The left-hand couch was taken by a newcomer to the emerging aristocracy, a young man whose father was the officiating priest at the earlier ear-piercing ceremony. Short, bandy-legged Beriah was next, and next to him, two brothers, both of them with severely-trimmed, pointed beards. Machir gained the couch next to Dekar, and next to him, leaving the end couch empty, was Abinadab's son, Hesed.

The chatter ceased as each man took his place, anxious to hear the new idea. Abinadab quickly called for Machir to speak.

"Thank you, Abinadab, for your wonderful party, and for allowing this interruption." He glanced from eye to eye. "My idea is simple, but effective, I believe. For all of Israel's history, farmers have observed the laws of gleaning. Never have we reaped the corners of our fields, nor have we retrieved the grain that was dropped, nor have we picked the olives and grapes the second time. All of this produce was left for the poor, that they might have food to eat."

He paused. His listeners were uneasy, he noticed, and they would respond cautiously to what appeared a call to break an old law that had been so assiduously honored.

"Now," he continued, being careful to force confidence into his voice, "we are in the midst of a drought. Not only the poor but the average farmer and worker as well secures his food with difficulty. We who know better how to stretch the produce . . ." He was interrupted with laughter. "We who know better how to stretch the produce must take the initiative for the good of all Israel."

Dekar shifted his weight, not trying to hide the worried look on his face. "You're speaking of breaking an ancient law of Israel, Machir. You put me in an awkward position."

"Let me finish, friend Dekar," Machir insisted. "Your part in the plan will be honorable."

Dekar gestured for him to continue.

"Elijah is a great and powerful prophet. He said there will be no rain and no dew until he pronounces Yahweh's word that the drought is ended. Perhaps Ahab will find him soon. Personally, I think not. Perhaps Baal is stronger than Yahweh, but Baal has not yet broken Yahweh's drought. We will be wise to assume that the drought will continue.

"We have been able to plant only near the streams that still flow. We will have little grain. The lentils will be like the grain. The olive roots and grape roots will find some water, but those crops will be slim. We must make the best use of what we have, and even at that we will have to buy food from Egypt.

"I propose," he continued, "that all of us reap every head of grain we can, that we send slaves behind the reapers to glean the fields, that we reap the corners, that we pluck every grape from every vine and every olive from every tree. This policy will accomplish two goals. We'll control the supply so that it will be distributed most wisely. Further, because there will be no gleaning for the poor to eat, they will give themselves to us to be our slaves."

"Machir," Dekar interrupted, "I cannot allow such disregard for the laws of Israel."

Machir held up his hands for silence. "Dekar, the poor will starve if the drought continues, and it will continue. We will show compassion if we make them our slaves, for a master is obligated by law to furnish food for his slaves. Many will live who otherwise would die. Should we not break the laws that some may live? Should we not put aside the law to show mercy?"

A chorus of approval greeted Machir's argument, no one caring to test the shallowness of the solution.

"And of course you will release them from slavery in the Sabbatic Year," Dekar said, "and return the land to them or their families."

"Of course," Machir smiled, "according to the laws of Israel. Naturally, if a slave marries during the time, his wife and children are not to be released. That is the law, is it not?"

"Yes," Dekar said softly. He looked at the other men to

study their reactions. Abinadab nodded. At his cue, the other men nodded their agreements.

Abinadab took charge. "Then it is done. To show mercy to the poor, and to provide the best distribution of the available supply of food, we shall reap cleanly and thoroughly. Now, back to the party." He clapped his hands loudly and the doors swung open. The eight men rose from their couches and made their way to the banquet table.

"Abinadab," Beriah complimented, "you set a table fit for a king." The men took their places, and the parade of food began.

Chapter Eleven

THE WOMAN was in the center of the room standing on the stretched out and disheveled sleeping pads when Elijah entered. Her son's ashen face lay still on her shoulder, his arms limp to his sides. She held him stoically, her arms locked under his buttocks.

"Bosheth is dead."

Elijah started to move toward the boy.

"Go away." The woman's voice was low and distant, as though the words were spoken from another part of the room.

"Let me look at the boy."

"No. Go away." The woman turned her back. The boy's mouth was open against the mother's shoulder. His closed eyelids were almost white, his lips dark. The woman was crying now. "What do I have to do with you, prophet of Yahweh?" she accused through her choking voice. "Have you come into my house to call your God's attention to my past sins? Are you here to call Yahweh's attention to me? Is this your God's punishment for the bad things I have done, to take my son's life? Is this really why you came to my house?"

Elijah quietly made his way to her. "Give me the boy."

The woman did not answer. Her shoulders were shaking now, though tears would not come. The prophet grasped the boy under the arms and pulled him from the mother. She did not resist, nor did she watch him as he went toward the door.

Outside, he climbed the stairs to the flat roof and made his way quickly to his loft. His own face was strained as he laid the boy on the bed.

He knelt beside the still body and looked up. He began to pray. "Oh, Yahweh Elohim, my God," he began, "have you brought even more grief to add to this woman's burdens, this woman who gave me, your prophet, a place to stay? Are you taking her son? Is this your will?"

Elijah felt a moving in his body, as though a wind blew deep in his bowels. He looked at the still body before him. The color in the boy's lips was darkening, the limp body becoming colder. With careful precision, he stretched the boy's arms straight out and up from his shoulders, then spread the boy's legs.

The prophet spread himself on top of the boy, his legs on the boy's legs, his arms on the boy's arms. His stomach and chest pressed against those of the boy, and he placed his mouth over the boy's mouth. He began to force his breath into the boy, breathing rhythmically, slowly and deeply, his chest and stomach forcing the movement of the boy's chest and stomach in sequence to his breathing.

After a few moments he moved away from the boy. The color in his face looked better, but the boy still did not breathe. "Oh, Yahweh Elohim, my God," Elijah called out loud, "let this boy's breathing soul come into him again."

The prophet spread himself again on the boy as before. Again he forced breath into the boy's lungs. Silently, he prayed that life would pass from his own organs to those of the boy, from his heart to the boy's heart, from his lungs to the boy's lungs.

Again he rose to look at the boy. Still he did not breathe. Elijah repeated his prayer aloud and again spread himself on the boy. This time he did not rise to measure his progress. He breathed long, carefully, deeply, forcing air into the boy, praying silently to Yahweh, willing with all his mind that his own life forces would pass from his body into the boy's.

He felt a movement under him, and quickly he rolled to the floor. The boy gasped, and his chest arched ever so slightly as wind moved into his throat. As Elijah watched, the breathing became less labored. The boy opened his eyes. They held a look of surprise, as though the boy awoke from a nightmare. He looked at Elijah with apparent difficulty.

"We almost lost you," the prophet said.

The boy smiled feebly. Elijah picked him up and carried him onto the roof. Bosheth did not speak, but he raised one arm weakly to place it around the prophet's neck.

The woman was lying on the pads when Elijah entered. She did not look up. He walked to her. "Bosheth is alive," he said. "Look and see."

The woman turned slowly, unbelieving, and looked up. "Bosheth?" she whispered cautiously.

The boy's voice was weak, but the mother heard him clearly. She whirled to a sitting position and held out her arms. Elijah laid the son against her bosom. She kissed his forehead and clutched him tightly.

"The boy needs fresh air. This summer heat will not aid his recovery. I will take him to my loft and leave the door open to catch the breeze from the sea." Elijah took the boy again from the woman.

The mother followed him as he climbed to the roof and laid the boy on the bed. She looked long at her son, whose skin fast was regaining its color, then turned to Elijah. "There is no doubt in my mind at all now. Bosheth's recovery can only mean that you are a man of God, and that the word of *the* God, Yahweh, is spoken by you."

Elijah turned to leave the woman and son alone. He had not wept in a long time, but he had to clench his teeth hard to fight back the tears. *Is it possible*, he thought, *that if a Gentile woman will believe in Yahweh, Israel also might believe again?*

The summer months passed hot even on the coast of the Great Sea. Elijah and the boy slept on the flat roof and left the upper chamber to the woman, so all three could feel the breeze, however slight, from the sea.

As severe as was the famine in Phoenicia, it was not so hard as in Israel. The Tyrian cloth, dyed from the Murex shellfish in shades of crimson and purple and delicate blue, provided a means of trade. The seagoing nation was able to buy its food from Africa and Asia Minor. Indeed, Tyre even resold food to those in Israel who could pay the price.

It was because of the commerce that Elijah heard news from Israel. No rain had fallen since his pronouncement to Ahab almost a year and a half ago. Nor had the heavy dew come, the dew carried into Israel on the wings of the Great Sea to touch the chill shoulder of Mount Hermon and fall heavy to cover the land, the dew that rises with the morning sun in a mist as heavy as fog.

But the people were not turning to Yahweh. Even more, they prayed and sacrificed and copulated and paid levies to Baal. *Even so,* Elijah thought again and again, *if a Gentile woman will believe in Yahweh, is it possible that Israel might again believe?*

They talked a lot, Elijah, the woman, and Bosheth. The woman was mystified that Israel would serve any other God but Yahweh, and the more so as she heard from Elijah the stories of Israel. He told her of Moses and the plagues that struck the Egyptian taskmasters. He told her of the crossing of the Red Sea, of the manna that fell from the sky to feed the wandering people in the wilderness, of the thundering voice of Yahweh from a smoking Mount Sinai, of the conquering of the land.

Was it not time, she asked the prophet, for Yahweh to send another sign, another miracle to prove his strength?

Yes, it was time. Elijah was convinced of that. But what was the sign to be? He prayed much about it. When the coolness of the winter came and the woman and son moved back to the lower room, the prophet spent long periods in the upper chamber thinking, praying, about the end of the drought and the sign of Yahweh.

It was a chance remark by Bosheth, a reminiscence, that gave the answer. The boy mentioned Mount Carmel to his mother. Had she not gone there to thank Baal for a boy-child? The woman was embarrassed, but, yes, she had gone, before she knew of Yahweh.

Mount Carmel. The ancient mountain that jutted out into the Great Sea like an aggressive guard that dared test the deep mystery of the waters, the god of the land in battle against the god of the waters. A sentinel home of the rival gods since long before Israel's conquest of Canaan, that mountain always had antagonized the prophet of Yahweh. *Even now*, Elijah thought, *Yahweh's shrine lies broken while Israelites worship at the squared-stone shrines of Melkart and Asherah.*

What better battleground of the Gods? Looking over the Great Sea, at its right hand the fertile Valley of Jezreel, at its left the fertile Plain of Sharon, its spine pointing to the fertile Jordan, it was a fit place for Yahweh Elohim, the God of Israel, to put to flight the false Gods of Power and Fertility. But it must be a decisive battle. No doubt must remain among the people as to which God is real.

The winter passed slowly with its dry cold. The people talked in the marketplace of the strangeness of Lebanon whose brown ribs showed hard where usually they glistened white against the winter sun. They talked, too, in the marketplace, of Israel, the land mysteriously cursed by Asherah, more angry at that nation of Yahweh than at them. The caravans of food merchants no longer went into that drier land without contingents of armed soldiers, for the growing numbers of bandits ambushed every caravan and stole every unprotected morsel.

There was no gleaning any more for the poor in Israel, and the famine was so long that the wealthy men no longer could accept slaves, hardpressed as they were to provide for those they already owned. The returning caravaneers talked of beggars by the way, who sometimes threw themselves into their paths in desperation. But the caravans dared not stop, and the soldiers drove their horses through the plaintive cries. Both poor and wealthy foraged or sent slaves to forage the land for food. Every cache of honey was sought out, every carob tree was stripped of its pods, locusts were caught and placed in jars, fowl were hunted by those who could hunt, and wild boar were chased dangerously into the wild marshes and tangled bush.

Yet the people prayed and sacrificed and copulated and paid levies all the more feverishly to Asherah. And the drought did not end.

Dew fell late in the winter on the narrow plain of Phoenicia and on the western slopes of Lebanon. Her people managed to break the earth and plant their crops, a gamble of precious seed that paid, but meagerly, with two light rains as the sparse crop neared its ripening. Yet no dew settled and no rain fell in Israel.

That summer, the third of the drought, was the hottest. Elijah and Bosheth moved to the open roof again, and the woman slept again in the upper chamber. Elijah prayed every day, his face toward Jerusalem, for a word from Yahweh. Yahweh had been silent for many months, save with that constant provision of the oil and meal. It was that constant replenishing that reinforced the prophet's faith during those months of silence.

And the marketplace continued to be a source of news. Elijah never went there himself, since every merchant and caravaneer, every soldier, every king's man was on the alert for the prophet, for Ahab had threatened reprisals against any nation that harbored the man of God. Bosheth, or at times the woman, brought the stories home. The priests and prophets of Baal reigned in Israel, they said. The desperate people paid their levies of precious food for incantations to Asherah, and the priests spilled the blood of now-scrawny lambs and goats, burned a few portions of the meat, and ate the rest. Smiling through jowls made fleshy by the sacrificial meals, they encouraged the people to sacrifice the more to elicit Baal's blessings. The people's eyes stared back at them from gaunt faces to gamble on a word of faint hope.

It was in early winter, two weeks after the early rains should have come, that Yahweh spoke.

Elijah awoke one morning at dawn and knelt in the crisp air on the open roof. As he faced Jerusalem to watch the sun break its way over the mountains, he felt a feeling grow in the pit of his stomach. The feeling burned as though his blood rushed through his veins with quickened speed, to spread throughout his body. The time had come. He could feel it, as though time itself had entered his blood.

He went downstairs to eat his last breakfast with Bosheth and the woman. The oil and meal, he told them, would continue until the earth blossomed in the spring.

The prophet adjusted his leather girdle about his waist, gathered his provisions, and bade good-bye. A few minutes later he passed through the gates of Zarephath and turned south.

"Obadiah is here, my king."

"Good. Show him in." Ahab sat on the smaller throne he preferred to use to conduct the business of the day. He watched his tall governor enter, this immaculately-groomed man who tenaciously but silently clung to his belief that Yahweh was the strongest of the gods. The king was glad Obadiah had done well during the crisis, for Jezebel detested the man. He would be one of Yahweh's martyrs, Ahab knew, were his services not so clearly valuable. "Good day, Obadiah," the king greeted.

Obadiah knelt on one knee briefly, and spoke as his knee touched the highly polished floor. "I trust all is well with you, my king."

"I can answer that when I hear your report."

"It is not good, King Ahab. That is why I requested an audience."

"Then let me hear the worst. Come, sit beside me."

Obadiah stepped up onto the dais and took a lower-backed chair next to the king. He drew a scroll from a fold in his tunic. "I have the records here of the levies from each administrative city since the drought began. Also, I have talked with each district collector of levies. I am prepared to give you as much detail as you wish."

"The details can wait. What is your assessment?"

"I do not believe we should exact any more produce for the royal table, or any more feed for the royal stock. My lord, the people are impoverished for food. Only the priests eat well."

"The priests." Ahab spoke contemptuously. "Asherah protects her own."

"The people are ripe for rebellion. They are not angry with you, but they are desperate. Another levy may well turn their anger toward the royal house."

"Yes. My advisors of state have the same opinion."

"My lord, the stock will die if we do not feed them. Another week and all provisions will be gone. Quite frankly, I do not know what we should do."

"We shall forage, Obadiah, as the people do."

"The land is well foraged already, my king."

"Yes. I have no doubt. But some grain may have grown again in the low places and by the water sources. We can do no other than try. We will organize two parties. I shall command one and forage to the south and in the Jordan Valley. You shall command the other and forage to the north. Go through the Jezreel Valley and then up to Dan. Return by the way of Jezreel and the Great Sea. Be sure to check the springs around Megiddo. Perhaps we can find enough feed for the stock to keep them alive until the rains come."

Ahab caught the look of discouragement in Obadiah's eyes. "The rains will come, my governor. Yahweh will not let his people perish from the earth."

Obadiah glanced quizzically at the king. "You said Yahweh."

"Yes," Ahab answered. "I said Yahweh. I do not know the ways of the gods, but still I am an Israelite."

Obadiah nodded.

"Now go. Organize the parties. We shall leave in the morning."

Each party consisted of a chariot—a royal one for Ahab, a smaller one for the governor—and fifty horsemen. Each horse was fitted with twin baskets strapped together, one to hang on each flank. Each rider pulled a donkey fitted with similar but larger baskets. By morning, the two contingents were ready to depart.

The white Ladder of Tyre glared fiercely under the strong sun. Elijah squinted his eyes, shielding them with his hand until his arm grew tired. When night fell, he continued his journey, thankful even with the chill that he had to face the glare no longer.

It was well past midnight when the prophet slept under a tamarisk tree, covering himself with his heavy mantle. The next noon he crossed into Israel at the base of Carmel, to follow the road that ran along its northern shoulder. Even Carmel—this mount of perpetual growth—was brown except for a few scattered evergreens.

Now walking at a brisk pace, now jogging, Elijah passed Megiddo late in the afternoon, then left the road to cross the spine of Carmel's tail, where the mountain dissipates into a broader range of hills to cut southeast toward Samaria. He traveled late into the night, slept fitfully in the cold, and resumed his journey before sunrise. By dawn he gained the road just north of the city. The white limestone walls shone white, catching the early morning sun before the brown earth did, as though Samaria itself rose early to capture the first light.

A column of riders led by a chariot rounded the northwest corner of the city wall, and soon the company stretched along the north wall. Elijah watched the procession, visible over the top of the Baal temple Jezebel had erected. Reaching the road, the column turned north, moving toward the prophet.

Within minutes, Elijah recognized the man in the leading chariot. It was Obadiah. The prophet stood to the side of the road and watched the company approach. As it neared, he raised his arm. "My friend, Obadiah," he called loudly.

The governor pulled his reins hard. The two horses stopped quickly, snorting in protest at the interruption. Obadiah's tunic was pulled up from his legs, and its folds were tucked into his jeweled linen girdle. "Elijah," he called, "Elijah, is that you?"

"Yes, my friend."

Obadiah dropped the reins across the front rail of the chariot and stepped to the ground. He knelt in front of the prophet and touched his forehead to the earth, his tunic dragging on the ground. "My lord Elijah," he said.

Elijah made no effort to call the governor to his feet. His voice was deep, with a powerful resonance that rose from some inner part to emerge as though it belonged to the wind. "Go to Ahab," he commanded. "Tell your lord that I am here, waiting to see him."

The governor remained on his knees and kept his head slightly bowed. His hands were on his thighs. He did not look at Elijah, nor did he answer.

"What is it, my friend?" Elijah asked, surprised at the silence.

The governor raised his eyes then. He spoke accusingly. "You ask me to do a thing that may bring about my death." He stood up to face the prophet. Looking down at the shorter man, his clipped beard jerked as he spoke in a tone that bordered on anger. "I am glad to see you, Elijah. We have searched for you, at the king's command, with great effort. Now you want me to tell King Ahab that you have appeared and wait for him beside this dusty road. Why must you be so demanding? Why do you not allow me to take you to the king?"

Elijah's eyes flashed angrily. He spoke with sternness. "Because Ahab must show that he has some respect, however slight, for Yahweh, the God of Israel."

"And suppose you are not here when I return with the king? You will be nowhere to be found."

"I will be here," Elijah answered.

"What sin against Yahweh have I committed that would cause you to send me to my execution at the hand of my King Ahab? What have I done?"

Elijah shook his head in exasperation, surprised at the feverish response of his old friend. "You have not sinned against Yahweh," he answered. "Why do you talk like this?"

"I swear," Obadiah answered, "as Yahweh your God lives, that there is not a nation or kingdom on earth to which Ahab has not sent a delegation to inquire of you. Even after the kings reported that you were not to be found in their domains, Ahab demanded their oaths. You cannot imagine, hidden away in some place by the hand of Yahweh, how thoroughly Ahab has searched for you and how furious he has been that he has not found you. Now you tell me to go and announce that you are here. Suppose I do. And suppose that when I leave you behind, the spirit of Yahweh comes over you and drives you in your divine inspiration to some place I could not even guess. Ahab will search this countryside for you, and then he will kill me on the spot for not apprehending you when I had the chance."

The governor paused. He glared at the prophet, his breath rapid and short, his usually unruffled face strained. "Elijah," he said, "I have been a follower of Yahweh since my youth, and have served him ever since then as well as I know how. Has no one told you how I hid one hundred prophets in the caves of Samaria's hill? Has no one told you how I fed them with breadcakes and water, which I gathered and took to them at great risk? Now you tell me to go to Ahab, playing on our past friendship, and tell him you are here." He shook his head firmly. "Elijah, perhaps I have seen too much of this war between the Gods, but neither you nor I can know what Yahweh will do next. You do not belong to yourself. Perhaps he will call you away.

I cannot take such a foolhardy chance. I shall take you to Ahab."

"You shall *not* take me to Ahab. He will come here to see me or by the word of Yahweh the drought will not end in Israel." He caught his friend's arm. "Obadiah, as Yahweh lives, the God of all the forces of heaven and earth, whose prophet I am and by whose voice I speak, I tell you that I will most certainly show myself to Ahab today."

The governor stared a moment at the prophet, then turned to his chariot and stepped into it. He looked down at Elijah. "So be it. You have sworn by Yahweh that you will see Ahab today. You are bound by your oath, and if you are not here, may Yahweh do to you what Ahab does to me."

"I am bound."

Obadiah signaled for the column to turn around, then he turned his chariot back toward the city. He snapped the horses into a run, leaving a cloud of dust to choke the riders who struggled to get out of his way. Ahab would be only a short way along the road to the south.

Elijah sat down by the roadside and watched the retreating column return toward Samaria.

It was but an hour later when Ahab arrived, mounted on a horse rather than in a chariot, and riding fast. He had only five mounted horsemen with him. Obadiah had remained behind. The prophet had not moved, not even to approach closer to the city.

There was a wild but uncertain look about the king's eyes. He spoke angrily, but his voice betrayed a sense of astonishment toward the prophet. "Are you the one who has brought trouble to Israel?" he demanded.

Elijah rose. He did not bow, but walked quickly to the chariot. His voice was as loud and angry as the king's. "I am not the one who brought trouble to Israel," he said. "You are that one. You and your father's house, for in your rule you have turned your back on Yahweh and his commandments, and in place of the God of Israel you have followed the Baals."

A soldier kicked his horse toward the prophet in protest at the tone, but Ahab's gesture stopped him.

The prophet's eyes flashed angrily, as they had two and a half years earlier when he last stood before Ahab. "Now, king of Israel, Yahweh will show himself and his power. By the command of Yahweh, I tell you to send out runners to every city of Israel and gather the people to the top of Mount Carmel. Gather there all of the prophets of Baal-Melkart, all four hundred fifty of them, and all of the prophets of Asherah, all four hundred of them. Gather all of the prophets who eat at the table of Jezebel to Mount Carmel. There Yahweh Elohim, the only true God, will work a great work that will astonish you, and there all Israel will see who is God."

He paused, and the king and the prophet glared into each other's eyes, one man with the armies of Israel at his command, the other with the forces of heaven at his call. Neither man flinched. Then Elijah spoke again. "Gather them there at Carmel, all the prophets and all the great men of Israel. I speak at the command of Yahweh. If you do not gather them, the drought will not end. If you obey, Yahweh will work a miracle that will astound you, and then the drought will end."

Ahab stared down from his horse. Twice he started to speak, but each time he thought better of it. Finally, he said quietly, "The drought must end. I do not know the ways of the gods, but one of them must win. I will do as you say. I will send runners throughout Israel. In seven days, the people will gather on Carmel. The leaders of Israel will be there, and all who want to come from among the people. The prophets of Melkart will be there, and the prophets of Asherah. And I will be there." He wheeled his horse around, then turned back to the prophet. "We shall see who controls the heavens. And if the drought does not end at the word of Yahweh, if Yahweh does not show himself, you will die." He gouged his horse hard and broke into a gallop toward Samaria.

Elijah smiled. Seven days. "Yes," he said softly, "Yahweh will show himself." He laughed and called after Ahab's party, though they likely could not hear. "Yahweh will show himself, Ahab." He watched the dust from the horses' hooves spread thin and settle, until the party disappeared out of sight around the corner of the wall and toward Samaria's entrance. He stood with his hands on his hips, staring toward the distant walls of Samaria. His voice was quiet again. "Yahweh will show himself. And all Israel will know who is God."

He felt excitement grow in his stomach and send its tingle through his body. Seven days. How could he contain himself for seven days? But it was good. All Israel would know that the lone prophet of Yahweh, one man, would stand against eight hundred fifty of Baal's best prophets. "Yes," he repeated again, "Yahweh will show himself."

Elijah turned to scan the land. Where would he go to wait? There was the Great Sea, far down the Vale of Barley to the west, hidden by the range of low hills that rose from the Plain of Sharon. There was Jezreel, the fertile valley to the north, and Judah to the south, with the holy city of Jerusalem. He looked northeast, as though he could see Bethshean, set in the Jordan Valley where the Valley of Jezreel spills by terraces down into the Ghor to widen its low plain. He missed Rejab. *That is where I would go*, he thought, *if Rejab still were there*.

He was a lone figure, standing between earth and sky, his heavy mantle draped across his shoulders and loose at his neck, his disheveled hair and unruly beard blowing easily with the occasional breeze, as though he were brother to the wind.

There was a family, he recalled as he mused, that Rejab mentioned several times, a friend who was faithful to Yahweh, a man from whom Rejab purchased produce. Shaphat was the man's name, and he lived in Abel-meholah. The prophet's eyes brightened. That is where he would go. The town was closer than Bethshean, at the southern end of the same Jordan plain, where the hills of Samaria press in to narrow the valley. He could make the journey before dark.

Elijah left the road and started directly east toward Tirzah, once the royal city. Beyond Tirzah, he turned northeast on the narrow road called The Way of the Diviners' Oak. The road followed a wadi bed down a wide valley. A few miles later, well before dusk, he was in the Jordan Valley.

The valley narrowed at this point, stretching wider toward Bethshean but closing into its deep, three-mile-wide Ghor shortly to the south. He had been here before when the meadow was green. The inspiration for the town's name was apparent then: Abel-meholah, Meadow of Dancing. Now the area was brown and parched.

Shaphat was a leading man of Abel-meholah, Elijah learned, owner of a very large field and several oxen. He easily found the house. It was large, with four lower rooms and a commodious upper chamber.

The prophet rapped on the door. His knock was answered by a tall, intense young man, dark-skinned and wiry. To Elijah's surprise the man's hair hung below his shoulders, though it was not unruly like his own.

"Are you a Nazirite?" he asked without introducing himself.

"I am," the man replied. "I have taken a vow that no razor will touch my head as long as one shrine to Asherah remains in Israel, and as long as one stone of the cursed temple to Melkart stands on another."

Elijah whooped. He leaped into the air and turned completely around, landing on his feet. "Praises be to Yahweh. I did not believe such faith still could be found in Israel."

"And you are a prophet, sir, I perceive. Where do you hail from, and how is it that Jezebel has not found you out?"

"I am Elijah, friend of . . ."

Elijah's introduction was cut short. This time it was the young man who whooped, though he did not leap into the air. He grasped Elijah firmly and pulled him forcibly into an embrace, kissing both bearded cheeks in the process. He pulled back, his eyes shining. "You are Elijah, truly? You really are Elijah?"

The prophet laughed. "I really am Elijah." But the young man already had turned to call his father and mother. "Excuse me," he said to Elijah, "I have not invited you in. Please, enter."

As Elijah walked through the door, the parents of the young man approached. "Father, mother, this is Elijah," he introduced excitedly, "the prophet Elijah."

The man and woman moved forward quickly, the man throwing his arms wide to embrace the prophet. Tears glistened in their eyes. "I am Shaphat," the man said, "and this is my good wife, Deborah." Then he beckoned Elijah to a seat, a pillowed chair with a back to it, one of two set in a corner with a low table between them. Shaphat took the other chair. He was tall like his son, and thin, but his skin hung loose at his neck and arms, and his hair, trimmed straight across the back above his shoulders and tapered from front to back below his ears, was white.

As Deborah hurried to the kitchen to pour wine, the son pulled up a stool to sit with his father and the prophet. As the son seated himself, Elijah asked him, "You have not told me your name."

"I am Elisha," the young man answered.

"Elisha, 'God is salvation.' A good name."

"A name I am proud to bear."

The days passed pleasantly, more than pleasantly, for Elijah found that Elisha's knowledge of Israel's history and his zeal for Yahweh matched his own. His zeal, in fact, was more exuberant, at times bordering on violent anger. The young man clearly had the cast of a prophet.

Elisha and Shaphat were well informed of affairs in Israel. The seven days were well spent in long discussions. Elijah learned from them that Jezebel found the prophets Obadiah had hidden in the caves. They were slaughtered at her order and, Shaphat surmised, the queen would have contrived Obadiah's death, too, were he not a clear favorite of Ahab's. Elisha talked excitedly of the embarrassment of the Baal prophets that they could not break the drought imposed by Yahweh, but he talked more somberly of the many babies, even occasional youths, who were sacrificed to the Baals by despairing parents advised by desperate priests.

The drought had done its work. Every Israelite knew of Yahweh's curse at the mouth of Elijah. Most of them sought to propitiate both of the gods, going first to one shrine, then to another—reciting the laws of Moses at home, and embracing zonahs at the high places. Elijah grew angry hearing of it, though he already knew of the practices.

As the days neared an end, Elisha began to pressure Elijah to take him along as a servant. They talked long about the matter. Shaphat was in favor of the arrangement one moment, reluctant the next. The famine had hit him hard —though being near the Jordan he was able to load jars of water onto ox-drawn carts to keep alive a small field—and he needed Elisha's help.

But it was Elijah himself who was most reluctant. "Always I have worked alone," he said. "I move quickly from one place to another. I don't know that I want a servant." Finally he agreed, because of the great work to be done on Carmel but especially because the young man had qualities the prophet wanted to develop.

Chapter Twelve

PEOPLE CAME from all over Israel for the amphictyony, the assembly of the nation. They camped all along the small Kishon River that flows along Carmel's base and into the Great Sea. Even on the great day, a few latecomers still straggled along the footpaths in the Jezreel Valley, and from across Jordan along Carmel's caravan route, and from the south along the ancient seacoast highway, and from the hill country—the Shephelah—across the Plain of Sharon to climb Carmel's flank.

Elijah and Elisha arrived a day early. They found the Baal prophets already camped under a cluster of terebinth trees near the sacred ground. The two men sought a more congenial place in a ravine to the south.

Ahab arrived at dawn, having spent the night at his summer home in Jezreel. Jezebel had excused herself, angered that the king had interfered with the authority he had granted her over religion. He left his chariot with attendants at the foot of the mountain and climbed like a pilgrim to its crest. The prophets of Baal thronged around him as he neared Melkart's shrine.

Elijah watched the greeting from higher on the hill, then with Elisha he made his way to the sacred ground. A Baal priest heard his approach and turned to speak to his companion. The men laughed.

The sun had risen high enough to break through the chill of the night air. Not a leaf moved in the stillness, as though nature itself held its breath for the day's happenings. Elijah beckoned his servant to wait at the edge of the sacred ground, and he strode forward. The clearing was of soft soil laced with rocks. Its north side melted into a ledge of rock that fell sharply for more than two hundred feet toward the Kishon. Near the cliff was a heap of stones, the altar to Yahweh that Jezebel had ordered destroyed. The other three sides were gradual slopes capable of supporting a large audience. A peak rose to the west to block the view of the sea, but to the north, across the Kishon, the Jezreel Valley lay in full view. The brush and bushes that generally grew in patches and clusters in the soft earth of the sacred place had been cleared away. Only a few gnarled old trees remained to draw attention from Melkart's waist-high altar of dressed stone. That altar stood in the center of the clearing. Elijah stared at it in contempt, then looked toward the crowd of prophets.

He called out loudly, "Where are the prophets of Melkart?"

A spokesman stepped out from the group and answered in a voice that equaled Elijah's in force, "We are here."

"And where are the prophets of Asherah?" Elijah called. There was no response.

"Where are the prophets of Asherah?" Elijah called again.

No one moved. The Melkart prophets murmured among themselves in low, surprised tones.

"King Ahab of Israel," Elijah shouted, "where are the prophets of Asherah?"

Ahab stepped into the clearing, his bearish head held regally high, and walked slowly toward the prophet until he was a few feet away. "Elijah, I did as you asked," he said in a normal tone. "They knew of the assembly. I cannot explain their absence."

Elijah turned slowly in a circle to look at the crowd which was gathering quickly at the sound of his challenge. "Let all Israel know," he shouted as he turned, "that Asherah is not God, and her prophets are cowards. Nor do they dare test her power against Yahweh's."

The people did not answer. They continued to take their places as near the holy ground as they could, the lesser personages giving way to the greater. The Melkart spokesman stepped forward. "But we are here, Elijah, prophet of Yahweh." He wore a prophet's mantle, closely woven of fine wool and dyed with the purple of Tyre. "We are four hundred fifty gathered here to show that Baal is as much stronger than Yahweh as we are superior to you in numbers."

"So be it," Elijah answered. "You shall stand, all of you, for Baal, and I shall stand alone for Yahweh." He turned to the crowd, his arms outstretched, his mantle hanging in a triangle from each forearm to drape to a point below his knees. "People of Israel," he shouted, "how long will you limp from one crippled leg to another, as a lame man who faces a fork in the road and cannot decide which way to go? Make your decision now. If Yahweh is God, follow him. But if Baal is God, follow him."

The people were silent. Some of them smiled, satisfied that the entertainment promised to be worth the journey.

Elijah lowered his arms, but his voice rose in crescendo. "I stand alone, one man, the only living prophet of Yahweh. Only I remain, one, to stand for the God of Israel." His arm swept toward the men of Melkart. "But there, Baal has four hundred fifty prophets. Yet Yahweh dares to challenge Baal."

Still looking at the unimpressed crowd, turning to address all the people, he pointed at the cluster of prophets. "Let those prophets furnish two small bulls. Of the two, they shall take first choice, so their sacrifice will surely be acceptable to Baal. Let them cut it into pieces as the ritual requires and lay it on the wood of the altar. They shall not set the wood afire, but rather call on their gods to send fire. Afterward, I shall do the same. The God who answers by sending fire from heaven, he is the true God."

The people murmured among themselves, many heads nodding in approval. Ahab, stoic, stood surrounded by court attendants. Obadiah had joined him. A voice called out from the crowd, "Well spoken, Elijah." The leaders of Israel, gathered closer by rank, echoed the call. "Yes, Elijah, it is a good test. Well spoken." Voices came more loudly from the crowd, and laughter, until Elijah's voice pealed above the tumult.

"Choose then, you prophets of Baal. Choose a young bull for yourselves. Call first on your god, for there are many of you. Dress your sacrifice and call on the name of your gods. But do not put fire into the wood."

Elijah turned and went to the edge of the clearing. He threw his mantle on the ground, sat on it, and pulled its folds over his legs. The people near him drew back to avoid being close to the strange man.

The Baal prophets, certain that animals would be required for some sort of sacrifice before the day was out, had brought several young bulls with them. Their spokesman called to his servants to fetch two of the best ones. Quickly, the two were brought forward, both of them well-muscled, with shiny coats. It would not do to give Elijah a poor specimen, for the people surely would react to any unfairness on their part. The spokesman looked the animals over carefully, feeling the withers and flanks, checking the skin for imperfections, inspecting the eyes and mouth. He made his choice.

At his signal, six prophets came forward. One of them struck the animal hard between the ears with the flat edge of an axe. The animal dropped to its knees without a sound. Another prophet thrust his sword into the bull's heart. While the seven priests dressed him, other prophets arranged wood on the stone altar.

The heart and kidneys were placed on the altar, along with all of the choice cuts of meat. Then the spokesman began to pray. With no memorized prayer available for such an occasion as calling down fire from heaven, he called for Baal to have mercy on the people who served him, to show to all Israel that Baal was God. Other prophets joined him, and soon all four hundred fifty prophets crowded in a cacophony of sound into the clearing and around the altar.

The people watched with easy acceptance, for all of them had seen sacrifices before, when voices rise as long fingers from the earth to point to the sky, when blood runs full over an altar to entice the life force of water from the skies to join the life force of living things to wet the earth, when the prophets or priests cry to the gods to accept the dead sacrifice as though it were the people themselves laid on the altar to die for the gods.

But the heavens did not answer. The prayers droned on, now loud and demanding, now pitiful and begging. The prophets' eyes soon were rimmed with the dark earth, which they threw in handfuls onto their hair, and the ground grew powdery under their constant pacing. The sun hung at midday. It glared down through white circles in the blue sky to draw upward the stench from spoiling meat. The prophets called to the silence through hoarse throats. When the silence did not answer, some leaped onto the altar itself. They lay across the meat and heart and kidneys and wood until one man was pushed off by another, while those who fell rolled with their blood-stained cloaks in the choking dust.

And still the sky was silent.

Elijah watched. Occasionally he laughed quietly but audibly to the people around him, who moved still farther away from this wild-haired man who dared defy the Baal, this unruly prophet under some exotic protection of Yahweh.

Finally, the prophet rose to his feet. Bare-armed in his tunic and standing on his mantle, he shouted at the men of Baal, "Cry louder, you prophets of Baal, for Baal is a god, is he not! Cry louder, for surely a god can hear!" He laughed derisively, a wild laugh that knifed its edges in horror through the crowd. "Perhaps he is thinking through some new invention for the people of Tyre, or talking over some new idea with Asherah. Perhaps you need to cry louder to draw him away from his work."

Elijah walked along the edge of the clearing. As he passed the people who had managed to gain the favored vantage points, they moved back instinctively from him, catching their breath at the brazen blasphemy of his words.

"Cry louder," he yelled toward the already screaming prophets. "Cry louder. Perhaps Baal is excreting and he cannot hear you for the strain." He laughed as the prophets turned toward him in righteous, frustrated anger. "Cry louder," he shouted, leaning toward their contorted faces. "Perhaps he has gone on a journey to Spain with Tyre's new colony. You will have to cry louder for him to hear you from across the waters." Elijah's own laughter now was as loud as the wails of the men of Melkart. "Cry louder. Perhaps he is asleep and needs to be awakened."

Elijah's taunts, coupled with frustration of three hours of frenzied prayer, goaded the prophets to greater displays. Their voices rose, until not even Elijah's loud laugh could be heard. As they screamed out their prayers, they began the whirling dervish dance of Baal. Knees bent, with thighs outstretched, crouching, they leaped high, whirling into the air. Disorganized, yet moving in a circle around the altar as though some force stirred them like heavy brew in a caldron, they danced. Some rocked in slow rhythm from one bent knee to the other, crouching on one leg at a time, while at the same time they flailed their arms fiercely and shrieked out their prayers. Some in the audience pressed fingers into ears to gain relief from the awesome cries that rose in a deafening mass above the four hundred fifty prophets. Others in the audience joined in the cries and prayers, raising their arms upward, shaking them in rhythm to the ecstatic chants until they were hypnotized.

Then one prophet leaped onto the altar and drew his knife, sharpened on two sides. He held it high, with both arms outstretched. He screamed, then drew the knife diagonally across his chest. A ribbon of blood instantly appeared and he shrieked in homage to Baal. Again he drew the knife against his flesh to mark an x, which quickly was obliterated in the red flow. Again he raised his arms and screamed allegiance to Baal. Then his knife arm moved more quickly. He drew it across his abdomen, and across his arms, and across his legs, shrieking rather in ecstasy than in pain as his blood flowed from the shallow cuts to redden the dark, dried blood of the sacrifice.

His devotion was infectious. Other prophets drew knives and leaped onto the altar to join their companion, until no room was left and the altar itself could not be seen for the press of bodies.

Many of the prophets were naked now, their mantles long since thrown aside and their tunics cut loose from their bodies by the frenzied handling of the knives. With sticks picked up from the altar, some of them beat themselves, swinging alternately across their shoulders to pound their slashed backs until the blood flowed even more freely, until the skin and rough clubs were red with the liquid of their lives.

Even more loudly they screamed, in volume that was beyond the power of normal men. For three more hours beyond noon, until the time of afternoon sacrifice, they screamed, until they fell to cover the sacred clearing in exhausted, bleeding, earth-caked heaps, until only five remained, who still opened silent mouths that uttered only throaty hoarseness. The five moved around the altar still, their muscles refusing to obey the dancing command of their frozen minds, their throats cauterized by the screaming and chill air and dust, their legs shuffling where they should be leaping, their arms limp where they should be flailing.

Elijah left them and moved to the edge of the cliff. He gazed down on the latecomers and women and poorer classes who could not get to the slopes, who could only listen to the cries from high above and catch reports that were passed down from the more fortunate who could see the spectacle.

He turned to face the audience. All but a few sat in stony silence, their senses seared by the display, their minds unable to register the horrors any longer. They were mute. Heads lay bowed into knees. Backs were turned to the scene. Unseeing eyes stared at the altar. A few were drunk, blessedly drunk.

Elijah called to the stupored crowd. "Come," he called. "Come closer to me." Eyes looked his way, and heads shook loose from their hypnotic stares. "Come near. Come close to me," the prophet repeated.

Ahab was the first to respond, followed by Obadiah. The king's stoic look had melted into shocked disbelief, disbelief at the excesses of the Baal prophets. He was a military man, an administrator. He had seen less of the Baal religion than the common man, and what he had seen was tempered by the dignity of the court. He wondered about Jezebel.

The people followed their king and clustered close around Elijah. He looked at them for a moment. Then, without a word, he turned to Yahweh's broken-down altar and selected a large undressed stone. Grunting under its weight, his muscles straining against the thin cloth of his tunic, he moved it to a level place near the cliff but still on the soft earth. He laid it flat and straight. Then he moved to another stone of equal size. Then to another. And another. Finally, he had arranged twelve stones side by side and end to end to make a low, flat altar. He looked at the crowd. Twelve tribes of Israel, divided now politically but never to be divided spiritually. They quickly caught the significance of the number.

The prophet called to Obadiah to fetch a digging tool. Elisha watched his mentor work hard at the menial task and wished he could help. But Elijah dug the trench himself, several inches deep into the soft earth, all the way around the improvised altar.

This task completed, as the people watched in rapt silence, Elijah gathered armloads of wood. This time he beckoned Elisha to help. Together, they arranged the wood on the altar. Then, on command from the prophet, Elisha brought forward the young bull he had tied to a tree. Elijah killed the bull, cut it into pieces in much the same way of the Baal prophets, and laid the proper pieces on the wood.

"Now," he said to the audience, "fill four large pots with water." At his first spoken word in over an hour, several young men hastened to obey. They found the jars among the supplies of the Baal prophets and clambered down to a pool at the bottom of the cliff. In a matter of minutes they returned, sweating from the strain of carrying the jars up the steep ravine that led from the pool. Word had reached the throngs of people below, who now craned their necks toward the cliff even though they could see nothing of the activities on top.

The men looked at Elijah, waiting for his word. "Pour the water onto the sacrifice."

They glanced at one another, not believing they had heard the command rightly. "Onto the sacrifice?" one asked.

"Onto the sacrifice," Elijah answered quietly.

The men obeyed. In teams of two, the men lifted the large jars. The water splashed on the sacrificial meat and wood and ran down into the cracks between the altar stones. The next team followed, and the water ran onto the ground. Then the next team followed, and the next. The sodden meat lay red on the wood; and the wood, pink-tinged from the watered blood, lay dark on the wet altar. The soft dry ground below quickly soaked up the excess water. Elijah's act was so extraordinary that no one thought to question the impropriety of pouring out precious water during the drought.

The eight young men stood by their four large jars. "Do it again," Elijah ordered. Incredulous but obeying, the men hoisted their jars and worked their way to the pool. When they poured the water the second time onto the altar, the earth no longer could hold the wetness, and the water trickled on all sides into the ditches.

To the astonishment of the young men, Elijah ordered them a third time to fill the jars. Low, subdued conversation moved throughout the audience.

The men returned, sweating profusely now, their legs aching from the threefold climb, their shoulders and biceps burning from the weight of the threefold burden. They did not question Elijah this time, not even by so much as a glance, when he simply pointed to the altar. Each team in turn, they poured the water onto the meat and wood. It ran in quick streams down the altar and across the soaked ground into the surrounding ditches. The fourth jar filled the ditch to its brim.

It was done. Four jars, the number symbol for the world with its four winds and four corners. Three times emptied, the number symbol for the divine Yahweh. The message was clear to the people. Yahweh controls the earth.

Elijah motioned the men away and cautioned the crowd to move back, then he stood near the altar, his face up-turned. His voice was loud but even, and the people below could hear the words from the prophet they could not see. "Yahweh Elohim," he called, "God of Abraham, God of Isaac, God of Israel. Let it be revealed today, and known to all, that you are God, the only God, in Israel, and that I, Elijah, am your servant. Let all Israel know that the drought spoken by my mouth and all that happens here today is not my doing, but is done at your command and by your power."

The people, the leaders of Israel, the great men of the nation, stood straight and silent as the prophet spoke.

"Hear me, O Yahweh," he continued, his hairy arms out-stretched, "hear me, that all these people, all the people of Israel, may know that you are the Lord God. Let them know that by this act you turn their hearts from Baal back to you."

Elijah moved backward toward the cliff until he stood at its edge. He raised his arms upward. The people below could see him now, a lone figure small against the sky. The audience nearer him hardly breathed, so electric was the contrast between the lone, calm prophet and the frenzied Baal multitude.

The sun was over the Great Sea to the west. Without a trace of cloud, the clear sky was a blue expanse that stretched as far as the eye could see. The people followed Elijah's gaze upward. All nature was silent, without a breeze to rustle a leaf. Then it happened. Lightning streaked from the cloudless blue to touch the altar. The thunderclap was instantaneous and awesome, the thundering voice of Yahweh in answer to the prophet's prayer. The whole area exploded into flames. A blue fire rose in a roar from the wood and meat and altar, as if sucked upward into an invisible chimney. Electricity crackled like fire among the trenches, and on the wet ground the white-hot flame burned the water from the blackened ground in frightening, fast-moving streaks. The flame burned still on the wood and meat, and between the stones hot electricity sizzled with its white flame.

All was over in a moment, even before the people recovered from the horrendous shock of the thunderclap. The intense heat left the stones broken into small pieces, and the wood and meat were completely consumed.

The people fell to the ground and pressed their faces against the earth. The people below, too, saw the lightning and the leaping flames. The thunderclap jolted them as sternly as it did the people closer to the altar, for they saw the lone prophet standing with upraised arms against the backdrop of fire. They, too, fell to their faces, even before word passed down to them of the total destruction of the altar. The chant started almost immediately from the mountain, but it spread quickly to the people below. "Yahweh, the only God. Yahweh, the only God." The people said it with their heads still bowed to the earth, then as they recovered from their shock they shouted it louder still. "Yahweh, the only God!"

Elijah had not moved, but he lowered his arms and pointed toward the Baal prophets who lay amid their mumblings, still dazed. He shouted above the din, "Take the prophets of Baal. Do not allow a single one to escape." A few closer men heard the command and quickly obeyed. As others watched them move, Elijah screamed out the command again, and a mass of men moved into action against the prophets.

Exhausted and still hypnotized by their ecstatic dancing and screaming, the prophets offered little resistance as the horde of men caught them up bodily. The servant Elisha led the way, mercilessly shoving a naked, bleeding prophet down the ravine past the pool and on down the steep slope to the Kishon River. Sliding down the rocky path, rolling and tumbling, the prophet of Baal was a mass of lifeless bruises and torn flesh by the time Elisha plunged a borrowed knife into his heart and threw the body into the narrow, muddy river.

The men followed Elisha in the orgy of slaughter. Mangled bodies, with arms and legs at grotesque angles, their throats slashed or stabbed through the heart, were piled into the Kishon until the muddy water turned brown-red. The path was clear from the sacred ground of Carmel down to the river, the slope marked with blood left on the trees and rocks. And the reddened Kishon flowed sluggishly toward the Sea to regurgitate the contagion of the land into the home of the Tyrian god.

Ahab, with Obadiah at his side, had not moved throughout the massacre. Stunned by the enormity of God's display of fire, he was mute to the slaughter. He thought instead of Jezebel.

Elijah had not moved, either, but his face held a glow of victory. Though he had expected God to answer, even in his certainty the loud and thorough response was a shock. He felt as though his soul was outside his body, observing with joy the purge of the land, watching with anticipation the proclaiming of Yahweh. But there was more to be done.

He called to some older men who still remained, "Go and slay and prepare a young bull for a feast. Your king must eat." Then he shouted across the demolished altar to Ahab. "Follow the old men higher up on the mountain. They will prepare a feast. Eat your fill and drink deeply of the good water. Celebrate the end of the drought, for my ears ring with the sound of a great, abundant rain."

Ahab turned without a response and moved lethargically in the direction Elijah pointed. Obadiah walked silently at his side, the royal train following close behind. Thoughts whirled in the king's mind, thoughts of Yahweh as the God of Israel, thoughts of the drought's end, thoughts of Jezebel.

Of all, Jezebel loomed most important. What would she do? Would the slaughter of the Baal prophets cause Tyre to break their alliance? How could he promote Yahweh worship in Israel without breaching the terms of his marriage to Jezebel? The development was not a religious problem to Ahab so much as an administrative one. How would he administer the zeal now toward Yahweh and hold together the pieces of the mutually profitable alliance with Tyre?

Elisha returned as Ahab's company disappeared among the trees.

"Come with me," Elijah ordered.

The two men walked up to the crest of Carmel. The sea still was not visible when they stopped, hidden by another peak a few minutes to the west. Elijah sat on the ground. He buried his face in his drawn up knees and clasped his hands around his legs. "I will pray," he murmured to Elisha. "Go up higher and look out to the sea."

With quick obedience, Elisha broke into a run. The climb was not overly steep, but the winter air held enough chill to bring pain to his throat from the exertion. Even so he ran with excitement, his own head dizzy with the sudden and decisive victory. On the peak, he looked beyond the yellow-sanded gulf shore below him and out to the western horizon. He cupped his hands over his eyes to break the late afternoon sun, and for several minutes he looked, with increasing disappointment. As far as he could see, the sky was clear.

He descended the peak at a disappointed walk and reported to his master. "There is nothing. I don't see a thing."

Without looking up, Elijah waved his hand toward the sea. "Go, look again."

The servant nodded, unseen by Elijah, and returned to the peak. Again he searched the sky. He squinted against the bright sun and looked carefully. Still, the sky glared clear. Despondently, he returned to Elijah with his discouraging report. Again, Elijah motioned him back to the peak. Again, the sun-dominated sky glared with its dry stare.

Elisha made several trips. Each time, Elijah repeated his unspoken gesture for his servant to look again, with hardly an interruption of his prayers.

Below, by the Kishon, the wild excitement of the slaughter was over for the people. They talked of the spectacle of the Baal prophets, and spoke in tones of awe of the act of Yahweh, and laughed about the prophets' naked bodies that forced the river to work its way around them.

The sun sank lower toward the horizon with each of Elisha's trips. On the seventh trip the servant saw a cloud far in the distance. The seventh trip. Elisha felt a current run through his body. The number was fitting. Seven was the number most sacred to the Hebrews, the number made up of four plus three, the number to symbolize the perfect union of earth with heaven. He wiped his watering eyes to see more clearly. The cloud was there, tiny and far away, but it was there. The servant ran recklessly back down from the peak, the bushes and trees grabbing at him in his rush. He was breathless when he came to Elijah, and spoke his report through a heaving chest. "There is a tiny cloud far away," he reported, gasping, "no larger on the horizon than a man's hand."

Elijah arose. "It is enough," he said. "Now, go to Ahab at the feast. Tell him to hurry to his chariot and hitch up his horses. Tell him to get down from off the mountain and hurry to Jezreel so he will not be caught in the storm."

Ahab's laugh rang among the trees. Jubilantly, he clapped Obadiah's back, then rose to hurry to his chariot, leaving his governor to oversee the return of equipment and animals to their proper places, a difficult task in the rain, for the lava soil of the valley could become boggy with the wetness. Horses and carts would find the travel slow and laborious.

Elijah already had started down the mountain and was on Jezreel's plain by the time Ahab had his chariot prepared and ready to start. His tunic ends tucked into his wide leather girdle, the prophet ran hard toward the city, seventeen miles away at the foot of Mount Gilboa, across the hard-packed, thirsty valley floor. Asherah had a temple there, built by Jezebel to house the four hundred prophets of the goddess. They surely would claim credit for the breaking of the drought. He must outrun the rain, so it would follow close at his back, as though he delivered it in Yahweh's stead. The gatekeepers must see that the rain belonged to Yahweh.

The clouds gathered quickly behind him, dark and heavy in the late afternoon, and they brought dusk before its time. The thunder rumbled in the distance toward the sea. Its sound forced its power into his limbs. He ran in a straight line, cutting across the cracked fields, while Ahab's chariot followed the turns in the road. He ran with fury, accepting the challenge of the chariot, racing to see Ahab's face when the king entered Jezreel's gates. His short, muscular legs pumped rapidly to propel him across the wide expanse of the basin in short steps rather than in the long strides of a thin runner.

He arrived at the gates just before Ahab, with the storm pressing close behind. He stood at the side of the gate to wait for the king. The wind came in gusts now to announce the impending rain. It snapped the folds of his tunic and blew his hair wildly. His chest rose and fell with his heavy breath and he flexed the muscles in his legs to the point of strain to fight back the threatening cramps. Ahab's chariot careened toward the gate only moments after the prophet arrived, and Elijah raised his hand in greeting. Ahab pulled hard on his reins to stop the horses. He did not speak as he stared down at the strange, bare-armed, hairy prophet. The rain came with him, and it struck suddenly and with fury, a blowing rain that soaked both of them in seconds. Elijah raised his face and arms toward the rain, feeling the wetness wash away the dust from his skin and soak into his beard and hair and plaster his tunic against his flesh. He began to laugh. "Well, my beloved king," he shouted through the storm to Ahab, "Yahweh indeed showed himself today."

The king felt the rain pelt his face and back and rush at his sandaled feet to flow out the back of his chariot, but he did not smile. He wanted to tell Elijah how he felt, that as an Israelite he was glad Yahweh had won, but the burden of being king was the greater force within him. He could only think of Jezebel and the alliance with Tyre. Without speaking, he snapped his reins and moved through the gates.

He sent word immediately for the queen to join him. She had waited anxiously for word about the contest, and so came to his chambers quickly. Ahab was changing from his wet clothes when she was announced. He rubbed his hair and beard vigorously with a towel as she entered.

"The storm is ferocious," she said, her cheerfulness guarded and cautious.

"Yes," Ahab answered, "but it is not Baal who sent it. The rain is Yahweh's."

The queen's face revealed brief shock, but she quickly suppressed the feeling and asked evenly, "How so?"

"Elijah challenged your prophets to prepare a sacrifice and pray to Melkart to send fire from the sky to light the wood. They prayed all day, from morning until the time of the afternoon sacrifice. In all my life I have not seen such a display. Your prophets were frantic. They ended up by cutting their own flesh with knives and rolling in the dirt. They not only were tired, they were out of their minds. Either they are crazy or their god is."

Jezebel walked to two conversation couches set close together in the center of the room. She stretched out and propped herself on one elbow. Her face bore the look of casual nonchalance. "And Yahweh?" she asked. "Did Yahweh answer with fire?" She laughed. "I would like to have seen Elijah dancing around the altar. His frightful hair must have been a sight indeed."

Ahab slipped a tunic over his head and straightened it at his shoulders. "Yahweh did answer, and never have I seen a prophet so calm as Elijah."

The queen still feigned an attitude of polite interest, as though she were being given a report of some sporting event. She asked, smiling, "And how did Yahweh answer?"

"He answered with fire." Ahab's hands were on his hips and he stood squarely in front of the queen. "Jezebel, your prophets are beaten. Yahweh answered Elijah in an extraordinary way, a magnificent way. Never since the Exodus has our God spoken so clearly. The people fell on their faces and proclaimed their allegiance to Yahweh. Then, at Elijah's command, they slaughtered your prophets. Every one of them. Their bodies lie this moment in the water of the Kishon River."

Jezebel rose to a sitting position. She nervously twisted a fold of her dress. Ahab watched her quietly, half amused at the efforts she expended to maintain her control, but distressed that this queen he loved dearly must face the crushing of her dream. When she finally spoke, she could not keep her shoulders from shaking. "All right," she said, "tell me all that happened."

Ahab sat on the opposite couch and leaned toward her. He started from the beginning.

When finally he ended the account, Jezebel asked quietly, "Where is Elijah now?"

"He stood by the gate to greet me when I entered Jezreel." The king walked to his wife and stood behind her. He put his hands on her shoulders and kissed her hair. "Jezebel, to continue your battle with Yahweh is insane. The close alliance of Israel and Tyre is important to me, but this effort to unify our religions has gotten out of hand. I swore to you once that I would not allow you to persecute the prophets of Yahweh. Yet you have killed every one of them. Only Elijah is left. I let you have free rein because of their strong opposition to your building of the temples here and at Samaria. They could not be allowed to infringe on your right granted by marriage." He turned the queen to him. "Jezebel, I know little of gods. But I know from today that Yahweh is and always will be the God of Israel. You must be content to worship Baal alone, only with your court. That is all the marriage treaty requires. You must give up your efforts to convert Israel to Melkart and Asherah."

Jezebel gently pulled Ahab's hands to her face. She kissed his fingers, then pushed away. "I must think, Ahab. I want to be alone." She turned to the door.

Meor-baal, having heard the news from Carmel, waited for the queen outside her chambers. He dropped to the floor on his hands and knees as she approached, touching his head to the cold stone of the floor.

"Meor-baal, arise," she said quickly.

The priest stood. Jezebel turned to her two attendants, who stood respectfully behind her, and beckoned them to wait in her chambers. Alone with Meor-baal, she dropped her controlled pretense. She grabbed his arm fiercely and spoke through clenched teeth, her eyes burning. "Get this message to Elijah," she said. "Tell him that I swear by my Gods that I will have him dead and butchered by this time tomorrow. Tell him that his body will be thrown into the Kishon just as he did to my prophets." She pushed Meor-baal's arm, as if to propel him on his errand, but before he had time to move she grabbed his sleeve. "Wait, priest of Baal. Tell him that I swear this. Tell him that I vow the Gods to do to me, and more, what has been done to my prophets if I do not have his life by this time tomorrow."

The priest, trained in the art of royal manners, did not reveal his concern. "I will do as you command." He nodded in a partial bow.

Elijah was at dinner with one of the wealthy men of Jezreel when the word came. Meor-baal, afraid that the victorious prophet would call for his death, sent a neutral messenger to reveal the queen's oath. Elisha had arrived only moments before, wet and shivering, delayed first by the need to retrieve his master's mantle, then by his search for Elijah.

The host answered the knock, then called Elijah to the door. "A messenger for you, Elijah. He says he has a word from the royal court." The messenger, wide-eyed, whispered his message into Elijah's ear, then stepped back in fear that the unpredictable prophet might call down a curse from God. Elijah listened in shocked surprise. He closed the door slowly and turned to his host. "I must go," he said.

"Now?" the man asked. "Food is ready to serve. You must eat first."

"I must go now." Without explanation, the prophet threw his mantle over his shoulders and walked out the door.

The host stared after him. "Your master is a strange man," he said to Elisha.

Elisha did not answer. Without a backward glance, he grabbed up his own mantle and hurried outside.

"Now," he said to the audience, "fill four large pots with water." At his first spoken word in over an hour, several young men hastened to obey. They found the jars among the supplies of the Baal prophets and clambered down to a pool at the bottom of the cliff. In a matter of minutes they returned, sweating from the strain of carrying the jars up the steep ravine that led from the pool. Word had reached the throngs of people below, who now craned their necks toward the cliff even though they could see nothing of the activities on top.

The men looked at Elijah, waiting for his word. "Pour the water onto the sacrifice."

They glanced at one another, not believing they had heard the command rightly. "Onto the sacrifice?" one asked.

"Onto the sacrifice," Elijah answered quietly.

The men obeyed. In teams of two, the men lifted the large jars. The water splashed on the sacrificial meat and wood and ran down into the cracks between the altar stones. The next team followed, and the water ran onto the ground. Then the next team followed, and the next. The sodden meat lay red on the wood; and the wood, pink-tinged from the watered blood, lay dark on the wet altar. The soft dry ground below quickly soaked up the excess water. Elijah's act was so extraordinary that no one thought to question the impropriety of pouring out precious water during the drought.

The eight young men stood by their four large jars. "Do it again," Elijah ordered. Incredulous but obeying, the men hoisted their jars and worked their way to the pool. When they poured the water the second time onto the altar, the earth no longer could hold the wetness, and the water trickled on all sides into the ditches.

To the astonishment of the young men, Elijah ordered them a third time to fill the jars. Low, subdued conversation moved throughout the audience.

The men returned, sweating profusely now, their legs aching from the threefold climb, their shoulders and biceps burning from the weight of the threefold burden. They did

Chapter Thirteen

ELISHA, EXHAUSTED from the hard run, stared at his master as they both lay panting under the partial protection of an olive grove. Elijah had not yet acknowledged his presence, nor had he seemed to notice when his servant caught up with him just outside Jezreel's gates. They had run together, sometimes side by side, sometimes with Elisha a step behind. The stout prophet ran with his short-stepped, pumplike gait, needing three strides to his servant's two, yet even after running from Mount Carmel to Jezreel he had set the pace on their flight.

The fury of the storm abated only moments before the men sought shelter and rest under the thick, heavily-leafed grove of trees. They had run seven miles, around the foot of Mount Gilead, with the lava-red soil of the valley already marshy underfoot. They were at Engannim now, a respectable head start on any search party that might start out in the morning. Elisha could only speculate about his master's fearful and uncommunicative flight after his victory on Mount Carmel. Jezebel could be the only possible cause, unless the prophet had yet another miracle to perform, a possibility that Elisha discounted because of the look on Elijah's face when he bolted from the house.

The thick limbs above them tempered the force of the still steady downpour but did not stop the wetness. The limbs gathered the water to loose it in large drops that made irregular plopping sounds, as though the yellow grass beneath them were hollow. Elijah lay on his back, his thick chest heaving, his blank, immobile face catching the weight of the thick drops without flinching. His eyes were open, unblinking except when a drop landed directly on target, then he shook his head sharply and resumed his entranced stare upward.

Several times Elisha started to call the prophet's name, but Elijah's unfamiliar strangeness cautioned him each time against intrusion. Finally, he rose and took off his mantle. Carefully, he maneuvered its edge through the twigs and over a larger branch to form a tent over his master. The activity loosed a sudden and heavy shower onto Elijah, who shook his head violently and sat up. He rubbed the wetness from his face and looked at his servant, seeing him for the first time. Elisha finished attaching the edges of his improvised tent and sat down under the small covering.

Elijah still did not speak, nor did he return Elisha's smile. He shook his head slightly as though unable to formulate his feelings. The prophet pulled off his mantle and gestured to the servant to share his cover, looking now more despondent than Elisha ever could have imagined any real prophet to be. The two men lay down together, still without speaking. Elijah fell asleep on his back, but he grunted and mumbled throughout the night, waking Elisha time and again with his twitching muscles and nervous sniffing.

The rain stopped before dawn, but a heavy mist obscured the valleys. The two men walked toward Dothan, crossing over the low hill that descended gently into the plain controlled by the city, and arrived on its outskirts well before noon. There they turned southeast up the road to Tirzah. Elijah still was untalkative, and Elisha walked silently, pondering the extreme change in his master and mentor.

At Tirzah, Elijah stopped and motioned toward the road he had traveled to Elisha's house only a few days before. He spoke with finality, the first full sentence since leaving Jezreel. "You must leave me now, Elisha, and go to your home."

The servant looked down the narrow valley, then turned to look into the despondent face of his master. "And where will you go without me, prophet of Yahweh?"

"I go south."

"South?"

"Into the wilderness, where Israel found its God. It is fitting."

"What will you do?"

Elijah did not answer. He nodded good-bye and turned south on the Way of the Diviners' Oak. Elisha, without so much as looking toward his home, followed his adopted master. For nearly two miles he walked behind Elijah. Elijah stopped at a point where the road topped the mountain crest. He stared down a long, well-traveled wadi that ran east to the Jordan. He could see the deep cleft of the Jabbock River that flowed into the Jordan from the other side. That river marked the southern boundary of his homeland, Gilead. The high, rolling pasturage of the land was not visible, only the bluffs that rose much higher on the east of the Ghor than on the west where the two men stood.

The prophet turned to Elisha, who now stood silent beside him. He did not question Elisha's presence. "It seems a lifetime ago that I came out of those hills. A lifetime." He jerked his hand toward the valley floor. "And two years ago I walked that valley at night to avoid Ahab's search."

"Elijah," the servant ventured, "the years have been worth the cost. Why are you now so troubled? What message could break the victory of Carmel?"

"Yes, the victory," the prophet said softly. He squatted, groaning as the effort pulled his aching thigh muscles, then sat on the ground, his legs out in front of him. "The message, my friend, was from Jezebel. She promised to kill me by tonight."

Elisha knelt, facing Elijah's side. "Would she do such a thing? The people would not allow it. The act would be striking at Yahweh himself."

"Yes, she means to do just that."

"But Yahweh will protect you. He has protected you through these terrible months."

Elijah did not want to explain the realities of a prophet's life to the younger man; he did not just now feel like a teacher. "How many prophets of Yahweh are left, Elisha?" he asked.

The servant shook his head, his face blank with disbelief. "But you are Elijah. You are different. Yahweh protects you miraculously. And Mount Carmel. Elijah, that was one of the greatest victories for Yahweh in Israel's history. Can you walk away from such a victory?"

Elijah picked up a stone and threw it carelessly toward the valley. "Jezebel is a fanatic for Baal, even more fanatic than I imagined. The great victory did not turn her heart."

"You are weary, Elijah. You need rest. Then you will think more clearly."

"Perhaps."

"What are your plans now?"

"I'm not sure. I think I shall go into the land of our nation's birth."

"You still are determined to go into the wilderness?"

"Yes."

Elisha nodded in agreement, shaking off his first feeling of concern. "That may be well. The wilderness has a way of renewing a man's soul, though it seems to me that you leave at a strange time."

Elijah smiled wryly and did not respond. He moved to rise and grunted with the effort. Elisha sprang quickly to his feet and caught his master's hand to pull him up.

"Thank you," the prophet said simply.

The two men started down the hill, walking silently side by side. They arrived at beautiful, well-watered Shechem just before noon. Elisha went to buy food, with instructions to meet Elijah at Jacob's well.

The prophet found the well easily, and sat down on its rock-lined edge to rest. Deep rope marks were etched into the large stones where for centuries shepherds and women had drawn water for their flocks and families. Mount Ebal rose imposingly to the north, Mount Gerizim to the south. He thought of the Blessings and Curses read in solemn assembly from the twin hills during Israel's earlier days. *Even then*, Elijah thought, *four hundred years ago, this well was ancient.* How many times had the rope-scarred stones been replaced since Jacob dug the well another four hundred years before Moses?

The meal revived both men. Elijah had not eaten a full meal since the night before the Mount Carmel contest. They resumed their southward journey as far as Lebonah, some twelve miles farther, then left the main road on Elisha's impulse to sleep the night at the broken shrine of Shiloh. The impulse was a mistake. Elisha thought the touch with Israel's past would serve to revive his master's spirits, but the night was grim. The cloud-covered sky was dark, and the random array of stones reminded Elijah of the dark days of Israel's commitment. Shiloh, once one of Israel's most hallowed shrines, had been destroyed by the Philistines during Samuel's day, never to be rebuilt. Other shrines, more convenient, had taken Shiloh's place. Now other gods, more convenient, were replacing Yahweh himself.

With the experience of the night at Shiloh, Elisha dreaded the effect Bethel would have on the prophet, that ancient and holy shrine city where Jacob built an altar to Yahweh after his dream of the golden stairs. Jeroboam had placed a golden calf there to lure the newly seceded Israel from Jerusalem.

With the excuse that they would be safer from Jezebel's search, Elisha convinced the prophet that they should stay to the back road. The road was longer, winding among the higher hills, but it met the main road again at Gibeah, across the border in Judah. They could be in Jerusalem by late afternoon.

Elijah's spirits revived when he crossed the border into Judah. He stopped and breathed deeply. The Great Sea glistened in full view to the west, down the steep slopes of the mountain range and across the gentler Plain of Sharon. He turned to Elisha. "Would to God that I were a prophet to Judah, with a king that loves Yahweh."

"Yes," Elisha agreed, "that would be easier. But then you would need another name."

Elijah looked quizzically at his companion.

"What good is a name that means "Yahweh is God" in a land where the people already know he is?"

The prophet smiled. "Yes. But I would gladly change my name."

"Elijah," the servant spoke in a tone of serious piety. "Is it not a matter of great comfort that Judah is faithful?"

Elijah looked back across the border. "But to a prophet of Israel, the comfort is hollow." His voice lowered, speaking more now to himself than to Elisha. "Does it mean that Israel has given up her destiny? That Yahweh's efforts will be directed only to Judah now?"

"I share your love for Israel," Elisha replied, unaware that Elijah had conversed only with himself, "but still it makes me glad to know that King Jehoshaphat can be faithful to Yahweh and still build a great country. Ahab builds Israel by appealing to greed and power. Jehoshaphat builds Judah by setting up a system of justice for the people and commitment to Yahweh by the people. And Judah is doing well by such a policy."

"Judah is doing well," Elijah acknowledged. He turned full circle and took another deep breath. "And the air breathes better," he said.

Jerusalem was set on the crest of the mountain range, as impregnable a fortress as any large city could be. They entered Jerusalem through the Gate of Ephraim, one of three main gates on the north that led into the walled city. The Temple was not far inside. Quickly, they made their way to the great wonder.

Elijah and Elisha stood side by side to gaze in reverent awe at the Temple's entrance. Two huge, free-standing pillars rose thirty feet into the air, two-thirds as high as the front of the Temple itself. Jezebel's temple had similar pillars, but those represented the phalli of fertility worship. These two had names: Jachin meant "Yahweh establishes" and Boaz meant "In Yahweh is strength." Fire fluttered in gentle waves from huge bowls at the top of each pillar. Their significance was both historic and mystic, to recall the pillar of fire by night and cloud by day that led the Israelites through the wilderness, and to merge earth with heaven as the smoke rose to mingle with the sky.

To their right stood the massive altar of burnt offerings, measuring thirty feet square and fifteen feet high. It was placed over, and completely hid, the natural rock altar. A ledge ran below the top of the altar, on which priests stood while preparing and offering the sacrifices. A drainage system ran beneath the altar to carry the blood of the sacrifices underground to drain into the Kidron Brook.

To their left was the equally massive arrangement of the basin and lavers. A bronze basin, so large that it was called the Molten Sea, was lined on each side by five lavers. The Molten Sea itself was fifteen feet broad and seven and a half feet high. It was supported on the backs of twelve bronze oxen, seated on their haunches, in groups of three facing each of the four directions. The priests washed their hands and feet in the water of the basin before they approached the altar or entered the sanctuary. Each of the ten round bronze lavers measured ten feet in diameter and were supported by large, nine-foot-high bases, around and on which were placed and carved various forms of animals and plants. The basins were used by the priests to wash the entrails from the animals in preparation for sacrifice.

Without speaking, the two men walked between the altar and the Molten Sea to ascend the ten steps between the two pillars. They walked into the *ulam*, the vestibule of the Temple, and stared through other high doors into the *hekhal*, the holy place. Its dimensions were exact. The length of the room was twice its width, sixty feet by thirty feet, and the height was half again the width, forty-five feet.

Near the top of the side walls were windows that slanted upward through the thick masonry to catch the sun, which glistened with striking brilliance on the gold-overlaid walls. Intricate patterns of palm trees, flowers, and cherubim were carved into the cedar that lined the walls. The entire structure inside was overlaid with gold, every bit of wall and ceiling space, every implement and furnishing.

On each side of the wall stood five gold candlesticks, each one with seven branches, each one shaped out of pure gold. Three of the candlesticks burned even now, during the day, to symbolize the unbroken worship and unceasing light of God and his people. The flickering light from the candlesticks cast gentle and ever-changing light on the gold of the room.

On the right was a table made of acacia wood, also overlaid with gold. On it was placed in two neat rows twelve loaves of unleavened bread, each loaf to represent one of the twelve tribes, a double reminder of the wilderness provisions and of the constant provisions of the earth, all given by Yahweh. The altar of incense lay directly ahead of them, in front of the door to the *debit*, the holy of holies. Every morning and every evening a priest burned incense on the altar, prepared by formula from four perfumes and a temper of salt, to signify the adoration of Yahweh's people for their God. A trace of the odor, sweet to the nostrils, remained from the morning ritual when the smoke of the incense rose to the ceiling to escape through the slanted windows and to dissipate toward heaven.

Beyond the incense altar was the cedar wall of the holy of holies. Its two olivewood doors were, as all else, overlaid with gold. Few men in Israel's history ever had entered the perfectly square cubicle, thirty feet by thirty feet, for only the high priest could go into the dark chamber, and he only once each year on the Day of Atonement. Yahweh's presence dwelt intensely in the holy of holies. His *shekinah* glory was there—that awesome, almost visible presence of God that was in the pillar of fire and the cloud, that presence that descended on Mount Sinai when Yahweh's voice thundered from the cloud-bound heights of the mountain, that presence that threatened by its very holiness to overcome even the high priest who entered into the holy room.

Elijah spoke very softly, not particularly to his companion. "I would that every Israelite heart were a holy of holies."

The ark of the covenant was in the room, the acacia wood chest that housed the stone tablets hewn by Moses' own hands and on which Yahweh himself had inscribed his Law. Every devout Israelite knew the placement and design of the holy of holies. The ark was the central object, but it was not the largest. Its lid, the mercy seat of Yahweh himself, was of solid gold. Joined to the lid in one unbroken piece were two large cherubim, facing each other and looking down to the mercy seat, each with wings that touched the wall on one side and the wing tip of its companion in the center. In the space between the two cherubim and just above the mercy seat was the holiest spot in the holy of holies. The mercy seat was the seat of God, his special abode which, for all its sanctity, was unlike the shrine of other gods. It was much too small to hold Yahweh, whose presence permeated the universe.

Feeling small, yet honored, the two men turned back from the outer door and walked slowly out of the Temple area.

Two hours yet remained before dusk, and Bethlehem lay but five miles farther.

The road to Bethlehem ran along the crest of the range. To the left the barren hills descended in a bizarre array of yellow-brown nakedness to the Dead Sea, broken by a faint haze of green that lined the banks of the Kidron Brook, now flowing with the winter rains. To the right the hills were greener, though the fields that supported barley and wheat now were bare. Men still toiled feverishly in the downward-terraced, stony plots to break up the rain-softened earth. They would work until nightfall, so late were the rains in coming.

Do they know, Elijah thought, *of the contest on Mount Carmel—that Yahweh broke the drought and that his prophet walks even now so close by?*

The hard land in the region was rich but troublesome, not so easily tamed as Ephraim's valleys. Stones dominated the fields, littered across the landscape as though a giant trickster cast new ones from his hand each time the farmers cleared the old ones. The toil was ceaseless. Low walls built from the troublesome rocks so laboriously gathered marked the boundaries of individual fields. The walls criss-crossed each arable valley and terraced hill, yet other stones remained, to the farmers' unending consternation. The limestone hills broke through the earth in places, like the bald heads of old men, and at other places ran just under the soil, unseen but treacherous to the farmer.

Elisha, more the farmer than his master, explained to Elijah how the plants sprout early and promising from the shallow earth that covers the underlying stone. The sun heats the earth quickly in such places, causing the seed to germinate and the shoot to grow rapidly. But the plant is unable to break through the stone to send its roots deeper. Soon, it shrivels and dies.

The servant was sorry the moment the explanation passed his lips. Elijah stopped and looked over the fields. Then he turned and said, almost inaudibly, "Israel is like that." He resumed his walk, head down, watching only the ground directly in front of him as despondent men do when they walk. "I cannot understand, my friend Elisha, how Israel can be so hard to reach. Our country is richer than Judah. The land gives of its bounty so much more easily than here. And we are richer in commerce. Yet here the people give Yahweh credit for the toil of their lives and the yield of the earth."

"It is partly leadership, is it not, prophet of Yahweh? Jehoshaphat is just, and he knows that only Yahweh truly teaches justice. Ahab knows only the power of arms and treaties. Religion is a mystery to him, so he allows Jezebel free rein to teach the people what appears to work, the worship of the Gods of Power and Growth."

Elijah did not respond. He felt strange to be taught by the younger man, impressed by his insight yet chagrined that he, the prophet, was not teaching the servant.

The prophet slept fitfully again that night, even amid the comfort purchased with Elisha's money. His life did not make sense. The Mount Carmel scene reconstructed itself minutely and vividly, despite his efforts to push it out and go to sleep. He tried to relax his muscles, starting with his fingers and working to his shoulders and neck, but each time the scene forced its way into his consciousness. The Baal prophets played out their drama of ecstatic screams and wild gyrations again and again. The onlookers' faces came into focus individually, and the prophet's mind recalled expressions he had not consciously noticed two days ago on Carmel, expressions that changed through the long day from excitement to disbelief to stony rejection by minds seared with what they could not accept.

He woke out of his semi-consciousness from time to time to ponder the events more controllably. The people did not really accept Yahweh. They were overwhelmed by him. They obeyed the command to slaughter the Baal prophets as they would obey a victorious general at the moment the tides of victory turn his way; and they would as quickly desert Yahweh as a mercenary soldier would a losing cause.

The morning broke under partly cloudy skies, and at his servant's prodding Elijah woke from the deep slumber that comes in the early morning after a sleepless night. Elisha tried to be cheerful. He had ordered breakfast already, and he joked about the downhill road from Bethlehem to Hebron.

By the time they resumed their journey Elisha had given up his efforts to cheer his master. Though concerned about Elijah and mystified at his behavior, the servant knew that some problems can be worked out only by the man who is troubled. Outside help, though appreciated, rarely touches the nerve of the concern, a nerve the troubled man himself may not know.

The men had started late in the morning, and it was early afternoon by the time they reached Beth-zur. They climbed the hill to refresh themselves and refill their water-pouches at the city's copious springs. No cattle or sheep were present, since it was midday, but hollowed-out stone troughs encircled the fountain for watering the herds and flocks. After resting only a few minutes the prophet and companion clambered down the hill to the road.

Hebron was but an hour ahead. From tales told over campfires and under flickering oil lamps over the years, Elijah knew that soon they would come upon a grove of oak trees, the Oaks of Mamre, where Abraham lived several times during his travels over the vast land. In spite of the beauty of the location, no tent was pitched among the thick trees. The spot was sacred.

They did not stop at Machpelah, northwest of Hebron, though Elisha wished strongly to visit the cave tomb Abraham had purchased from Ephron the Hittite when Sarah died.

Nor did the two travelers stop for the night at Hebron as planned. Elijah insisted they continue, in spite of the cold that would settle on the desert night. Elijah hastened his pace. He walked like a man obsessed, and soon talked so incessantly of the wilderness wanderings of the Israelites that the tired Elisha longed for the tranquility of the former silence.

Elisha's stomach protested through the night for lack of food. He had not eaten since the late breakfast in Bethlehem, and Elijah had eaten little even then. Yet the prophet showed no sign of hunger and little sign of discomfort from the cold. *He is a single-minded man*, Elisha thought, *and now he thinks only of the wilderness.*

Halfway to Beersheba the road and wadi left the infertile chalk and entered a stretch of softer alluvium. The hills were low, rolling gently toward the desert. An occasional small, unwalled town nestled silent and dark on the side of a low hill, always next to a smaller wadi that fed into the Khalil.

The road turned to sand as the travelers approached Beersheba, placing tension on their calf muscles as their toes pressed ineffectively into the loose soil. Their steps were shorter, and the cold night air parched their throats as they breathed more deeply with their effort. Still, they reached Beersheba by midnight.

The city had light fortifications, but no encircling walls except around a small portion. Settlements were spread out instead all along wide wadis.

In the marketplace, travelers huddled in doorways or sat back to back in the open night each to protect the other, their mantles pulled over their heads and double wrapped around their bodies, sleeping lightly in mild fear of being molested or robbed. They waited to join caravans that might take them across the treacherous desert to their destinations. Some of them would wait for days.

Elijah and Elisha passed through the scattered sleepers as silently as they could. Some of them, no doubt, awoke to watch them carefully, but not one of them moved perceptibly. Beyond the marketplace they came to the trickling Wadi es Seba. Elijah stopped and spoke softly to his servant. The prophet's voice was firm. "Elisha, I want to go into the wilderness, alone."

Elisha had expected his master to say that, though he had hoped all during the journey that he would be able to stay with him, to help him through the period of discouragement. But Elijah had worked alone as a prophet all of his life, friendly toward the coenobias but independent of them. Even more than most prophets he drew strength from the solitude of the wilderness. But the servant could not hide his concern, for the southern desert was unfamiliar to Elijah.

"You should eat first," he cautioned.

"No. I shall go now."

"You don't know the wilderness, Elijah. At least wait until morning to ask directions."

"No."

"Then where shall you go?"

"Where the Spirit of Yahweh leads me."

"You are being foolhardy to leave now, in the night, and without food. You must be hungry even now."

Elijah did not respond to his servant's challenge. "Stay here, Elisha," he ordered. "If I am not back in a few days, return to your home."

Elisha nodded, having learned more during their journey of the unswerving single-mindedness of the prophet. "I'll wait a few days. Shalom. Yahweh be with you."

Elijah looked toward the sky to get his bearings from the stars. Then he knelt and filled his waterskin from the narrow, shallow stream. Rising, he crossed the water in two steps and began his walk due south. Elisha watched him for several minutes, as his master made his way among the low-built houses that littered the wide valley. Soon Elijah disappeared in the darkness. The servant stared after him, into the void that he could feel in the air. Worried, he forced his mind to recall the prophet's last gestures and his scanning of the sky. *He went due south*, Elisha concluded. *Because he does not know the way, he went due south. He will not swerve.*

Chapter Fourteen

WITHIN AN HOUR after leaving Beersheba, Elijah left behind him the fertile soil of the broad valley. The low hills became harder and more barren, with rocks strewn promiscuously over the surface. They were anathema to him in the dark, as he kicked them or stepped on them with the sides of his feet.

By sunrise Elijah approached Mount Haleiqim. The journey would not have been particularly hard during daytime, but in spite of the bright moon he fell several times. His forearm was scraped painfully from one of the falls, and he walked with a limp, the result of striking his knee against a small, sharp stone. Though he did not feel hungry, the loss of strength had slowed him considerably. As he dragged his feet, the toe of each sandal pulled a tiny trough of dirt upward with each step.

Determined to go farther, and now with the daylight to aid him, he followed the foot of Mount Haleiqim toward the southeast. The land was treeless, but looking west to the lower region he could detect an occasional ribbon of winter-dulled growth, and sometimes a clump of tall cypress trees.

By the time he found a pass through the forbidding ridge he could see no sign of life anymore, though the pass itself gave evidence of rare travel. Once again he was almost due south of Beersheba. He turned east into the pass and then, shortly, north up into a deep valley between two high ridges. After an hour of climbing he came to a small level flat. In its center, fed by the bit of water that the level could hold for awhile, grew a single broom tree. It was leafless, but its myriad of thin branches broke the sun to offer a gray shade. Elijah lowered himself slowly to a sitting position, careful of his aching muscles and sore knee as he shifted his weight, and stretched out his legs in front of him.

He sat for a long time that way, moving only a hand occasionally to relieve an aching wrist or stretching his legs to fight off the ache that dominated his calves and thighs. He looked carefully at his bruised knee, but decided to ignore the dull pain since he could do nothing about it.

He wanted to cry, but he could not remember how. Instead, the despondency tightened in his throat. He sat in a stupor, unable to formulate words with which to pray away the despair. For more than an hour he stared at the bluffs that rose on either side and down the valley that stretched beyond his feet. The land and rocks were brown, austere in the desert sun, their rock-hard slopes and ridges speaking both of timeless peace and of timeless anguish. They reflected his soul, his deep certainty that Yahweh was God and that he was his prophet against the despair that his life had accomplished nothing.

He had laid his faith, never mind his life, on the line on Mount Carmel. Never had Yahweh granted a greater, more viable, more convincing sign that he was God. Not even the parting of the sea when Israel was led by Moses from Egypt, not even the manna in the desert, was a greater sign than the fire from heaven. Yet Jezebel was not convinced. And if she were not convinced, Israel would not be.

A sense of antagonism toward God filled his breast. Not doubt. He did not doubt God. He was angry with God—angry that Yahweh would lead him to perform such a magnificent miracle, then withhold from him his legitimate expectations of the results. The Israelites crossed the Red Sea on dry ground and they believed in Yahweh, at least for a while. They ate of the manna in the wilderness and they believed in Yahweh, at least for a while. But they saw fire descend from heaven to devour the offering, and the altar, and the water itself, and they did not believe, even for a while.

Elijah's daydreams of years past gathered in the crevices of the mountains and permeated the air around the tree. They were the haze that hung in the desert sky and that rose in shimmers from the hot stones of the valley. For all those years of preaching in marketplaces, of meditating in the trackless regions of Gilead, of talking passionately under flickering lamps, he had dreamed of standing one day beside Ahab and from the palace balcony to announce to the assembled crowd below that from now to forevermore Yahweh was God, the only God, in Israel.

If ever that moment should have come, the miracle on Mount Carmel should have brought it.

Elijah lay back, the weariness of his body spreading into his soul until, like his leaden arms, his spent spirit lay prone on the earth. He had failed, and in his failure culminated the failures of all who came before him. Moses failed in him, and Samuel, and David, and Nathan, and all those myriad nameless thousands of faithful spokesmen for Yahweh whose names were known only to God. He was the end of the line of witnesses. Their success was worthless without his success. All of that effort had come to this end. Yahweh was rejected, with finality and in the face of a great display of his power.

Thought clings tenaciously to the exhausted mind, and the stories of Israel's history poured in quick succession into his consciousness, filtering through the hazy disillusionment that hung in the sky.

Moses' face, as he often had pictured it, large and square with long beard and bushy eyebrows, loomed in his vision. But now that face did not hold a fierce, prophetic determination. Now the skin hung more loosely and the eyes were hollow.

Samuel's eyes stared at a throne, and his downcast head was shaking slowly back and forth, for what he had warned about a king, should Israel continue to demand one, had come to pass.

David, large-boned and muscular, tall and fair—his poet-warrior, warrior-poet's face was the most agonized of all. That face reflected hurt more than disappointment, for the kingdom he pulled together through a lifetime of brilliant leadership and commitment to Yahweh had broken in two, and the larger and richer of the pieces was drifting from the rock-hard mountains into the cavernous sea.

David's face disappeared, and in its place paraded a sea of faces. Most of them were blank and featureless, but he recognized Caleb and Joshua, and Abijah and Nathan, all with features he had assigned to them as a boy listening to his father tell him the stories of Israel. All of them, to the last man, had lived for nothing. Their leadership, their suffering, their prayers, their commitment to Yahweh was wasted. And why should he, Elijah, a lone prophet among an apostate people, suppose himself able to turn a tide that had engulfed so many valiant and determined lives?

He spoke then, aloud but low, to the God he could not feel but who he knew was there. "It is enough," he said slowly. "Now, Yahweh, take away my life. I am not better than my fathers." Then his eyes closed in sleep, and his last thought was that he would not awake.

The sun crept higher to cast its full fury into the valley, to filter through the leafless branches of the broom tree to shine on the prone body of the prophet. He lay flat on his back, his arms wide above his head, his face turned to one side, the tangled shadows of thin branches criss-crossing his body. He did not move as the sun passed from view beyond the western bluff, nor as the shadow deepened in the valley. Night fell, and with it the winter's desert chill, and still he did not move.

At dawn, while the early light of the pre-morning reflected in bright pastels of orange and pink and red and purple and blue on the ridges that enclosed the valley, Elijah felt a tug at his shoulder. A voice broke through his deep slumber, as though from far away, the voice of a messenger of God, the touch of an angel, speaking and touching with the gentleness of love.

He woke slowly, climbing from a deep pit of slumber, making his way toward the sunlight at its top. The voice spoke, "Arise and eat." And then the voice was gone, and the tug ceased.

He raised himself on one elbow and opened his eyes toward the soft smell of hot breadcake. A small fire smoldered only a few feet away, smelling of thornbranches. Baking on a flat stone placed in the midst of it was a large breadcake. Nearby was a cruse of water.

Elijah pushed himself to his hands and knees and crawled to the fire. He cautiously pulled the breadcake from the hot stone and shifted it back and forth quickly from hand to hand until it cooled enough to be held. He ate slowly, washing down each bite with the clear, cool water from the cruse, wondering at the providence of God, yet wishing that God had taken his life instead.

After he ate, he lay down again in his place under the broom tree and quickly fell again into his deep slumber.

The sun moved as hot as before into the valley and beyond it to the west. The night fell as chilled as before on the desert floor. Elijah slept through it all, still, his body and soul quiet, without visions or dreams of Israel's yesterday or his today. At the moment of the predawn's most vivid painting, again he felt the tug at his shoulder, and in his cavern of sleep he heard the distant and gentle voice calling again to him, "Arise and eat." This time he thought he heard another phrase, "because the journey ahead is too great for you."

Waking was not as hard as the morning before, but even so the climb from the deep was as though he had been in the belly of the earth.

Three breadcakes this time baked on the flat stones in the midst of the fire. He retrieved them and ate them slowly, drinking in small swallows the water from the cruse.

The voice had said, "because the journey is too great for you." Elijah pondered the words. *Yahweh did not want me to die yet, but what is the journey? Surely it is not to return to Israel, after Jezebel's threat? What then?*

By the time he took the last bite of breadcake and drank the last bit of water from the cruse he had decided. He would go to Mount Horeb, the Mountain of Yahweh in Sinai where Yahweh gave the Law to his people. There either he would hear God as vividly as Moses did or he would die.

Elijah laid the empty cruse aside, rose, and started down the valley. He struck a course due west when he emerged from the valley, walking at a fast pace, his route being for the most part downhill. Somewhere to the west, he knew, a road ran from Beersheba to Kadesh-barnea.

He left the barren chalk hills soon and entered a stretch of desert that supported rare clumps of scrub and even, in the wadis, more aggressive growth. But though the small trees and winter-dead grass of the dry wadis appeared as oases in comparison to the desert's bleakness, the region was forbidding. The bare stretches of rock-littered gray and tan wilderness shouted its awesome warning to travelers to seek directions before journeying into the great and terrible Sinai Desert.

Those who survived the wilderness sought those directions carefully at one of the towns or cities that lay on its perimeter, like Beersheba or Kadesh-barnea. The traveler would question until he knew every landmark, every trail, every watering place, every controlling Bedouin tribe and its leaders. The prophet, then, had double reason for going through Kadesh, to seek directions and to start his pilgrimage at the site where Israel itself languished for much of her forty years of cursed wandering.

By the time Elijah reached the sprawling town dusk was dissolving into darkness. He was disappointed at first at the smallness of the ancient settlement until, the next morning, he discovered that the city was spread in wide-ranging clusters up and down the wide Wadi el Qudeirat and its tributaries, each cluster concentrated near or around a rock-sided well. The town had no strong buildings to form a center, only a ramshackle marketplace that, later in the morning, was filled with desert Bedouins and the almost-alike Judeans of Kadesh. They were desert toughened, darker than their kinsmen to the north, due surely to the ferocity of the sun.

Kadesh was on the very edge of the terrible wilderness, the last outpost between the vengeful desert and the dew-tempered hills and wadis that stretched north and west. His forefathers lived on the edge of existence for forty years. *Now,* he thought, *they have chosen again to live on the edge of existence in their wanderings of the spirit.*

To the south the wilderness began in earnest. Elijah looked out toward the Tih, the Wilderness of the Wandering, shielding his eyes from the glare. That is the hardest way to Mount Horeb, though the shortest. *Perhaps,* he thought, *the harder way is the better way for the wandering soul. Forty years Israel wandered, ten times four years.*

The holy significance of the number was apparent. Ten was the number of human completeness; four was the cosmic number to symbolize the world. The forty-year period then had its divine purpose—to bring God's people to completeness.

Elijah started down the north slope of the hill into the Wadi el Ain. His journey, the journey that would be too great for him without the sustaining food provided by God, would be in that great wilderness. He would stretch his journey to Horeb to last forty days, a day for a year. Perhaps Yahweh would do in his soul what he did with Israel.

Once in the valley the prophet sought out an elderly Judean for directions. They sat for more than two hours under a terebinth tree. The old man was glad to share his knowledge with a traveler, especially with a prophet of Yahweh on a pilgrimage to Mount Horeb. He described the wilderness in great detail. When Elijah bade the man good-bye, he started his journey with confidence.

Elijah spent the days exploring the region. He examined every slight valley and camped beside every waterhole, forcing his mind back into the minds of his forefathers, to think as they thought, to see life as they saw it. He struggled to grasp the secret of the disbelief and weakness that forced their wilderness wandering; then he struggled to grasp the secret of the faith and fierce commitment that made their children a conquering nation.

He walked the trackless expanse of the Tih, the vast plain west of the Wilderness of Paran, and wondered at the black flint, worn glass smooth by the wind-driven sand, thickly strewn across the gravel plain, a mixture of black against harsh white. He felt the flint slip underfoot and cut into his sandals, and his legs ached from the short, ineffective steps he was forced to take.

He scooped dirt from wadi junctures to uncover the hidden water of the *temails*, and filled his waterpouch time and again with the yellow, brackish fluid that appeared when the sand was scooped from the right place. He wandered over the Tih for hours at a time without seeing a single shrub. He wondered at the tiny snails that sealed themselves airtight onto the rare plants that grew erratically along wadis. At the appearance of the equally rare rainy season the snails would come to life again.

The prophet traveled east to explore the Wilderness of Paran, part of the terrible plateau that broke farther east into eerie, craggy mountains in their plunge to the Arabah. He tried to guess where his forefathers may have traveled, where they pastured their flocks, and where they pitched their tents. He felt the hardness of the arid region, and felt the sun burn into his already deeply tanned skin. When he ran out of water he felt the spittle dry salty on his lips, to leave them swollen and cracked. He felt the fiery burning of a parched throat and the heavy weight of disobeying limbs and the fear of hallucinations in a land that did not care.

He watched the colors of the gray and white desert turn to hues of reddish browns and more distinct grays, and saw the sandstone hills turn into rainbows brushed by the rising and setting sun. He felt the breathtaking heat of the still *hamsin* and shivered under the heavy and penetrating cold of the nights. He looked forward each day to the relief of the late afternoon breeze that rarely failed to come.

He ate sparingly, to allow the fast to do its work in his soul. When he did eat, it was the pleasantly acrid, fleshy-leafed *gataf* plant.

The days were too agonizing to pass quickly. They lingered long, the nights longer, to melt one into the next with an ever-increasing sameness. Toward the end he knew he had discovered the source both of weakness and strength that drained one generation and shaped the next. The desert that proved too hard for a generation of slaves formed of their children a generation of warriors.

He found that secret, but he did not find the answer to his own life. Mount Carmel still loomed as one of Israel's great miracles, and the Israelites still followed other gods.

During his wanderings he had worked his way farther south into the wilderness, so that on the morning when he determined to move on to Mount Horeb he stood on the southern rim of the Tih. The air was quite cold, and the prophet shivered even under the warmth of his mantle. The enormous plateau cut its triangular point through the heartland of Sinai. Then it stopped, with abruptness, to fall away all along its cliffs to a wide sandstone plain, the Debbet er Ramleh. Its mountains were low and rare, broad at their tops, with bizarre shapes, its valleys sheer-walled and narrow.

Beyond the sandstone range rose the blue-hard granite mountains, the majesty of all Sinai. They were a chaotic mass, with sharp ridges and snowcapped peaks that clawed upward to tear at the sky. Mount Horeb was straight ahead, two days' journey away, the highest point on the peninsula. The slightly lower but unbowing Mount Serbal rose to dominate the range to the west of God's mountain.

Elijah was thinner now, his skin looking older from his fast, with slight hollows under his cheekbones. His limb muscles were sinewy rather than rounded, his dark eyes and hair more prominent even than before. He moved down the trail with resolute determination, his mind forcing his body, his body obeying with strength drawn from the mind, obeying because the mind would not let the body stop. The body was beyond fatigue, unfeeling, a vehicle only to carry the mind.

But the endurance of the body passed into the mind. The mind would not be still. It darted catlike from thought to thought, finely tuned by the desert fast to recall details of the prophet's life and of Israel's history. Yet for all its discipline and recall it could not quiet the prophet's foreboding spirit. The soul was as exhausted as the body, forced on to Horeb only by the dominating mind.

He was in a different world now, the sickly-green herbage of the valley that wound through a maze of barren ridges looking rich in comparison to the Tih. Large thorny trees grew spasmodically along the bottom and lower sides of the narrow valley. The walls rose sharply on both sides, perpendicular at places.

By late afternoon he arrived at the large Wadi Feiran, the route the ancient Israelites followed inland from the Red Sea during the Exodus. The floor was of white sand, smooth in places, stone-littered in others. The mountains rose in irregular patterns from each side, their height tempered by the wadi's wideness.

He turned east. His mind projected into the valley a scene, almost a mirage in its reality, of thousands of newly-freed slaves shuffling along the path of dust and stone, their fear dominating their hope, their bickering eclipsing their faith, led by a man determined to free them against their will. It was here, in Sinai, not many miles up the wadi, that Moses had faced some of his most trying hours. But in those hours, Elijah's mind insisted to his sick soul and tired body, Moses heard God most decisively.

By midafternoon of the next day the prophet could contain his excitement no longer. He broke into a run, his sandals kicking up spurts of dust where his toes propelled him forward. He ran hard for a few minutes, then settled into an easier stride. The valley was splotched with vegetation, thin-trunked acacia trees with their flat tops of tangled branches, palms ringed along their bottoms with wild new growth from fallen seeds, and gnarl-trunked terebinths. He passed all of it without notice, nor did he notice the peaks, rising ever higher and more imposing as he moved south. He ran erect, his legs pumping in their short-stepped way, his arms moving in rhythm to his stride, his eyes fixed only on the wadi as an obstacle to surmount.

Elijah maintained his pace for four miles, then, as he rounded a bend, Mount Horeb came into view. He stopped, his hands at his sides, his breath coming in deep, fast gulps. The base of the mountain was hidden by outcroppings and turns of the wadi, but the bald ridge rose in steep precipices all the more imposing because the prophet had not noticed the increasing height and strength of the range.

He fell to his knees, his arms limp to his sides, still with his face raised to the Mount of God. Its high crags scraped hard knuckles against the sky. The Mount of God indeed was awesomely majestic, powerful, immovable, but it did not speak. No thundercloud hung over its blue-shouldered height. No crevice opened up to speak. No message was etched on its rocky cliffs. The excitement drained from him then. He felt empty, unable to express either his sense of shame or his anger. Yet he knew from a lifetime of experience with God that Yahweh often does not speak when the servant expects him to. Disappointed, yet confident that Yahweh would speak in his own time, the prophet rose to complete his journey.

In thirty minutes he came to the plain where Israel assembled to hear the reading of the Law. The prophet looked up the two-mile length of the Plain of Rahah. The whole nation could be accommodated by its wideness.

He turned to face the Mount of Safsafeh. It was not the highest peak in the range, but it was imposing. Elijah surveyed the holy mountain carefully, trying to set every detail in its proper place in history. Moses could have stood on any of a number of ridges on the lower part of Safsafeh as he read the Law to the assembled Israelites. And a select group of tribal leaders could have stood on the semicircular mound that ran along the base to form an amphitheatre, a favored position from which to hear the solemn words.

A peaklike ridge caught the prophet's eye. It was a miniature of the whole mount itself. Though less than halfway up, it claimed a majesty of its own. *A perfect place for a golden calf,* he thought, *a limited view but an easier climb. It is the nature of men to settle for less than Yahweh can offer.*

His sense of despondency returned. How must Moses have felt at that moment when he came down the mountain with the stone tablets heavy in his arms, only to see the golden calf standing on that lower hill? Moses had his miracles, too, and yet his people worshiped other gods.

Elijah stared at Safsafeh into the evening, until its sunset-pinked walls turned dark and he turned with a shiver to find his shelter for the night. All of those miracles and more did not keep the Israelites from abandoning Yahweh for their golden calf.

Chapter Fifteen

During the next several days Elijah explored the region. Water was plentiful, perhaps more than anywhere in Sinai. He found running streams in four of the valleys that ran in and around Mount Horeb. A wide basin, beautiful and rich, dipped high up into the center of the mountain. The range had several basins, in fact, with a variety of grass, herbs, and trees, all unseen from below.

On successive days he climbed the various peaks, each time expecting a message from Yahweh, each time caught only in his own thoughts. He scaled Mount Safsafeh first, trying to recapture Moses' experience. There was a small basin part of the way up, where Moses may have left the elders of Israel to continue his climb alone.

The long, high ridge behind Safsafeh, Elijah concluded, was where Moses must have received the Law. A small cave would offer protection to the lawgiver during his forty days on the mountain, and not far away was a cleft large enough for a man to crawl into. Perhaps the cleft was where Moses caught a glimpse of God. The summit itself rose even higher, precipitously, from the ridge; perhaps at its peak Moses received Yahweh's Law.

The prophet did not climb the highest peak until spring, after the snow and ice had melted. The cold was bitter on the other peaks, too, with hard winds. He would not have exposed himself to the region at all except for his impatience to survey the places of Israel's beginnings as a nation.

Yahweh's voice was silent during the days of exploration, and silent still after Elijah had examined every point except the highest of the mass of Mount Horeb. The prophet was silent, too. He could not pray, though he often tried. He simply could not express the rumblings of his soul. His life was too impractical, too misused, too wasted on a people who would not respond. He had not dreamed of being the last prophet in a line of faith, but of rousing success in his efforts to bring the people back to Yahweh. The hiding, the loneliness, the austerity, the taunts, the fear, the anger of rulers all were worth bearing if the end brought success, but not if the battle were lost.

The immobile mountains spoke to Elijah, but their message was not clear. One day the barren crags spoke of hard, barren hearts; and another day the green ribbons of valley spoke of hearts that yielded fruit. One day Elijah saw visions in the wadis of Israelites who made a golden calf; on another day the visions were of a people who did, ultimately, follow Yahweh.

As days passed into weeks Elijah spent long hours staring from high ridges at the great mass of gray granite peaks, and their hardness came into his spirit. He could feel the steeling of his nerves. The food of the basins and valleys gradually filled out the muscles of his body, too, so that he took on once again the hard, healthy stockiness he had before his fast. His eyes lost their bewildered look, and took on again the prophet's piercing depth.

Yet Yahweh did not speak.

Elijah became restless. He thought of Israel more. As March broke up the winter, he recalled images of Baal altars once again, and felt the anger rise again in his chest. But the renewed sensations only frustrated him more, for Jezebel had won. Yahweh no longer had a foothold in Israel.

It was in early April that Yahweh spoke. Elijah sat on a ridge below his adopted cave, watching the granite peaks that shone in the spring sun like burnished copper. The voice startled him, so abruptly did it break into his thoughts. He jumped to his feet and looked around. The hard mountains looked the same, with the shadows of their crevices etched deep into their sides. The voice had not been loud, and he wasn't sure whether it came from Mount Horeb or from within his own breast. The voice asked simply, "What are you doing here, Elijah?"

The prophet answered out loud, with an edge of anger such as when one lover feels wronged by the other. "I have been zealous for you, Yahweh, knowing that you are Lord of all the hosts of heaven." The prophet's voice was strong, louder than the voice that spoke to him. "I have fought hard for you, because the children of Israel have turned away from the covenant you made with them to be their God and they to be your people. They have thrown down your altars and slaughtered your prophets." Elijah gazed upward toward the summit he could not see. Surely that was where the voice had come from. "I am the only one left, God, I alone, and I am marked for death, too. They are looking for me to kill me."

The answer from God came quickly. It rose from within Elijah's soul and from outside, too. It sounded from inside his head and from the rocks and trees of the mountain. He felt it in his limbs and heard it from the valleys below. The voice was soft, but commanding. "Go and stand on the mountain in my presence."

Elijah started immediately up the mountain, climbing up a fairly easy trail that ran along towering precipices. Once on the ridge he made his way quickly to his cave. Inside, he turned to face the opening, his heart beating more rapidly from his awe of Yahweh than from the climb.

He had stood only a moment when a loud, whirring sound began. It quickly grew louder. The day darkened with surprising suddenness. Soon a wind of gale proportions sucked at the mouth of his cave and whistled in the crevices of the rocky ridge. Elijah fell prone to the cave floor and buried his head under his arms. The sound grew louder still, the terrifying storm of rainless wind whipping and snapping with wild fury at the mountain, trying to rip the rock skin from the Mount of God itself. Loud screeches echoed in the cave as the wind twisted trees around on their trunks, then horrendous cracks like thunder tore into his cave as trees were roughly severed from their bases. Torn trees plummeted down the mountainside, joined by boulders knocked loose by the weight, to fill the air with horrifying crashes, scraping against the rock sides of the slope on their way to the valley below. In the midst of the screaming sounds of the stricken earth an even louder crack sent chills along his spine as a large boulder crashed into an outcropping to force it loose from the parent mountain.

The storm lasted almost an hour, then a deep quiet settled over the peaks. Elijah rose cautiously and moved slowly toward the mouth of the cave. He looked out. The sky was clear. He inched out to find a better vantage point. A large boulder lay a few yards from the cave. Below, down the valley where he had heard God's voice, other boulders had cut tracks of destruction. Outcroppings that had become familiar to him were sheared off, their jagged edges left strangely lighter in color than the weathered pieces that lay broken below. Shallow trenches were cut promiscuously down the steep slope by the plummeting and tumbling rocks and trees. Below, the tree trunks and boulders and stones were heaped together in a wild tangled mass. Branches of bruised bark and torn leaves littered the slope and the valley floor. Bare trunks jutted out from the downward slope, their torn splinters shining yellow-white in the sun. The stumps were bare and pitted, their bark stripped away and lying in tiny bits below them. To the right, not far away, a part of the mountain itself was torn apart from the range, standing alone as a sharp uplifted hand separated from its body by a deep chasm. The howling and crashing and wrenching screeches still echoed in Elijah's head. A throbbing fear forced heavy thumps in his chest.

The mountain was silent now. Not even the faintest breeze broke the quiet, now almost as ominous as the sudden storm itself.

Elijah surveyed the destruction for many minutes. Surely God had called him to the mountaintop for this experience. Surely in it Yahweh had a word. Perhaps this is the message the prophet should deliver to Israel. Yahweh will tear them with the vengeance of a mighty storm.

But Yahweh did not say that. Was that not the message the prophet had preached all of his ministry? He could not deliver again such a message of wrath without divine certainty that it was from God. But Yahweh was as quiet now as the air itself.

Elijah walked slowly through the destruction back to his cave. He sat in the cave's mouth and looked out onto the torn scene. Chills broke out on his arms several times as the terrifying sounds forced their way back into his mind. He listened to the day, expecting at any moment that Yahweh would speak again. But as the sunset touched the mountains again with color, ignoring the destruction below, Elijah still waited for that new word. Gradually, the colors on the granite lost their tone and the night fastened its grip on Sinai. A soft breeze began to blow then, its whisper a contrast to the wildness of the storm. The prophet nodded his thanks to Yahweh for the breeze and went into the cave for the night.

He awoke the next morning and went again to the mouth of the cave. Nothing had changed. The desolate scene was untempered from the day before. He sighed and shook his head. He started out of the cave, but in midstep the earth beneath him began to shake. He leaned his back against the cave wall and pressed his hands against its roof. The tremor increased. The hard, dirt-covered rock floor under him vibrated in quick, short movements, then with increasing tempo. There was a rhythm to it for the first moments, then the shaking became more erratic and violent. Elijah fell to the floor again and crawled in panic farther into the cave. Dust fell from the roof to fill the air with its choking fineness. The earth roared now, a long, rending, scraping, sliding sound of rock on rock, and the noises of yesterday tore the air, louder than before, built on and carried by the shaking of the mountain. The thought flashed through his mind that Yahweh was going to take his life now as he had requested weeks before. It was fitting that he should die in Mount Horeb. But the cave roof held, and the quake was over in a few moments.

The dust in the cave filled Elijah's nostrils and throat. He coughed, trying to expel the choking particles, then sucked in more of it as he gasped for air. He ran for the cave opening, coughing with such force that he had trouble with his footing. Outside, the floating dust formed a sheet above the earth as it was caught by the wind and pushed away.

The boulder that yesterday was deposited near the cave was gone. The broken hand of mountain that had been separated by a crevice from its parent was split away. It lay in a thousand pieces up and down the mountain, leaving its destruction behind it. The mass of tangled tree trunks and branches in the valley reached out their shredded limbs in grostesque gestures for help, broken by the weight of monstrous boulders released onto them by the quake. To the right the ancient crevice that had mystified him for days with its clinging bits of hardy growth between its jaws had opened wider, a chasm now whose bottom was lost in darkness.

Elijah could breathe now, but a taste of dust still lingered in the air, and the sun filtered through its haze to cast a dismal glow onto the mountain.

The prophet looked around carefully, half expecting a message from Yahweh to be etched in the newly-created crevice, or in the tangled mass of tree and rock below, or written in the dust that hung high in the air. But again he was met by the silence of God. Even the light wind that followed the earthquake had died away. Now, as yesterday, the day was bathed in quiet, as though nature had to catch its breath after the destruction before she could speak again. The newly rent rocks rested unmoving in their new places. The severed stumps suffered their stigma of death silently. The light litter of leaves from torn trees lay serenely where they fell.

The day wore on and Elijah did not leave his place. He paced up and down the ridge beyond his cave. If God did not want him to die, what then was his cause to live? What message did Yahweh have for his prophet?

Yahweh did not answer.

Evening came as before, ushered in by the same faint whisper of breeze that yesterday had cleansed the air and swept away the heat. As yesterday, Elijah thanked God for the gift, then continued his vigilance for the word from Yahweh.

Night came and Elijah ate of his stored provisions before stretching out to sleep. His mind raced unremittingly as he lay on his bed of leaves and twigs, his mantle spread under and over him. He could recall only two phrases from Yahweh, one question and one command. The prophet had answered the question and obeyed the command. What indeed was he doing here? Waiting for a word from his God. And Yahweh's command to go to the top of the mountain surely was a preface to some word to come. Was there a message in Yahweh's question? Were the cataclysmic events a warning that he should not be here? But, surely, there was more.

The next morning Elijah trembled as he left the mouth of the cave. His fright was mixed with a sense of anticipation to see what God would do next. A slight breeze blew, warm, not cool as the morning breeze usually was. He looked to the east, expecting to see the approach of dark storm clouds. Sure enough, they formed beyond the peaks, out toward the Gulf of Aqabah. Elijah watched them, entranced, as they thickened. They built up quickly, their thunderheads rising higher into the sky, gathering together in a great mass as they moved over the Sinai range. The mountain peaks looked blue and purple under them, dark colors, as dark as the clouds themselves, majestic and awesome in their shrouded fury. Lightning flashed from them, and in moments grand thunderclaps reached Elijah's ears. The storm moved west, toward Mount Horeb, and soon the wind blew in hard fits around the prophet. His hair blew into his eyes and he felt the whipping of his beard against his neck. He watched and felt it, feeling as if he stood inside the voice of God, until the rain started. A few large drops fell first, irregularly, blown ahead of the clouds by the wind. By the time he ducked into his cave the storm had come in fury, blowing its rain so hard that he had to move farther back into the cave's interior.

The sound of the thunderclap invaded the hollow sanctity of the cave simultaneously with its flash. He did not see where the lightning struck, but it was nearby and, he knew from its force, destructive. The rain fell only for a few moments, but its force was furious. Then it passed over the mountain to the west. Before Elijah could make his way out of the cave the sun was out again.

He was surprised that the fury was so short and ineffective. He made his way out to the cliff edge to survey the storm's effect on the torn valley. Then he saw it. The mass of tangled trunks and branches in the deep wadi below was burning. He watched the flames, curiously for awhile, then with alarm as they spread rapidly along the huge pile of nature's trash. Soon he could hear its roar, even at his distance, burning with the white heat of a smelter's fire. Bits of bark and twigs, still burning, rose on the hot waves of the flames to be carried by the wind all along the valley. Within an hour the unchecked flames spread throughout the wadi, the floating bits of fire igniting clumps of trees and bushes up and down its length. The smaller clumps of growth burned rapidly, the larger ones more slowly but more fiercely, their own fires throwing off faggots to ignite other trees and bushes. The fire roared with the sound of a thousand chariots into the afternoon before it began to die.

Elijah watched in amazement and listened again for God's voice in the destruction. By evening the valley was black, the fires gone but smoke rising from bare black trunks that stood like violated sticks in the battleground of nature. Every tree and bush within his sight was burned. The valley walls around the clumps and clusters of now-destroyed growth were carbon black. The rubbish pile still smoldered, sending the acrid smell of its smoke, thicker now in the aftermath of the fire, to burn Elijah's nostrils. There was not the slightest doubt in the prophet's mind that somewhere in the destruction and power of the last three days Yahweh had a message.

He watched the smoldering pile below, pock-marked with boulders sent down by the quake. The destruction was terrible, he thought, but with the passage of time the dead roots would decay and the burned growth would come back greener than ever. The broken mountain would accept its scars, and later visitors would point with admiration at the awesome formations as surely as he himself had pointed to other ones before the storm and quake. Nothing really was changed.

As he mused, the breeze began again, like the day before and the day before that. It was only a whisper, a gentle movement of air, so faint that he could hardly tell its direction. But soon the smoke-filled air freshened and the evening sky became clearer and the sun's rays once again touched the bare mountain walls with copper and pink and gold. *In the end*, Elijah thought, *it is the gentle breeze that most inspires a man to give thanks to God.*

A shudder passed through the prophet's body, and a prickling sensation lingered in his chest and arms. He looked up and asked aloud, "Is that your message to me, Yahweh?"

The prophet's eyes were wide with surprise. He began to pace toward his cave, then back toward the scene below. His mind raced back to Mount Carmel, to the miraculous display of power, to the sight of the fiery bolt streaking from the clear sky to ignite the sacrifice and altar, to the muffled cries of the astonished people, to the loud screams of partylike delight as they slaughtered the prophets of Baal, to the bloodstained Kishon River and the heaps of bodies that raped its waters.

The breeze began to speak. "My ways are not your ways. I work mysteriously in the hearts of men to win their love." The breeze spoke softly, in a tone barely audible but that came from every direction, whispering from the sky, and from the valley, and from the mountain, surrounding the prophet with its truth.

"Did I do wrong on Carmel?" Elijah asked out loud. He repeated the question more loudly, turning slowly to speak to the gentle voice that surrounded him. "Did I do wrong on Carmel?"

The voice responded in its quiet strength. "My ways are not your ways. I work gently in the hearts of men."

Elijah fell to his knees, oblivious to the hard rocky shelf, his arms outstretched, his mind whirling. Mount Carmel did not work. The miraculous display of power did not bring the immediate change in Israel he had dreamed it would. But surely the strong methods of Jezebel called for such bold action. Surely strength should be met with strength.

"My ways are not your ways," the faint breeze repeated.

The prophet lowered his arms. He still was on his knees, but his body was straight, his faced turned upward. The breeze did not pass with the coming of dusk. It stayed and whispered its message again and again until it came into Elijah's body and took up a rhythm with his heart. He could not speak. He felt that he stood at a moment of great revelation, yet he could find no response to Yahweh. In his silence, his months-old sense of despondency returned. How could he change his ministry? Did he have it in him to change? Where would he start? How does a hard prophet speak softly to the hearts of men?

Yahweh did not allow him too near the precipice of his doubt. As Elijah's unspoken questions spilled into his soul, God spoke again. He asked the question he had asked three days before. "What are you doing here, Elijah?"

Elijah looked beyond the rocky ridge to the uprising summit of Mount Horeb, but even as he looked out he felt the question from inside. He repeated his answer of three days ago. "I have been zealous for you, Yahweh, God of all the hosts of heaven. Your people have ignored the covenant you made with them. They have destroyed your altars. They have slaughtered your prophets. I am the only one left, and now they seek my life."

The breeze died away for a moment. Elijah rose to his feet, breathing heavily. He put his hands to his face. The breeze must not stop now, not on the verge of an answer. Then the breeze began again, gentle, as before, and he heard his name. "Elijah." He lowered his hands and looked around. "Elijah," the word came again, carried to his heart on the whisper of wind. "Go," it said, "turn around and journey to the wilderness of Damascus. When you get there, anoint Hazael to be king of Syria. And anoint Jehu the son of Nimshi to be king of Israel. And anoint Elisha the son of Shaphat of Abel-meholah to be your successor as prophet. And it shall happen that whoever escapes the sword of Hazael shall be slain by Jehu, and whoever escapes the sword of Jehu shall be slain by Elisha." The breeze repeated his name then. "Elijah," it said, and again, "Elijah." He looked up and turned to survey the air above. "Elijah, you are not the only Israelite faithful to Yahweh. I still have seven thousand souls in Israel who have not bowed to Baal and have not kissed his idol. Go. Your work waits to be done."

The breeze died away. Elijah listened for a moment longer, then turned toward his cave. *Hazael is to be king of Syria. Jehu is to be king of Israel. Elisha is to be my successor.* Inside the cave, he pondered the message from Yahweh as he selected his evening meal from his stored provisions. *If Yahweh speaks gently to the hearts of men, how is it that Hazael and Elisha and Jehu will slaughter the enemies of God?*

The prophet finished his meal and retired early to rest for the long trip he would begin in the morning. As he lay waiting for sleep to come, though, he could not erase the contradiction between Yahweh's message to him and the predictions of violence. What kind of God was Yahweh? He speaks gently to woo the hearts of men, yet he punishes obstinate men who turn themselves loose to sin. He is a God of love and a God of judgment. In the twilight of sleep Elijah felt a voice speaking yet again. It came from inside his soul, and spoke from inside his mind. "My ways are not your ways. My ways are past finding out. Your task is to be faithful to what you know to do."

Naboth rose from his knees, smiling with satisfaction. The shoots were growing well; the canes were tied properly to the trellis. The three years of drought had not dulled his sons' knowledge of vinedressing.

He was a small man, slender, with a flat stomach and narrow chest. His two sons were larger, thankfully, like their mother. The early spring work of clearing out the fall prunings was exhausting; each harvest was more difficult with the heavy lifting of the rich clusters. But he enjoyed everything connected with the land, even the aching tiredness that stayed with him throughout the busier seasons. His vineyards were good. Each trunk was as familiar to him as each sheep is to a shepherd. He watched the vineyard carefully, supervised the pruning and tying and harvest. He walked up and down the rows during the hot summer to gauge the amount of heavy morning dew, guessing with the knowledge of generations behind him at the effect of the wetness and of the sun on his harvest.

Life hardly could be better, now that the drought was over. His family was healthy, his daughters married, his sons a credit to any father. He was the representative of an ancestral family that helped settle the city, an honored member of the council of Jezreel. Naboth looked up at the sun. The year had gone well so far. The crop should be a good one.

He was pulled from his reverie by Ahab's voice. He looked toward the palace. The king made his way alone among the vines, waving as he approached.

The vinegrower returned the greeting and started toward Ahab, who waited patiently while Naboth went through the amenities of kneeling and entreating God's blessing on the royal house.

"Naboth," the king said, "I have not seen you much lately. How have you been?"

"Good, King Ahab. Very good since the drought ended."

"Your vines look good, as usual."

"Yes, they are coming along well."

"Naboth, I have come to make you an offer." Ahab spoke carefully, but took pains to sound pleasant. Naboth watched him quizzically. "My friend, I have great need for a garden where I can grow herbs and food for my summer home. Your vineyard is next to the palace. There could be no better field for me."

Naboth's eyes narrowed. He looked out over the vineyard and then gazed up intently into Ahab's eyes. "My king, this is my ancestral land. It would be wrong for me to give it up."

"I shall be more than fair with you, Naboth," Ahab pressed. "I own other fields, some of them better and larger than yours. I will give you better land for your vineyard." He laughed, seeking to ease Naboth's growing tension. "Or if you fancy the life of a merchant, I will pay you well for the field."

Naboth's response was quick. "No, my king. I cannot sell, nor can I trade. The field has belonged to my family for many generations. No price can make up for that. My roots are here, as surely as the roots of my vines."

"Vines can grow as well in other fields. Transplanting is no problem, not with vines and not with people, so long as the vines are in good soil and the people are with their friends."

"I cannot give you the land."

Ahab stared at Naboth sternly. "You are being unreasonable, Naboth. No other field will do for me. Your land adjoins mine. Surely there is a price that would be honorable for you and your sons."

"No, my king. I cannot sell."

Ahab felt a rising stab of anger. He held himself in control, but he studied Naboth's face indignantly. "You refuse even to negotiate?"

"I am sorry, King Ahab. My loyalty to you is well-known,

but this field is my life. It means more to me than anything in the world. By law, an Israelite is within his rights to keep his ancestral land. It is holy to him. I hope you understand. I cannot leave my field."

The king did not respond. He turned toward the palace, then faced Naboth again. The vinegrower's face was set. Ahab stalked away heavily. Naboth watched him cross the field. He had known Ahab for a long time. Often the king invited him as an honored guest for summer parties at the palace. They had talked together, even at times about policies of state. *I would do anything for him*, Naboth thought, *but I cannot leave my land*. Troubled, he turned toward his own house.

Ahab stormed into his summer palace without acknowledging the greetings of the door guards. His footsteps rang on the hard stone floor and he took the stairs two at a time. Jezebel stopped to watch him pass her without a word and slam the door to his bedroom chambers. She followed. Entering the room softly, she called to him. "Ahab?"

The king did not answer. His face was buried in his pillows, his back to her.

"Ahab, what's wrong?"

He raised an arm and waved the queen violently from the room. Jezebel slipped out and closed the door quietly.

Ahab did not come to dinner that evening. Jezebel had seen him angry before, but never so sullen as now. She ate in silence. Well before the court finished their meals she left the banquet hall and went to Ahab's bedroom.

The king lay unmoved with his face to the wall. She sat on the bed. "My husband and king," she asked with tenderness, "why are you so distraught?"

He did not move.

"My king, surely nothing has happened that cannot be remedied. Why have you shut yourself off from me?" The queen laid her hand on his shoulder. "Ahab, please. Don't be sullen. Uncover your head and tell me what is wrong."

Ahab pulled the pillows away and threw them violently against the wall. "Naboth refuses to sell me his field."

Jezebel laughed softly, but she caught herself as Ahab

turned toward her, his face flushed and angry. Quickly she asked, "Why did he refuse to give you the land?"

"I made him every offer. I told him I would trade him a better field or pay him more than it is worth. He would not even bargain."

Jezebel rose and walked to the center of the room. She turned toward him and spoke sternly. "I fear that you are following the way of Yahweh."

Ahab swung his legs over the mattress and blurted his words. "Naboth is within the law. It is his ancestral land. He has the right to keep the field." He slammed his fist into the bed.

The queen did not speak. She felt a sense of indignation rise in her. "Ahab," she called with a tone of authority, "who is king of Israel?"

"What kind of question is that?" Ahab responded angrily.

"Are you king of Israel or not?" Jezebel asked.

Ahab looked at her hard.

"Come and eat," the queen smiled. "Melkart has ways of serving kings and queens. I will get the land for you." She extended her hand to Ahab.

His look softened and he shook his head. "How can you be so cocksure?"

"Because I know my God." She waved her fingers to offer her hand. "I will get you the land, then I will give it to you as a gift. Now, come with me and eat."

Ahab shrugged his shoulders and rose from the bed.

The next morning Jezebel went to her business chamber early. She called for parchment and wrote a single letter to be circulated to the leading men of Jezreel. She handed it to the courier with express instructions to wait until each man on the list read the letter, then to carry it to the next man. Naboth was not on the list.

Within a week, the men on the list had called a three-day fast for Jezreel. The people responded with obedience. They had no real choice but to trust their leaders. Such a fast as this announced that the city stood in danger of calamity. The unknown cause must be discovered and rectified during the fast.

In each home, under candlelight, each family talked of the fast's meaning. Who had breached God's law so severely as to bring the entire city into danger? Did the councilmen think Ben-hadad was going to attack? Was the drought to begin again? They mused over past events. They searched their own lives. They looked at their neighbors with suspicion. Their stomachs growled with hunger. The men gathered in the marketplace to argue the possibilities. The women gossiped at the city's wells. Through it all, the councilmen maintained a glum silence, while Naboth wondered why he was not consulted before the announcement.

On the evening of the third day the men of Jezreel met in solemn assembly in the judgment hall. To his surprise, Naboth was given the seat of high honor at the center of the head table. He wondered why. Yet had he not been a leading citizen for years? Perhaps he was to be honored for past service.

Other councilmen took their places on either side of him up and down the long table. The townsmen crowded into the room to sit on the hard benches. The bustle of robes and low chatter was subdued by solemn concern, for tonight the impending crisis would be announced, or perhaps discovered, and solutions would be sought.

A priest rose and began his chant.

> Happy is the man whose disobedience is forgiven,
>   whose sin is put away!
> Happy is a man when the Lord lays no guilt to his
>   account, and in his spirit there is no deceit.*

The assembled people responded with a loud, "Amen." The priest continued, his monotonous chant hardly changing in pitch, reciting every inflection just as it had been determined by long custom. The people knew every word well, and where to interrupt with the proper response.

> While I refused to speak, my body wasted away
>   with moaning all the day long.

*Psalm 32

2 3 4

For day and night
thy hand was upon me,
the sap in me dried up as in summer drought.

"It is true, O God," the people shouted, filling the brief time space allotted by the priest.

Then I declared my sin, I did not conceal my guilt.
I said, "With sorrow I will confess
my disobedience to the Lord";
Then thou didst remit the penalty of my sin.

"We confess, O God."

So every faithful heart shall pray to thee in the
hour of anxiety, when great floods threaten.
Thou art a refuge for me from distress
so that it cannot touch me;
thou dost guard me and enfold me in salvation
beyond all reach of harm.

"God is merciful."

I will teach you, and guide you in the way you
should go.
I will keep you under my eye.
Do not behave like horse or mule, unreasoning
creatures, whose course must be checked with
bit and bridle.

"Heal our hearts, O God."

Many are the torments of the ungodly;
but unfailing love enfolds him who trusts in the
Lord.
Rejoice in the Lord and be glad, you righteous men,
and sing aloud, all men of upright heart.*

"Rejoice in the Lord, for he is merciful."

The priest paused and raised his hands upward. The people joined him immediately as he recited the Shema,

*New English Bible

his voice pitched higher than usual. All of them spoke in monotone, dropping their voices at the end of each phrase: "Hear, O Israel, Yahweh is our God, one Lord."

The priest sat down. An elder seated beside Naboth rose. He spoke as though his words were memorized. "People of Jezreel," he began, "we have met here in solemn assembly to seek the word of Yahweh as to our sin, to purge our sin and petition our God to remove the calamity that faces us. But before we proceed, the council has determined to honor a man who has served our city well." He caught Naboth by the arm to beckon him to his feet.

As if on signal, two men rose from the back of the hall and started forward. One of them shouted, "A moment, my lord."

The elder feigned surprise. Naboth looked at his host in anticipation. The two men sat on the bench in front of the table, as accusers were required to do, directly across from Naboth.

"This man deserves no honor, my lord," one of them said.

Naboth sat down, his brow wrinkled, but satisfied to let the elder handle the interruption.

The accuser continued. "My companion and I are here to tell the whole assembly the cause of the fast. It is Naboth who brings threat of disaster to Jezreel."

"You have an accusation to make against Naboth?" the elder asked. He glanced nervously at the accused.

"Naboth has cursed Yahweh and the king. By law, he must be stoned. This is the cause of the calamity."

"Your charge is serious. Are you certain?" the elder interrupted.

"In the presence of my companion and myself, after King Ahab talked to Naboth about buying his vineyard, Naboth cursed the king. To curse God's anointed one is to curse Yahweh himself."

"You need not inform the council of the law. Do you swear to the truth of your charge?"

Naboth pulled himself to his feet and leaned angrily toward the men. "You lie!" he shouted. "Never have I cursed the king. I do not know you!"

"We heard him in the marketplace. This man is not worthy of honor. He is worthy only to be stoned for his blasphemy."

The elder shouted his question again over Naboth's protests. "The law requires two witnesses to such a crime. Do both of you swear you tell the truth?"

"Yes, we swear," the men answered simultaneously. "We are witnesses, both of us."

Induced by the fast and the tension it created, the pent-up emotion of the people exploded. Yahweh had given the answer to the distress. Naboth was the guilty one. "Stone him!" someone shouted. Several young men pulled the table out of the way and rushed at Naboth, whose screams of protest were lost in the din. He flailed at them, but a blow by one of the larger men sent him sprawling. Naboth's sons struggled toward their father, screaming at the young men to leave him alone, swinging indiscriminately at all who caught at their clothing.

The hysteria spread. Other men joined the melee. Naboth whimpered with disbelief. His sons were surrounded by men who caught their legs and arms and pummeled their faces and bodies. The crowd moved toward the door and out into the street, carrying the dazed Naboth and the struggling sons with them. Someone shouted that the law required the whole family to be stoned. Another voice took up the call for Naboth's wife. A crowd of men moved toward the house to fetch her.

The scene lasted only minutes. Naboth and his sons were carried by their arms and legs outside the city walls and thrown into a gully. The first stone caught the back of Naboth's shoulder, then another one broke his hand as he covered his face. The three men were unconscious by the time their wife and mother was shoved headlong down the low hill to join them. Her clothes were ripped away, shamefully exposing her aged breasts. The men aimed their rocks at her exposure. She pulled herself mutely to her knees, the screaming gone, and called her husband's name.

The crowd paused for a moment. She tried to crawl toward him. A man shouted and threw a rock with deadly aim. She collapsed. A pool of blood quickly formed under her head. The rocks continued, thrown with all the strength the men could muster as they tried to outdo their fellows in zeal and marksmanship. Soon the bodies were half covered with the sharp stones. One son's cheek was torn back in jagged red edges over one eye. Blood streamed from a severed artery in Naboth's neck. The soft thuds continued long after the cries had stopped.

The last sounds were of rocks clattering on rocks, thrown with less fury and less aim than before. The crowd grew silent. Slowly, men turned toward the city gates. The shocked ones left first, the more morbid later. The last man threw the last rock with all his fury, as though to confirm the righteousness of his cause.

Naboth's daughters cowered in their homes, crying hysterically, their doors guarded by their husbands against the mob that had forgotten them.

An hour later Jezebel received word that the deed was done. She went to Ahab. "See, Melkart wins his battles. Naboth and all his heirs are dead. The vineyard is yours."

Ahab looked at her, his brow wrinkled. His smile ignored his heart.

Chapter Sixteen

THE GULF OF AQABAH stretched long and deeply blue between two rows of incredibly desolate hills. The eastern range across the gulf was higher and shut from sight the ugliness of the Arabian desert. Elijah stood in the mouth of the Wadi Sa'deh, where it emptied out from its narrow, deep ravine onto the mile-wide gravel plain that sloped gradually to the sea. He could see as far north as Ras el-Burka, the small headland that jutted a few yards into the gulf.

It was the fourth day since he left Mount Horeb. He was used to the southern wilderness now, so the journey was not difficult, though unpleasant. He had followed the route of the Exodus, as described to him by the old man of Kadesh, but he moved much faster than his forefathers could have done with their herds and children and belongings.

He was glad to be out of the hills, able to travel now on level land beside clear water. The sun still was hot, the glare from the white beach was unpleasant, but the way was infinitely better than the soft, dry dune sand and the incessant climbing in and out of wadis.

A cluster of palm trees at the edge of the water marked the fountain the old man had told him about. Elijah started toward it, leaving the larger rocks near the cliff. As he neared the water the rocks became smaller until, near the palms and along the shore of the gulf, the soil was composed mostly of fine gravel and sand.

The well was eight or ten feet deep, the water brackish. Its mildly sulfurous odor teased his nostrils, but he lowered the attached vessel anyway to fill his waterpouch. The old man had cautioned him that he would find no more good water until he came to Ezion-geber.

Elijah slung the waterpouch across his shoulder and turned north. He walked along the shore, feeling the coolness of the waves as they wrapped around his feet, then retreated to gather themselves for the next onrush. To his left the western hills rose high, their gray granite cliffs dismal in the midday heat. He had tried all during the four days of travel to reconcile the conflict between God's judgment and his announcement that he would speak gently in the hearts of men. God's judgment was a prophet's stock in trade. He could understand that. Sin must be dealt with. Moreover, sin led to the wrongs that permeated Israel now. Men who tread on other men, who live from their agonies, must be stopped. Israel's history with God had shown that Yahweh's way was the way of repentance. But the people would not repent, so judgment was the only recourse. Yes, he understood judgment.

But what of the quiet, tender voice? Can a prophet proclaim judgment to the unrepentant and speak gently to the rest? Can people understand gentleness in the midst of judgment? The question was imponderable. The prophet had little in his experience or in Israel's history to weigh the effectiveness of gentle dealings. At last, he thrust the problem from his mind. Perhaps time would explain the paradox.

The next morning was brilliant. The gulf waters were transparent in the sun; the eastern peaks were jagged, massive shadows and crags rising above the sea. Ahead, on the west side, the granite hills were aflame with the dancing colors of their minerals. The walls of the Tih shone yellow in the distance. They tumbled down toward the shore but were blocked by the copper granite cliffs, capped by sandstone that burned red in the dawn light.

Elijah enjoyed the ease of travel. Seashells, from the tiniest size up to several pounds in weight, lay all along the shore.

Late in the afternoon he came to the Bay of Taba. Four slender Sudanese palms rose to a height of sixty feet above the sandy plain. Young palms, dwarfed by their parents, were scattered around the taller trees. Perhaps the Israelites had camped here, but if they did, Elijah thought, they must have brought water from somewhere else. The water of Taba's well was too brackish to drink.

Soon Elijah could see the opening of the Arabah, the Valley of the Smiths, the deep cleft that ran south from the Dead Sea for one hundred miles to the Gulf of Aqabah.

A heavily traveled road from the west touched the narrow gulf at its northwest corner. The several caravan trails that crossed the Sinai converged at that point to complete their journey to Ezion-geber. Several roads met at the smelter city. Elijah would take one of them, the important caravan road that ran the length of the Arabah.

The road was packed hard by the hooves of donkeys that carried the ore from the scattered mines. Elijah frequently met them as he traveled north. They were scattered all along the road, traveling singly and in twos, driven by dirty, sweaty men who walked alongside them. The drivers were mostly Israelites whose luck or birth had put them at the lowest rung of Judean life, but they were free. The mining itself was done by slaves, expendable beings who had been captured in warfare.

Elijah passed the main mine, at Timneh, late in the afternoon. The entire operation was enclosed by strong walls to keep the slaves from escaping. Even the black slag was emptied inside the walls, for the ore was partly smelted in numerous small stone furnaces to reduce the weight and bulk that had to be carried to Ezion-geber. Guards were frequent and cautious all through the area, but occasionally one waved at Elijah in recognition of his prophet's garb.

The prophet reached the fountain of Gharandal by nightfall. A few palm trees clustered around the spring. The water was warm but drinkable. The day had been hot; even the wind that blew down the Arabah was hot. Elijah's tunic was sweated through, and his mantle, which he had carried on his arm or slung across his shoulder, was streaked with salt. He bathed his face and arms in the warm water, then drank his fill.

The night was hot. Elijah slept on his back on his spread-out mantle, his arms and legs outstretched to avoid the sweating contact with his own skin. He rose early, unrefreshed but less tired, to resume his journey.

The wadis on the west became more frequent now, each one dry except for rare fountains known to the caravaneers and travelers. Occasionally a donkey driver passed with his ore-laden donkey, his clothes smudged with black and red dirt, his eyes heavy and watery, his face sullen. Elijah could not help but feel a twinge of conscience for Israel and Judah. Even Judah, with its good King Jehoshaphat, known for his justice, allowed men to labor their forgotten lives away in the oppressive heat until the old ones died or the young ones ran away to join the bandit gangs that roamed the hills. And the slaves, shut up inside the walled enclosures where the heat was even worse than that of the valley itself, their lives must be hideous beyond words.

Shortly past noon Elijah came to the southwest corner of the Dead Sea. To his left the salt hill of Jebel Usdum rose nearly six hundred fifty feet. It was six miles long, a wind- and storm-carved array of fantastic mounds and pillars. The old men taught that Usdum was the destroyed Sodom, city of evil, companion to Gomorrah, and that one of the strange salt pillars was Lot's wife.

At the north end of the salt hill Elijah came on a party of salt diggers. There were four of them, all stocky, all naked, with dark brown skin. They stopped their work to stare at the prophet. Their eyes were wild and despairing, their muscles bunched in prominent sinews about their shoulder sockets. Sweat rolled from every part of their bodies. Their hair was cut well above their shoulders; all of them had shaved two or three days before their journey into the valley and now supported stubby beginnings of whiskers.

"I am Elijah, prophet of Yahweh," he announced. "Where can I find water?"

The four men stared at him without expression.

"Where can I find water?"

One man laughed. He pointed to the large skins near the hobbled donkeys. Elijah moved toward the skins, nodding his thanks. He pulled the waterpouch from his shoulder and knelt down, but then was interrupted by a loud "No," growled fiercely by one of the men. He looked around. "You want water. You pay us with salt." He pointed to an iron spearlike rod. "There. Dig for your payment."

Elijah shrugged. The men were Judeans, but of the same poor class that drove donkeys in the Arabah, unafraid of a prophet's curse because their lives already were cursed. He walked past the four men and picked up the tool. He shoved its point against the hard salt hill and scraped. Slowly, he etched out a two-foot square block as his iron dug out a narrow trench around it. Then he scraped under the block shape to free it at the bottom. The task required an hour to complete. Already sweating in the furnace heat, he found that the added labor pulled perspiration in rivulets from his body. His tunic was plastered against his skin and stained heavily with rings of salt. The powder from his tool settled in his hair and beard, which itched fiercely from the heat. In spite of himself, he licked the salt from his cracked lips occasionally, an act that added greatly to his thirst.

Finally, he lifted the shaped block and laid it on the stack beside the donkeys. He turned to the waterskins. The men laughed and moved in front of him, blocking his way. Elijah fought back his rage. "Give me water for payment," he said. The men laughed again. The prophet's anger prodded him almost to the point of pronouncing a curse on them, for an affront to a prophet was believed

243

everywhere to be a direct affront to the god he served. But he recalled the watery eyes of the beaten donkey drivers in the Arabah and thought, *These men at least still have spirit.* He turned without speaking to pick up his mantle and waterpouch. As he walked away he heard the low laughter of the salt diggers.

Elijah did not attempt to drink from his waterpouch until he was out of sight. Then his fears were realized. While he was at work cutting out the salt block, one of the men had emptied the little remaining supply. The nearest fountain was at Engedi, twenty-five miles farther, and his throat already screamed for water. Not even on the Tih had he felt the intensity of thirst that he felt now. The salt dried on his body and clothes. His lips cracked in the heat. His tongue swelled to fill his mouth with thickness. His eyes burned from the salt he had brushed into them, and he could not keep himself from further aggravating the constant, painful itch.

The night was dark. He scarcely could see the lines of cliffs on his left. The sea, too, was dark, but the white, salt-crusted shore marked a distinct ribbon in the moonlight for him to follow. He grew more angry as his tiredness and thirst increased, more angry because of the affront to Yahweh than to himself. Had he not been a prophet the salt diggers might have attacked him. He was thankful for that much. But what must the four men think of Yahweh now? They would boast of the incident to their friends. Rather than recognize the compassion of Yahweh for his refusal to retaliate, they would talk of God's weakness. *What now*, he thought, *of the gentle voice?*

Elijah reached Engedi long after midnight, slowed by his fatigue and thirst, having to force his legs to function over an unfamiliar and dark road. His throat scraped with each breath. His lips bled from wide, wrinkled cracks. He knelt at the edge of the wadi and lapped the water from his cupped hands. He drank slowly, and only a little. An urge to gorge himself rose like a sheet of fire inside him. The water stung his lips terribly, but the wetness on his swollen tongue was the greater sensation. He swallowed with difficulty. Only slowly did his throat open to receive the warm water.

After a short drink, Elijah sat by the brook to wait for his stomach to accustom itself to the relief, then he drank again. Fatigue, held back desperately during his eight-hour march for water, swept over him now like a wave. He rose before the tiredness took complete command, hoping to make his way up the dark wadi toward its source. The fountain was not far from the sea, but it was up a long, steep, rocky bed. He struggled only for a few yards, then gave up the climb. He laid his mantle, girdle, and pouches on the rocks, waded into the water, and sat down. The water flowed around his groin and legs, its warm wetness washing the caked salt from his lower body. He lowered his face forward into the water and shook his head vigorously. The wild hair flowed out and down. He raised his head and gasped. Then he lowered it again and rubbed his hair, scalp, and beard with his fingers. Some of the anguish passed from his fatigue into the stream, to be replaced with a more relaxed weariness. He struggled out of his tunic and held it in the water in front of him. The current stretched it flat beyond his hands. He waved it in the water to shake loose the caked salt, then he struggled naked to his sandaled feet, wrung out the tunic as best he could, and put it on again. He would wait until morning to clean his mantle.

The darkness blotted the growth of trees and bushes into an indistinguishable mass on the sides of the wadi. Elijah settled for the open rocks, at least until dawn, and arranged a reasonably smooth area near the stream. He was asleep in moments. His mantle protected his still-wet tunic from becoming soiled again and the wet cloth tempered the heat of the valley. The prophet slept until after dawn, but soon after sunup the heat caught in the red rocks and built rapidly. Still tired and groggy, Elijah moved to a sheltered area of acacia trees, taking care to avoid their thorns.

He slept for two more hours, but the breezeless heat then made comfort impossible. He threw his mantle over his shoulder and fastened his girdle around his waist, then went to the brook to fill his waterpouch. The ordeal of thirst and fatigue left him with a fierce headache that throbbed in his eyes and at the base of his neck. Scabs had formed along the cracks on his lips so that every change of expression brought stabs of pain.

The daylight revealed that Engedi was the most copious oasis along the west side of the Dead Sea. The fountain sprang from the limestone mountain several hundred feet to the west and cascaded down terraced shelves to the sea. Tall cane and acacia thickets formed a luxuriant jungle along much of the stream's course, interspersed with other trees and low bushes. The apple of Sodom grew profusely in various spots along its length. Elijah started to laugh, but jerked at the pain his smile brought to his lips. The apples were like the Baal religion. Round and smooth, yellow when ripe, they hung in delicious clusters of three or four. Inviting in appearance and soft to the touch, the apple beckoned the hungry Elijah to a feast. But he knew that when its sides are pressed in an attempt to open it up, it bursts in a puffy explosion. The rind protected only a slender pod of silk and seeds. The hungry man would find nothing in it but air.

Water would be no problem during the rest of the journey, for two major public fountains lay along the sea. Elijah could reach the north end of the sea by midafternoon, then cross the valley plain to reach Jericho well before dark. He determined to walk at a comfortable pace.

By late morning Elijah passed the Kidron at his left, the holy brook that flowed by the Jerusalem Temple and down through barren brown hills into the perpendicular Valley of Fire on its way to the Dead Sea.

He could see the north shore easily now. Across the north end of the sea a ridge, looking from below like a mountain in its own right, jutted out from the Moabite plateau. It was Mount Nebo.

Moses was old when he stood on Nebo, one hundred twenty years old, with the vast nation of Israel behind him, but he was not infirm. He gathered all of Yahweh's laws together and had them taught throughout the camps. God's warning was austere and prophetic. Though he dealt generously with his people, they would turn to other gods as soon as they settled into the new land. And so they had; even still they did. The pattern had not changed; the warning had not been heeded.

Moses' last act was to appoint a successor, Joshua. Then he walked from their sight into the land of valleys and gullies and crumbling rocks and slopes and silence and thistles and moaning wind. He walked into the hand of God, never again to be seen, his body never to be found.

The walk across the plain to Jericho was dismal, untempered by the intriguing bleakness of the wilderness hills that had been companion to Elijah all along the Arabah and Dead Sea. The city had lost its greatness long before, yet still it was paradise to the traveler coming out of the wilderness. Huge date palms towered over the dwellings, and smaller palms filled the city's gardens. The marketplace teemed with caravans trading for dates and balsam and buying provisions for their journeys.

Elijah knew the city best for its school of prophets. He wondered if any of them had escaped into Judah, and if they had returned. He made his way to the marketplace.

Some of the stalls already had closed; other small merchants loaded their merchandise onto their donkeys while larger merchants pulled their produce and wares inside their stalls to lock them away for the night. Elijah was shrugged off by one merchant who said he knew nothing of a school of prophets. Another merchant heard that the school had been established again, but the prophets moved around in fear of further persecution. No merchant knew where they were now. Finally, a Yahwist offered the prophet lodging for the night.

The host was kind. His wife gave Elijah some salve for his cracked lips, which greatly relieved the pain, and she provided a soft mattress for the night. The rare dinner of meat, served as an honor to the celebrated prophet, was a proclamation to Elijah that he was back in civilization. The sleep was good, and after a breakfast of dates, berries, and wine, he left Jericho in high spirits.

Neither the host nor his wife knew much about the return of Yahweh's prophets. The woman had heard talk that Macaiah had escaped Jezebel's slaughter, but she knew no one who actually had seen him. Perhaps, she ventured, he secretly sought to locate and organize the prophets who survived. Surely Jezebel could not find every prophet of Yahweh. There were too many of them and too many caves in the wilderness.

Elijah raised the waterpouch and caught its stream in his mouth. Yahweh said seven thousand persons had not bent the knee to Baal. He had met two of them.

The road to Abel-meholah ran over barren land. The occasional run of tangled bushes fortunately was kept trimmed away from the road by command of the king, but still the road was not traveled as heavily as the better watered one east of the river. The lack of growth added a glare to the oppressive heat and accented the monotony of the trip. The prophet was forced to his thoughts.

God would speak to men with a gentle voice. Yet Yahweh would cause Hazael and Jehu and Elisha to slay the Baal worshipers. Elijah knew that the three men would not necessarily wield the swords of execution themselves, but they would be as much the agents of slaughter as he himself had been on Carmel. Was his own slaughter of Baal prophets a mistake? The lesson at Mount Horeb made it seem so. Yet did not Yahweh commit himself to the same course of action? Perhaps there was a point at which God's gentleness turned to vengeance. Yes, perhaps that was the answer. God speaks gently until the mind grows so calloused that it will not respond to truth, so warped that it becomes one with evil, so inextricably tangled with delusion that it renders justice impossible. Then God must cut out the diseased tissue.

The burden of the problem shifted. *What man can make that judgment?* He thought. *Who can decipher the love and anger of Yahweh? Who but God himself can tell when men are beyond repentance?*

Elijah shuddered. The sword was so much easier an answer than gentleness, so much more in tune with the vengeance men would wreak on their adversaries, or on God's. In the end, he determined that the man of God must make gentleness, not indignation, his stock in trade, and must be a prophet of judgment only at the overwhelming insistence of God. He knew fear then, for he knew himself.

The sun set an hour before Elijah reached Abel-meholah. By the time he arrived at Shaphat's door, the night was settled well in the valley. Shaphat's broad smile and Deborah's meal restored the prophet's tired spirit. Elisha came in later from his social meeting with some friends in the city. His hair remained long; he had not given up his Nazirite vow.

Elijah's lips still were puffed and sore, and his back ached from the long day's walk. The family postponed their questions and allowed him to retire early.

Deborah heard Elijah come downstairs the next morning and greet the men. She removed the top from the cone-shaped mud oven and reached inside carefully to remove the breadcakes from where she had stuck them on the hot side. She laid them on a platter and went inside. Elijah greeted her with a kiss on the cheek. Shaphat and Elisha already had engaged him in conversation, but the three men moved to the stools around the table while Deborah served the cakes and honey, figs, raisins, wine, and—for the Nazirite Elisha—slightly soured goat's milk.

The young man interrupted the conversation to ask Elijah about his pilgrimage. Elijah told about the bleakness of the Tih and the hard wildness of Mount Horeb. Shaphat listened with great interest, while Elisha became more impatient for the prophet to describe his spiritual journey.

"Did Yahweh speak to you?" he finally asked point-blank.

Elijah paused and dipped his breadcake into the bowl of honey. He ate slowly, thinking over his response, while the men waited in anticipation. Deborah stood by the table, her arms clasped above her waist. "Yes," he finally answered. "Yahweh spoke to me." He paused again. "His words were not as before. I do not understand their meaning fully."

"What did Yahweh say?" Elisha blurted.

The prophet shifted on his stool. He told them, with some reluctance, of the wind, the earthquake, the fire, and the gentle, soft voice of God in the wind. He did not reveal his new instructions.

Shaphat broke the silence that followed. "What does it mean? Is this a new revelation?"

"It is a new revelation," Elijah answered. "I have wrestled with the meaning. I believe I understand Yahweh's instruction, but I do not know yet how to live by it."

"Do you not live by it simply by obeying?" Elisha countered. "What does a prophet do but obey?"

Elijah smiled at the young man's innocence. "Surely," he said, "that is true. But a way of life is hard to change. Even a prophet is bound in what he does by how the people think, and by how he has thought before. Will the people listen to a gentle voice when they are used to loudness?" He sighed. "Every man is bound to his time. He can think above the people only to a small degree. He is one with them. His thinking will follow their response. Surely Yahweh's way is to speak gently to men's hearts. But what if they do not listen? How will Yahweh speak then? What will a prophet do then?"

"I still say a prophet simply will obey," Elisha persisted.

"And does Yahweh speak to a prophet as though time does not exist? As though people are not what they are? No, my young friend, the lesson is great, but it is not simple." Elijah's words were spoken with finality, to end the conversation. "Now," he continued, "tell me of events. I have heard that Macaiah may yet be alive."

Shaphat answered. "We have heard that, too. No one in Abel-meholah has seen him, though. Perhaps Obadiah helped him escape."

"And what about Jezebel?"

"Ahab must have stayed the queen's murderous hand," Shaphat continued. "We were fearful for Elisha's life. He hid in the wadis for a while, but no soldiers ever came to search him out. He lives openly now. Perhaps the danger is past."

"Then the miracle on Mount Carmel did some good," Elijah said softly.

"Yes. It did some good."

Elisha interrupted his father. "Elijah, people still talk of the mighty act. Some of the people do not sacrifice to Baal anymore. Jezebel finds it difficult to entice new priests from Phoenicia. They are afraid to come to Israel." His tone became glum. "But the temples to Melkart and Asherah still stand. My vow is not complete."

Deborah, silent until now, broke into the conversation. "Shaphat, tell Elijah about Naboth."

Shaphat's smile disappeared. He leaned on the table toward the prophet. "Elijah, a tragedy occurred in Jezreel just yesterday." He told of Ahab's desire for his neighbor's vineyard and of the trumped-up charge against Naboth. "His sons and his wife were killed, too. It was Jezebel's doing, surely. Ahab never would flout the law of Israel so openly."

"But he allowed her to do it," Elisha shouted. "He is as guilty of Naboth's blood as Jezebel. His greed was stronger than the Israelite blood that flows in his veins."

Elijah stared blankly as the conversation continued. He rose while Shaphat was in the middle of a sentence. "I must go to Jezreel," he said.

The men grew silent.

"I must go." He turned to the wife. "Thank you, Deborah, for everything. I would stay longer, but Yahweh calls me to Jezreel."

"Let me go with you," Elisha asked.

"I go alone."

"I still want to be your servant."

Elijah turned to him. "No, I go alone. I will come back to you later." He took his mantle and girdle from the chair where he had draped them the night before. Deborah already was filling his waterpouch and gathering nuts and breadcakes to put into his foodpouch. She handed them to him at the door.

Elijah ran the distance to Bethshean, nine miles up the valley from Abel-meholah, then he turned west up the wide

Jezreel valley and settled into a fast walk. Jezreel was another thirteen miles. He arrived at the city three hours later. The palace was on its west side, with Naboth's vineyard below it on the slope toward the Great Sea.

Elijah arrived at the vineyard shortly after the hour of the noon meal. He could see Ahab walking up and down the rows, the custom for laying claim to land. He approached quietly, at the king's back, and waited for Ahab to turn toward him.

The blood drained from Ahab's face when he saw the prophet. The two men stared at each other, Elijah with a terrifying look of judgment in his eyes, his clothes sweaty from his hurried journey, his hair matted and in disarray. The king's face was blank, waiting.

The prophet raised his arm to point a finger toward Ahab. "So you have killed your man," he said sternly, "and now you walk his land to take possession."

Ahab, already conscience-stricken, answered in a low voice, "Have you found me out, my enemy?"

Elijah's tone did not soften. "I have found you out." His voice lowered but did not lose its hardness. The words, spoken evenly, without shouting, pierced Ahab's ears with their curse. "You have sold your soul, Ahab, king of Israel, to do what is wrong in the eyes of Yahweh. By the word of God, I tell you that Yahweh will bring disaster on you. He will sweep you away and destroy every son of every mother in Israel who is of the house of Ahab, no matter how they are protected. Yahweh will deal with your family as he did with the families of Jeroboam and Baasha. You are guilty beyond measure of leading Israel into sin. You have provoked Yahweh's anger by your actions and you will pay for your sin." The prophet gestured toward the palace. He gritted his teeth. "Jezebel will be eaten by dogs by the walls of Jezreel." He pointed to Ahab again. "Those of your house who die in the city will be left unburied as food for the dogs, and those who die in the country shall be left unburied as food for the birds."

Ahab's face drained. The prophet turned to leave the field. The king stared after him until Elijah was out of sight. He raised his trembling hands to his face. "My God," he said, "what have I done?" Tears welled into his eyes and spilled through his fingers onto his purple robe. He sank to his knees and raised his bearish head toward the sky. "My God, what have I done?" he shouted. He bent over and tore handfuls of dirt from the earth, throwing the red soil onto his head and shoulders. His voice carried over the field to the palace, screaming again in anguish, "My God! Yahweh! What have I done!" The guilt boiled from his bowels to flow through his body. He lay prone on the earth, beating the land with his fists, ripping up the earth to throw it over his body and into his hair until exhaustion drained all his remaining tears. He rose slowly. Tear-formed mud caked his cheeks and neck. The red soil appeared as blood against the purple of his robe. Hair from his beard stuck under his fingernails. He looked toward the palace. "Damn you, Jezebel," he shouted. He slapped at a growing vine with his soiled hand. "Damn you," he screamed. "Damn you, Jezebel! Damn you! Damn you! Damn you!"

Chapter Seventeen

ELIJAH CUPPED his hands to his mouth. "Macaiah!" There was no answer. He moved east below the ridge of the hill, not knowing exactly where the cave was, pausing occasionally to repeat his call to the prophet. Macaiah watched Elijah cautiously from behind a bush-covered formation of large rock. Not until the hairy prophet was near enough that Macaiah could see his features clearly did he step out into Elijah's path. He called the name with surprise, "Elijah?"

The two men faced each other, smiling broadly, before they embraced. "How did you find me, my brother?" Macaiah asked.

"By accident," Elijah responded. "By a happy accident. I passed through Engannim on my way from Jezreel. A priest there told me you were hiding on this hill. He did not know where your cave was located, though. Did my shouting frighten you?"

"I have long been beyond fright," Macaiah answered, "but not beyond caution." He laughed and slapped Elijah's shoulder. "But the danger must be over if you travel so boldly in daylight."

"Perhaps," Elijah smiled. "Perhaps. But the battle is not done."

Macaiah shook his head soberly. "No, the battle is not done." He caught Elijah's arm. "Come. Let's go to my cave where it is cooler. We can talk there."

The two prophets moved down the slope for a short distance. Macaiah led the way behind a small myrtle bush that only partly hid the cave entrance. The men had to squat to enter the low, wide opening. They sat near the mouth of the cave to wait until their eyes became accustomed to the darkness. Macaiah offered his waterpouch to Elijah, who shook his head and pointed to his own. "But this is wine," Macaiah said. Elijah smiled and reached for it.

"Now," Macaiah asked, "tell me what has happened to you since Mount Carmel."

The prophets talked until late in the afternoon, each one sharing his insights of Yahweh's battle against Baal. The miracle on Mount Carmel was decisive, Macaiah insisted. Many Israelites had turned from worshiping Baal; other Israelites, whose loyalties had been silent, spoke openly now of their allegiance to Yahweh, their fears dispelled by God's strong proof of superiority on Mount Carmel. The two men wrestled with Yahweh's pronouncement to Elijah that his preferred way is the gentle voice. Macaiah's observations were the same as Elijah's had been. Yet, they agreed, they could not ignore the new revelation. Yahweh had spoken.

Two young prophets arrived at the cave near sunset, sweaty and covered with road dust. They stared at the hairy prophet incredulously until Macaiah assured them that the stranger indeed was Elijah. Overjoyed, they attacked him with their questions with such enthusiasm that they forgot their meal. Macaiah finally had to intervene to insist that they wash and eat. The interruption hardly slowed the fervent conversation, and the questions continued until late into the night.

Elijah's mind would not be silent, tired as he was from the journey and the long discussions. He lay on his mantle, oblivious to the sounds of sleep around him. The young prophets had stirred in his soul an answer to God's riddle. To speak gently was to speak in many voices, to speak in the marketplaces of villages and towns and cities, in the homes of Israel's families, in the streets and paths and highways, to challenge Baal in her groves and at her shrines, to proclaim the message of Yahweh everywhere, to permeate the land with his teachings.

Elijah stayed with Macaiah all through the summer months. The time was good, a time of thought, of reassessment. He did not feel alone in the battle anymore, and the turn of so many hearts to Yahweh and young men to prophecy convinced him of the value of Mount Carmel.

The early rains came in October. Immediately the fields were dotted with men struggling behind wooden, iron-tipped plows to break up the ground. Elijah watched them in the valleys and terraces as he walked the seven miles from Bethel north to Gilgal. *And it is time for me to plow my own fields,* he thought. *Elisha has the qualities of Macaiah, and the distinctives of greatness as well.* The plan had fashioned itself over the weeks of late summer and autumn. He would teach Elisha all he knew; Elisha would establish the schools for prophets.

He spent the night at Gilgal and rose early the next morning. Abel-meholah was twenty-five miles to the north, up the mountain ridge and then down the road that followed the wadi to the Jordan.

The valley bustled with shouting, sweating farmers who grasped their jerking plows with one hand and goaded their oxen with long poles in the other.

Shaphat's field was among Abel-meholah's largest. It lay near the wadi, a long, wide strip of some of the plain's richest land. Elisha was unmistakable. His long hair was well below his shoulders, matted now in long, sweaty strings below his turban. His work tunic was drawn up from his slender legs and tucked into his wide cloth girdle. Elijah laughed as the young man stumbled at a sudden lurch of the plow.

Elisha worked with two oxen. In front of him, laboring in

staggered rows, were eleven more teams, each worked by a hired hand. *The man is wise*, Elijah thought. *He keeps them in front so he can check their work.*

The prophet approached the working men from behind, each of whom intently watched his oxen, the depth of the plow, and the straightness of the furrow. Elisha's row was on the outside, the inside man a good distance ahead to set the row the others measured against, each man a few yards behind the one to his left. The prophet removed his mantle and readjusted the pouch straps to his shoulder. He walked up to Elisha. The young man still did not notice. Without speaking, Elijah flipped the mantle to spread widely above Elisha's head and come down draped onto his shoulders. Elisha jerked the oxen to a halt and spun around, surprised. Elijah glanced at him only for a moment, then turned back toward the road.

"Elijah!"

The prophet ignored the call. He continued toward the road, walking on the level ground beside the new furrow.

"Elijah!" The young man looked down at the cloak. It was woven thick and tightly of camel's hair, with a mild odor of perspiration. The significance of the prophet's action flooded over Elisha. He gazed at the prophet's retreating figure. The mantle was as much Elijah's mark of identification as his hairy body. He broke into a run, the mantle corners flapping between his legs. "Elijah!"

He caught the prophet at the road that ran along the wadi bed up to the western range. "Elijah. I am astonished," he puffed. "But I do not question the word of Yahweh. Let me but kiss my parents good-bye and I will follow you."

Elijah nodded. "Certainly. I would not restrain you from saying good-bye."

"Will you come with me?"

"No. The decision is yours to reconcile with your father and mother as you will. You are on your own."

"I will catch up with you. Are you going toward Samaria?"

Elijah nodded. Elisha bowed from the waist and ran

back into the field. The prophet recalled his own decision to leave the Rechabites and Jonadab. Even God's people find good reasons why their friends and children should not heed God's call. Shaphat, Elijah was certain, would prove more difficult than his young friend surmised.

The workmen had reached the edge of the field. They stopped to watch their young overseer's actions with growing surprise. Elisha pulled the plow piece from its hole to let the beam end fall to the ground, then he tied the piece flat to the beam. He moved to the front of the team and tapped the leader on the side of its head to turn the oxen toward the stable. Sensing the coming rest, the team broke into a trot, Elisha running behind to goad them to a faster pace.

He did not remove the yoke and plow from the team, but simply turned them into the pen, then ran to the house. He burst through the door, still wearing the mantle. Without speaking, he stood in front of his father.

"Elisha, isn't that Elijah's mantle? What is wrong? Is he here?"

"No, he is not here, father."

Shaphat stared at his son, his eyes narrowing. "What does this mean? Why have you left the field?"

"Elijah has called me to follow him, father."

Shaphat rose from his comfortable chair. "Deborah, come here." The wife entered wide-eyed from the kitchen, alarmed by her husband's voice. "Look at your son," he directed.

She stared at the prophet's mantle.

"Your son says he is to follow Elijah."

Deborah walked to the young man. With her head tilted back to meet his eyes, she asked, "Is it true, Elisha?"

"It is true, mother."

Tears began to form in her eyes. Shaphat put his arm around her waist. She buried her face in his shoulder. "Elijah is a good man. We love him. But he does not know what he asks. Nor do you."

"Yahweh calls me. Elijah is but his mouth."

"The field, son, the farm. I cannot run it without you. I am growing old."

"You can hire an overseer."

"Serve Yahweh, Elisha, as we do and as we have taught you, but do not take this course. Elijah's life hangs like a dying leaf in the autumn. The wind will sweep you away with him."

"The safest place on earth is in God's will."

"I forbid you to go."

"Yahweh has called me. I cannot refuse."

The two men faced each other without speaking. Deborah broke away from Shaphat's arms and clutched at her son. "Elisha, do not go. Do not defy your father."

Surprised at the ferocity of their objections, Elisha pulled away from his mother. He walked into the kitchen and picked up an iron axe and a long-bladed knife. An oblong oil lamp stood on a table, its small flame flickering from its pinched end. He picked it up and walked back into the main room.

Deborah raised a hand to her mouth. "Elisha?"

He went out the door and toward the oxen he left untended in the pen. Shaphat hurried after him. Elisha set the oil lamp and tools on the fence and began to unfasten the thick wooden yoke. He dragged it and the plow to the fence, slipped the knife into his girdle, and picked up the axe.

Not until he raised the axe over the head of one of the oxen did Shaphat realize what he was about to do. "Elisha!" he called too late. The flat end of the axe came down hard on the ox. It slumped immediately to its knees and rolled onto its side. The other ox watched uncomprehending as Elisha moved toward it. Shaphat called out again. "Elisha! Stop!" He ran toward his son, but already the second ox lay dead on its side. "What's wrong with you, Elisha? Have you gone mad?" The father grabbed the axe from his son's hand, but its use was past.

Elisha pulled the knife from his girdle and began to skin the animal. The men arrived from the field just in time to see the second animal fall. Elisha called to them, "Tell the villagers there is a meat feast. Tell them to come now. Everyone is invited."

Shaphat, struck dumb by the quickness of Elisha's actions, did not object. He stared unbelieving at the two dead oxen.

Elisha worked with feverish quickness. He cut a long line down the ox's underside and along its legs to lay open the hide, gutted the animal, then began to cut sections of meat from the carcass. He carried each piece to the stable area and hung it by a hook to drain. Last, he cut the head from the ox and dragged the carcass on its hide, tied a rope to its hind quarters, and winched it over a beam to hang neck down.

Shaphat stood in his path as he approached the second ox. "Elisha, you are destroying my property," he said simply.

Elisha walked around him. "Take it from my inheritance," he answered.

Shaphat tried to talk to his son as Elisha carved the ox. The son worked swiftly, as before, ignoring the pleadings of the father. A few early arrivers stared wide-eyed across the fence, jesting with one another and calling for Shaphat to explain the occasion. Other villagers approached from three directions. The eleven workers who had been with Elisha in the field stalled their oxen securely and joined the crowd. Immediately they were assailed with questions they could not answer. Shaphat, at last, walked through the crowd, ignoring their questions and shaking off their friendly tugs, to make his way to the house.

Elisha retrieved the axe his father had dropped. He picked up the heavy end of the plow and moved between the pen and the house. He heard his name called amid the gasps of the crowd as he raised the axe and brought it down the first time on the precious plow. Someone in the crowd noticed that his mantle looked like Elijah's.

The new prophet chopped the plow into eighteen-inch pieces, which he stacked into a pile. He went to the pen, picked up the yoke, and placed it across his shoulders, his arms outstretched to balance it by each end. He dropped it to the ground near the newly cut wood and looked toward his friends. "As I shed this yoke," he said softly, "so I shed this life."

The announcement revealed to the crowd the seriousness of the feast. The people grew quiet, watching with wonder as the thunk of Elisha's axe into the thick yoke set a somber pattern of sound.

Perspiration had soaked through the shoulders of the mantle by the time he completed the task. He dropped the axe and walked into the house, to return in a moment with a long spit and its braces. Shaphat and Deborah followed him to the door and watched, arms around each other's waist. Their son set the spit properly, then arranged the wood under it. He gathered some thorn twigs from near his mother's outdoor oven, stuffed them under the wood, fetched the oil lamp from the fence, and ignited the twigs. The fire spread quickly along the dry wood.

Elisha waited until the flames passed their high point and a hot bed of ashes began to form underneath. He returned to the stable to select three large, choice cuts for the spit. Only when the meat was set in place to roast did he speak again.

The men, each one his friend, stood in the foreground, the women in a semi-circle behind them. "My friends," he began, "all of you know that I swore a Nazirite vow not to touch a razor to my hair nor wine to my lips so long as the temples to Baal stand in Samaria and Jezreel. My heart has been heavy for Yahweh. My greatest dream has come true this day." He grasped the mantle at arms' length to hold it out. Its shape formed a triangle from each hand to a point at his knees. His long black hair and beard set his face out fearsomely at the top of the straight line of his arms and shoulders. "This is the mantle of Elijah," he said. He lowered his arms. "Today, while I plowed in the field, Elijah cast his mantle over me. Yahweh has called me to follow the prophet, to be his disciple. I go gladly." He gestured toward the roasting meat and fire. "The flames burn away the yoke and the plow, and the meat of my ox team will pass into your bodies. They are symbols of my life. Now that life is ended. I will return to it no more."

His friends were silent, each one embarrassed that he could think of nothing to say. Most of them had worshiped at Baal shrines; some of them no more after Carmel. All of them knew well of Elisha's zeal for Yahweh. At last, a young man eased from the crowd and embraced Elisha tightly. He pulled away gently, bowing from the waist as he returned to the crowd. The act of endorsement and reverence brought tears to Elisha's eyes.

The crowd was immobile for a moment. Never had a prophet come from Abel-meholah. Then several men in front bowed to the ground, quickly followed by the others who stood behind them.

"By this honor," Elisha asked, "do you renounce Baal?"

A murmur ran through the crowd. Some of them shouted yes, others were silent.

Elisha did not press the matter. "Now," he said, "come and eat." He picked up the knife and cut generous portions, handing a piece to each man as he came by. The women sat in chattering groups around the perimeter to wait for the men to finish eating.

After he had served the men, Elisha turned to the house. Shaphat stood in the doorway, his arm still around his wife. "And my father," Elisha called. "Will my father eat a portion of the slain ox?"

For a moment Shaphat did not move. The crowd watched curiously. Then he made his way in slow steps toward Elisha. As he neared, his composure fell away and he broke into tears. He fell on his son's shoulder. Deborah ran from the house toward them. The three embraced unashamed before the crowd.

Elisha kissed his mother and father on each cheek and pulled away. "I must go now to catch Elijah," he said. He turned toward the crowd. "Even with tears of parting," he shouted, "the feast is for joy. Joy should flood the hearts of all when Yahweh calls a servant. Eat well." He turned to Shaphat. "Father, we would have wine." Shaphat nodded and started for the house. "Be happy, my friends," Elisha repeated, "for I am happy." He put his arm around his mother and guided her to the door.

Inside, he packed nuts and parched corn into a food-pouch and filled a waterpouch. His father handed him a small bag of coins and went outside with three skins of wine.

Elisha kissed his mother again.

Shaphat was waiting near the roasting meat. "Elisha," he asked, "will you cut me a piece before you go?"

The son smiled and went to the fire. He selected the best portion and cut from it a large serving.

Shaphat received it in both hands. He took a bite and chewed it slowly, then said to his son, "Elisha, I share in your new life. Go with Yahweh."

"Thank you, father." Elisha turned toward the road.

To the east the hills of Samaria rolled ever upward toward their crest at the ridge high above the Jordan Valley. To the west the dark gray alluvial soil of the rich Plain of Sharon dominated the slope to the Great Sea, accented by wide stretches of rich red soil and, along the shore, a spasmodic pattern of dune sand. Ahead, the Carmel range cut northwest toward the sea.

Dor lay on the coast fourteen miles south of Carmel, dominating the wide gray plain that lay between the sea and the mountain range. Both prophets carried their mantles across their shoulders—Elijah with his familiar one returned, Elisha with a newer one. After another ten miles the prophets left the Way of the Sea for the narrower Dor road. They arrived in the city late in the afternoon.

The elders watched the figures approach Dor's main gate. "It looks like Elijah," one of them said with surprise. Brows wrinkled as old eyes strained to see the men more clearly. "It is Elijah," the speaker said with more certainty.

The prophets entered the gate and approached the seat of the elders. The old men scrambled toward them, bowing as they came. "Elijah, we are honored," the chief elder welcomed. "What brings you to Dor?"

"If the prophet of Yahweh is honored, why then does Asherah's shrine still stand outside the city?" Elijah demanded sternly. Elisha stood quietly, wishing fervently that he could speak.

The elders shook their heads, embarrassed. "We do not wish it to be there, Elijah," one of them answered.

"Then why is it there?"

The chief elder approached the prophet until they stood face to face. His beard was a strange array of white, stringy patches, his head bald. He spoke in a hoarse, low voice. "We do not have the power we once had in Dor," he advised. "The people follow other leaders." He paused. "Would you speak to our people, Elijah?"

"I will speak. Gather them at six o'clock." The prophet waved toward Elisha and the two of them turned into the city toward the traveler's inn. The elders left in different directions to set the announcement in motion.

At evening, Elijah climbed the steps where the Baal prophet had stood several years before. A crowd already was gathered, having arrived early to gain better vantage points. He began to speak immediately.

"Men of Dor, how many of you were on Mount Carmel on the great day of God?" he called.

A multitude of hands joined the somber shouts in answer.

"You live on the plain," Elijah continued. "Yahweh challenged the rain goddess and showed Baal to be without power even on the plain. And now, tell me truly, did Baal deal with you well while you worshiped at the pagan shrine?"

A low, uncertain murmur spread among the crowd. Some of them turned toward Abinadab, who stood in his accustomed place in his carriage behind them, preferring to watch the crowd as well as the speaker.

Elijah recognized the challenge immediately. Baal had dealt well with Abinadab. "Some of you have become slaves since Jezebel was made queen," he shouted. "Yet still you dream of the promises of Asherah and Melkart. Has your chase been worthwhile? Do you still think that one day those gods will grant your wishes?" He pointed to Abinadab. "You are not slaves of that man, nor of any other. You are slaves to your own minds. You are slaves to the wrong dreams." He pointed to Abinadab. "Your slavery," he shouted, "came from your greed to be the kind of man he is."

He stepped higher on the stairway so all the people, now a large crowd, could see him better. His hair-covered, mantle-draped, leather-girded body stood in sharp contrast to Abinadab's well-groomed and immaculate figure opposite him.

"Why do you think Yahweh led you from Egypt?" Elijah demanded. "To lead you from one slavery to another? Why do you suppose Yahweh gave Israel new laws to live by? So that one man can cheat another? Have you not heard the laws of your fathers?" He stared at the crowd, pausing until the silence caught their attention more firmly. "Hear them!" he shouted. "Hear the laws of Yahweh! Did not Yahweh say through the mouth of our father Moses, 'You shall not do as they do in Egypt where you once dwelt, nor shall you do as they do in the land of Canaan to which I am bringing you. You must keep my laws without fail, for you shall have life through them.'"* The prophet drew a deep breath and leaned forward, as though to get closer to them. "My friends, the ways of greed of the Phoenician merchants are not the ways of God. Did Yahweh not tell us to leave unreaped the edges of our fields and not to glean the droppings nor strip the vineyards, to leave that food for the poor?"

Elijah noted with surprise the nodding heads and the nervous movements of the crowd. He wondered how the sacred law had been so openly broken, but he continued. "Hear the law of Yahweh. 'You shall not steal. You shall not cheat or deceive a fellow countryman. You shall not oppress your neighbor, nor rob him. You shall not pervert

*Leviticus 18:3, 4 (NEB).

2 6 6

justice. You shall love your neighbor as a man like yourself' "*

The crowd stirred more uneasily. Haggard faces glanced with growing contempt toward Abinadab and the line of chariots and well-dressed men who listened beside their leader. Elijah noticed that the rich ones maintained their looks of disdain and amusement.

The prophet continued his recall of Yahweh's laws, surprised that mere recitation of the simple commands aroused the crowd so easily. " 'When an alien settles in your land, you shall not oppress him. He shall be treated as a native born among you, and you shall love him as a man like yourself. You shall not pervert justice in the measurement of length, weight, or quantity.' "**

The murmurs of the crowd ceased. The people listened engrossed as he told them the near-forgotten story of the Exodus, made new and real to him by his own pilgrimage. He described the agonies of Egypt, and the worse agonies of the wilderness; then he told of the joy when the people of God came into the Promised Land. Every man was to have his own plot of ground, his own house, his own life. He told of the frequent lapses into idolatry and decried the lure of the licentious baals. He recited the history of retribution, as Yahweh had shaped them like clay toward a proper form, a form never attained and now horribly misshaped.

It was when he talked of the land that the crowd became restless; each time, as to a tooth that ached to be pressed, he came back to the laws of land and slavery, and the people whispered and stared. Both slave and free glanced cautiously but with hate toward the wealthy masters.

Elijah thought as he spoke, *How can a prophet teach both justice and compassion?* But he knew the answer. Men must learn compassion in those rare moments between angers.

He preached for nearly two hours, until the sun dropped

*Leviticus 19:9-18 (NEB).   **Leviticus 19:33-35 (NEB).

267

away and the shadow of the wall made the crowd into one shapeless mass. His throat was hoarse and dry, even though he drank occasionally from his waterpouch. Abinadab had left, along with most of the wealthy onlookers, but nearly all of the common people remained.

When at last he started down the steps, the crowd refused to disperse. Shammah elbowed his way toward the prophet. "Elijah, prophet of Yahweh," he shouted so the crowd could hear his question. "We would hear more of God's laws of servitude. When is a slave to be freed?"

"In the Year of Jubilee, or when he saves enough money to purchase his freedom," the prophet answered.

"Jubilee has just passed. It now is more than forty years away."

Elijah noticed the slave ring in Shammah's ear. "Are you a slave because you were tricked by your master or because you were tricked by your own greed?"

The crowd shifted uneasily. Shammah dropped his head for a moment, then raised it again to meet Elijah's eyes. "I chased after Baal," he admitted, but he added, "Should a man be condemned so long for one mistake?"

"One mistake?" Elijah asked. "Was your idolatry one mistake?"

Shammah stood his ground, determined not to be cajoled into submission to his tragedy. "I have sinned," he said. "But should Abinadab live like a king because of my sin? His sin is the greater!"

A man in the crowd shouted his approval of Shammah's words. Other voices immediately joined him. Elijah waited for the outburst to die away.

Baana made his way to his friend and caught his arm. "Shammah," he whispered, "what are you doing? You could be lashed for this." Shammah jerked his arm away without an answer.

"Yahweh will take vengeance on all who flout his laws," Elijah said. "As for you, you played the game of Baal and lost. Had you won, you would be like your master. You brought your tragedy on yourself. You seek now to use Yahweh as you once sought to use Baal, to gain your own

2 6 8

ends. Yahweh is not the cause of your misfortune."

"But the rich have power to work the law in their favor," a voice interrupted.

"Yahweh's justice is a heavier burden than man's folly," Elijah answered. "If the rich have sinned, correct the matter as well as you can, but see that you do not sin the more." Elijah motioned for Elisha to follow him. Voices called the prophet's name as he edged through the crowd toward the traveler's inn. He did not answer. The people pushed back to make room as he passed, but they did not disperse.

Shammah watched the two prophet companions move away. He felt a weakness build in his legs as the seriousness of his action flooded over him. Several friends inched toward him, pushing aside their fellows. Anonymous faces watched him silently, gauging their feelings toward his dangerous anger, fighting within themselves what their courses should be.

"Shammah," a friend said softly. He turned to see the man beside him. "Shammah, I fear Baana has informed Abinadab of your words."

The slave buried his face in his hands. "Baana is my best friend. He would not do that." He felt the companion's hand on his arm and looked up. The face reflected both concern and certainty. Baana, both of them knew, had become a different man in his quest to satisfy both Abinadab and Asherah. "What am I to do?" Shammah asked simply.

"You are not the only one," the friend answered. "Several of us spoke out. We will be identified in the end. Slaves are not brave for long."

Other voices surrounded Shammah, each one of whom was guilty of insurrection against their masters. Shammah knew that he was responsible, since he began the tragedy-bound discussion. "We must flee," he said in a low voice. "It is better to be a free bandit than a maimed slave." The others nodded. Six men slipped the bolt from the gate and edged through the narrow opening. They turned southeast, toward the hills of Judah.

Elisha lay on his back in the darkness of their room. "Elijah," he called, "are you still awake?"

"Yes."

"What will happen now?"

"Only Yahweh knows."

The young man raised himself on his elbow. "Elijah, the people are angry. They are ripe for rebellion."

"Yes, they are angry." Elijah spoke flatly, without emotion or real involvement.

"Should we not be with them? Shouldn't we teach them the right way to act?"

"And what is the right way? Has Yahweh given you such a word?"

Elisha lay back without answering.

"Teaching is not done in a night, Elisha. That is the first thing a prophet must learn."

"But what will happen?" Elisha asked worriedly. "Aren't we responsible for what might happen?"

"We are responsible for telling the way of Yahweh, and for telling it as clearly as we can to everyone. The wealthy ones heard Yahweh's word as clearly as did the poor and the slaves. It is up to those who heard to act. The wealthy should act first, for they have the power. If they do not, they will reap the whirlwind."

Elisha lay back. He was silent for a moment, then said simply, "I wish I could help."

Elijah smiled in the darkness. "That is why you're a prophet. It is in the word of Yahweh that the poor and distressed, and the rich, are helped." He spoke more intimately. "But, my young friend, you will not change Israel in a day. Men's hearts are more complicated than that. The clear teaching of Yahweh is that every man should have his own plot of land. When the poor hear that law they clamor for their share. But do you think they are different from the rich? No, one man is as greedy as the next, rich or poor. The rich and poor alike must be taught compassion."

The prophet rose from his bed and stood over Elisha. "Get up, Elisha," he said. "This is the time I must tell you all that Yahweh said to me at Horeb."

Chapter Eighteen

AHAB ARRANGED for throne chairs, one for himself, one for Jehoshaphat, to be placed at a large assembly area near Samaria's main gate. The two kings, contemporaries, were older now, but both remained in good health, especially the bear-headed Ahab.

The Judean king was as excited about his state visit as Ahab was, but his reason was different. Jehoshaphat's top officials had accompanied him. They were occupied in conferences with Ahab's advisors to establish economic and trade agreements. Ahab's reason was war. He needed Jehoshaphat's aid against Ben-hadad. To that end he greeted his southern neighbor with great regal pomp. He used well the promise of trade agreements, his chief bargaining tool, along with a convincing case that Ben-hadad soon would be at Judah's borders, too.

In the end Jehoshaphat agreed to fight. "What is mine is at your disposal," he said, "but first let us seek Yahweh's counsel."

The court prophets, always on call for advice, were summoned without delay, the entire retinue of four hundred.

Surely, Ahab reasoned, the dependable support of so many would offset the voices of a few dissidents. Their spontaneous answer came too quickly, though, too predictably: "Attack, Yahweh will give the victory."

Jehoshaphat shifted uneasily on his throne. The answer was patently man-made. He knew court prophets well and was surprised that, after Mount Carmel, Ahab still accepted the force of numbers as an indication of divine strength. He turned to Ahab. "Is there not some other prophet in Israel who may give us more dependable counsel?"

Ahab shrugged. The shallowness of the mass of prophets was as apparent to him as to Jehoshaphat. "There is a man," he answered. He ignored Elijah, whom he had not seen during the several years since the Naboth affair. "His name is Macaiah. But I tell you that I despise the man. He never prophesies good about anything I do, only evil."

"Don't prejudge the man like that, my friend," the king of Judah replied. "If he is a true prophet of Yahweh, let us hear him."

"Very well," Ahab agreed. He turned to an attendant, a eunuch, who stood nearby. "Go find Macaiah and bring him here quickly."

The prophets were unaware that their veracity was in question. They continued to moan incantations and prayers, dance their frenzied dances, throw small bones onto the ground to search their patterns for answers already determined in their minds, and send themselves into hypnotic trances to utter words they could have said as well—but less exotically—in their sanity. One prophet, Zedekiah, ingeniously fashioned a set of iron horns. Mimicking a charging bull, he ran at the other prophets and bystanders, who dodged adroitly out of his way. He turned to the two kings to announce, "This is the word of Yahweh. You will gore the Aramaeans as a wild bull gores everything in its path."

Macaiah, who had been preaching regularly in Samaria, arrived after the lunch hour, coached already by the eunuch on what the four hundred prophets had said. Macaiah had answered him simply, "As Yahweh is alive and real, I will prophesy only what he tells me."

Ahab immediately directed the question to him. "Shall we attack Ramoth-gilead or refrain?"

Macaiah smiled wryly. Most of the prophets were seated now on the ground, only a few of them still in states of ecstasy crying for Ahab to attack. "Why, King Ahab, you know the answer," he said in a falsetto voice. "Attack and win the day. Yahweh will deliver the city into your hands." He waved his arms in frivolous mimicry of the court prophets, who rose to their feet in anger. Jehoshaphat laughed heartily.

Ahab, not amused, slapped the arm of his throne. "Don't make fun of me, Macaiah," he said angrily. "I have warned you before about that. Speak what Yahweh says to you and say nothing more."

Macaiah bowed slightly and shut his eyes. He stood erect and quiet. His right arm rose several times, slowly, toward the sky, then lowered. His left arm stayed limp at his side. At last he opened his eyes and spoke in a natural voice. "I saw all Israel scattered on her mountains, like sheep without a shepherd, and I heard Yahweh say, 'They have no master. Let the warriors go home in peace.'"

Ahab turned quickly to Jehoshaphat. "Did I not tell you that Macaiah never prophesies anything good about me?"

Macaiah interrupted the king to continue his prophecy. "Listen now to Yahweh's word," he shouted. "I saw the Lord seated on his heavenly throne. A host surrounded him. All the hosts of heaven waited on him. Yahweh asked the host, 'Who will go and entice Ahab to attack Ramoth-gilead so he will fall in battle?' Many answers came from the host, but at last one angel stepped up and said, 'I will entice him.' 'How?' Yahweh asked. 'I will go out,' the angel answered, 'and enter the spirits of the court prophets to speak in lies from their mouths.' Yahweh answered, 'Your plan will succeed. You shall entice him. Go and do it.'" Macaiah gestured toward the prophets. "You see that the plan works well. These prophets have a lying spirit inside them. Yahweh allows you to go into battle because it is his will that you shall die."

The prophets began to shout at Macaiah. Zedekiah approached him quickly and slapped him hard across the face. "And how do you suppose that God speaks through you rather than through me?" he demanded.

Macaiah gritted his teeth to ignore the physical insult. "I will tell you how you shall discover who prophesies the truth. After the battle, when you run from one room to another to escape arrest for your false prophecy, then you will know that Yahweh does not speak through you."

Ahab rose from his throne chair. His loud voice interrupted the argument between the prophets. "Arrest Macaiah," he ordered sternly. "He must not spread this poison through the land. Take him to Amon, governor of the city, and to my son Joash. Tell them to lock him up and feed him sparingly on bread and water until I return safely from the battle."

Guards obeyed immediately. Two of them caught Macaiah's arms to pull him away. The prophet shouted back at the king, "If you return safely, then you will know that Yahweh does not speak through me."

Macaiah's prophecy worried Ahab. Yet the prophet did not predict defeat, but rather that the king would be killed. With a chill he recalled Elijah's prophecy made years ago in Naboth's vineyard. He convinced Jehoshaphat to proceed with the battle, but as a precaution Jehoshaphat was to dress in his royal battle attire to draw attention, while he himself would put on the ordinary armor of a charioteer.

A few weeks later the combined army camped on two sides of Ramoth-gilead, to the west and the south, to wait for dawn. The battle began at sunrise. Ben-hadad, well aware of the battle plans, came from Damascus to command his own army. While Ahab's engineers cut trees from the forests of Gilead to construct the heavier parts of siege machines, the armies of the opposing forces met on the plains and rolling hills outside the city.

Ben-hadad gave orders to concentrate on Ahab. All other priorities were low.

The Aramaeans directed their thrusts toward the regally dressed Jehoshaphat, mistaking him for Ahab, as planned. Within hours his contingent was isolated. Only when his Judean accent became apparent through his battle shouts and orders did the enemy turn away, disinterested in any save Ahab.

Ahab fought with his chariots on the wide flat below the city. On the wall and behind shields along its base, archers sent clouds of arrows toward the approaching Israelites. Ahab raised his arms high as he screamed a command to one of his captains. The gesture pulled his breastplate above the edge of the underlapping stomach armor. At that critical moment a chance arrow struck through the narrow slit with a soft thump. Ahab gasped in surprise at the sharp, sudden pain.

He did not fall. Clenching his teeth against the pain, he choked the command to his driver, "Take me to the rear. I'm wounded."

Behind the lines his armor bearer grasped the end of the arrow and jerked it hard from Ahab's body. The king muffled his shout of pain with his hand. The blood spurted from the wound to flow from beneath his armor and down his legs. Ahab recalled in a fleeting moment the prophecies of Elijah and Macaiah, but he forced away the thought of death and commanded his driver to hold him erect.

Only by sheer heroism did Ahab save the battle from disaster. His shouted commands to his captains renewed the army's courage. Word spread quickly. The king was alive. Past noon and well into the long day Ahab stood in his chariot. The driver wept and had to force himself not to look at the deepening pool of Ahab's blood that formed on the chariot floor.

Ben-hadad's army held. The siege machines were of no use, for the Israelites and Judeans could not force the Aramaeans back into the city. Ahab's shouts became softer and died into whispers. Two, then three men were required to hold him upright.

He died late in the afternoon, still held upright with strong arms at his back and under his armpits. The word was sent out, "Every man return to his home. The battle is over."

They were not pursued, for Ben-hadad's losses were great. He was content to save the city. The driver turned the king's chariot west. He drove carefully, determined not to jostle Ahab's unfeeling body, now slumped on the floor of the chariot between two soldiers.

They drove all night and arrived at the palace just after daybreak. Jezebel heard the news stoically. She ordered his body prepared for burial. After the driver and attendants left, bowing with deep respect out of sorrow and concern, Jezebel walked numbly to the window. The chariot was there in the courtyard, the royal battle chariot where her beloved had died. She opened the lattice and threw it back. The horrible sounds tore through the open air. Growling, greedy dogs surrounded the chariot, lapping the blood off its floor, snarling at others in the pack that struggled for the delicacy. Jezebel screamed at the attendants, just emerging from the outside door. "The dogs," she shouted, near hysteria, "get the dogs away."

The driver ran to the chariot for his whip and lashed at the dogs. Yelping in pain, they ran from the chariot and disappeared down a side street. Jezebel covered her face with her hands and slumped to the floor.

Three attendants mounted the chariot and drove it to Samaria's main pool. Prostitutes stood naked in the water, taking their morning baths. They stopped to watch the chariot back into the shallow end of the pool. One of them whispered, "It's the king's chariot." They splashed toward the attendants, shouting excitedly, "Is Ahab wounded?"

The men glanced at the women. "The king is dead."

The prostitutes, shocked, were silent for a moment. They watched the men begin to throw water onto the chariot. Then the water turned faintly pink around it. "I'm going to bathe in the king's blood," one said. She smiled. "Surely that will bring good luck." The prostitutes, their sorrow quickly over, jumped at the chariot. They rolled in the discolored water and splashed it at one another gleefully. The men, ignoring the trauma of the king's death for the moment, stopped to stare at the naked prostitutes.

Jehu bowed with practiced reverence. "My lord, king of Israel." The words came smoothly, with no trace of his turmoil. He rose and stepped back to his place to watch the continuing parade of high officials bow to the newly-appointed king.

Ahaziah looked as much like Jezebel as he acted. He was almost as short as the Queen Mother but had allowed his body to become fleshy. He was not yet fat, but his skin was soft and slightly puffy. He wore a closely-trimmed mustache and goatee, shaved under the lip to form an oval around his mouth. He sported the king's signet ring on his right hand, and on his left was a large emerald next to a wide gold band on his small finger.

The inaugural feast was a vexing affair, but Ahaziah did not notice. His personal enjoyment was immense, while his court officials feigned joy in his presence and frustration when by themselves.

He was not popular. Even Obadiah, Jehu noticed, bowed a bit stiffly. The new king looked on the ever-growing reform movement with disdain while he continued to indulge himself in the excesses of Baal. He was as fanatical as his mother, yet he had little of her discipline. Jehu could not imagine that his rule could be constructive. His talent lay in commerce, while tension with Ben-hadad and the rising power of Assyria called for a man of war. The leaders did not trust his competence, while the Yahweh prophets spoke sternly against his allegiance to the Baals. Ahaziah showed little concern that the people did not support him.

After a first flurry of effort, Ahaziah lost his enthusiasm and settled into the social routine of the court. Jezebel stepped into the vacuum, careful to work consistently through her son.

With a rich treasury at his command the king gave himself more and more to parties, letting matters take their course around him. Obadiah found it necessary to walk a narrow line between offending Ahaziah and maintaining fiscal responsibility. Jehu had less trouble, for the king cared little for military matters. The commander used the chance to build the army in his favor, toward the day when, possibly, the king might have to be dealt with for the sake of the nation.

It was at one of the court parties in Samaria that Ahaziah's reign of only a few months came to its end. He and some young companions left the main banquet room to take some dancing girls to private chambers upstairs. All of them were drunk. Laughing and joking, they shoved one another along the corridor toward the rooms. One of the girls stumbled. Gallantly but drunkenly Ahaziah tried to catch her. In his stumbling haste he crashed into a lattice wall that ran the length of the corridor. With a soft crunching sound, the thin wood gave way. Ahaziah grabbed at the framing, but it was as flimsy as the lattice itself. Clutching a broken piece of wood and screaming, he fell eighteen feet and landed on his side across a high stone curb that encircled a small garden.

His companions scurried down the steps to his aid, while the screams of the dancing girls brought the palace to life. When sober help arrived, Ahaziah's drunk friends already were carrying him by his arms and legs upstairs toward his room. A thin line of blood ran from the corners of his mouth. One side of his clothing was wet with blood.

The attendants took charge quickly. They placed him in his bed and stripped him. His side was badly skinned and abraded, but it was not pierced. He regained consciousness, groaning and crying out in his pain. The doctors cleaned the wound and bandaged the abrasion, but his throat continued to fill with blood. They propped him with pillows into a sitting position to keep him from choking and put a container by his bed for him to spit into.

The pain worsened. By the next day the abrasion was a deep purple-black. Ahaziah asked the doctors for their opinions. They could not hide the seriousness of the injury. Jezebel, by his bedside throughout the ordeal, asked his permission to send the doctors and attendants from the room.

The Queen Mother sat on the edge of the thickly-pillowed bed, careful to avoid aggravating his pain. "My son and king," she said gently, "the gods can do wonders when doctors are helpless. I implore you to call on Baal to heal you."

Ahaziah coughed into the container and leaned back on his pillows. He shut his eyes against the pain and nausea that dominated his midsection. "Tell me the baal that is best," he said.

"Baal-zebub, the god of Ekron of Philistia," she answered. "As God of Flies he can banish disease and injury."

The king, in a moment of desperate probing, responded, "My father put Yahweh's name in mine. Perhaps it is Yahweh I should seek now."

Jezebel took his hand. *He always was a weak son*, she thought. "No, my king. Your father called you 'Yahweh Possesses' before he learned of Melkart's strength. He himself would call on the god who specializes in healing."

"Very well." Ahaziah grimaced as he spoke. "Call the attendants."

The men arranged quickly for the trip. Ekron was fifty miles to the south, a very long and fast day's journey. They could not return in less than three days. In lightweight leather chariots, one man to a chariot and each carrying his own provisions, the attendants raced through the gates, circled the wall, and doubled back toward the west for ten miles to catch the north-south Way of the Sea.

Elijah was at Gilgal when word came of the king's accident.

"It is of God," Macaiah said promptly.

Elijah picked up his mantle and pouches, fastened his leather girdle around his waist, and turned toward the door. He moved more slowly now. The weathered skin was aged, but his body still was vigorous and well-muscled.

Elisha grabbed his belongings and ran after him, his two pouches swinging from one hand, his girdle from the other, his mantle across his shoulder. He fell into step with his master.

The two men walked north in silence for a short distance, then turned west on the Joppa road.

"Ahaziah serves Baal," Elijah explained. "If he is true to form he will send messengers to inquire from Baal-zebub whether he will recover. We will intercept the messengers."

The prophets walked rapidly, running when they could. By early afternoon they came to the marketplace of Aphek-on-the-plain. They learned from the villagers that no royal messengers had passed through. The two men started north toward Samaria from the city. After three miles, at a rise in the road, they sat down to wait.

Within an hour the chariots came into sight, their wheels and horses' hooves trailing a long line of dust. Elijah waited by the roadside until they were near enough to see him. They slowed a short distance away, eyeing him curiously in his prophet's garb. He stepped into their path and held up his hand. Elisha stood silent beside his master.

The drivers reined up their teams. The leader tied his lines to the chariot, dismounted, and asked cautiously, "Whose prophet are you?"

Elisha glared at the man. It was incredible that Elijah was known throughout Israel but not in the king's court.

Elijah answered sternly. "I am a prophet of Yahweh."

"You have reason to stop us?"

"I judge that you go to Ekron to inquire from Baal-zebub whether the king shall live or die."

The man looked back at his companions, surprised at the prophet's accuracy.

"I will tell you the answer to your inquiry," Elijah continued, catching their answer in the silence. His voice rose in force. "Go back now to Ahaziah and tell him that his choice of gods was a choice between life and death. Why should he send messengers to Ekron to inquire of Baal-zebub? Is Yahweh too weak to heal?"

Elijah looked hard into the leader's eyes and stretched his arm north toward Samaria. "Tell Ahaziah this word from Yahweh: 'Is there no God in Israel that you must send to Baal-zebub for an answer? Because you call on the baals rather than on Yahweh for help, you will not rise from your bed. You will die.'"

The messengers looked at one another. One of them ventured nervously, knowing he was out of line to advise the leader, "We should obey the king and proceed."

"Yahweh is God in Israel," the leader responded, inwardly pleased to be rid of Ahaziah. "We have our answer."

He remounted his chariot and pulled hard on the right rein, flicking his whip simultaneously to turn the horse in a short arc. The other men followed suit. The prophets watched them break into a gallop and disappear in clouds of dust.

Chapter Nineteen

AHAZIAH ANGRILY RECEIVED the messengers as soon as they returned, concerned at the quickness of their trip.

"We were met in the road above Aphek by a prophet of Yahweh," the spokesman reported. He fidgeted nervously, but continued, "Forgive me, my king."

"Speak quickly," Ahaziah snapped.

"The prophet gave us this word to you from Yahweh: 'Is there no god in Israel that you go to inquire of Baal-zebub? Because you did not seek Yahweh but rather the baal, you will not rise from your bed. You will die.'"

Ahaziah struggled to maintain his dignity. "What did the prophet look like? Describe him to me."

The messenger swallowed. "He was a stout man," he answered, "fairly old, and his body was covered with hair."

Coughing, Ahaziah waved the men out, then turned to the doctor. "Get the Queen Mother," he ordered.

Jezebel came quickly, already dressed in case her son's condition became worse. She noticed Ahaziah's drawn face and nodded for the doctor to leave them alone.

Ahaziah spoke loudly through his pain. "It's Elijah again," he blurted. "He says I will die."

Jezebel, not having seen the prophet for several years, was caught by surprise. She paled. Seeing the change in his mother, Ahaziah began to weep, coughing and clutching his side from the pain brought by his spasms.

Jezebel spoke gently but firmly. "Get hold of yourself, son. You are a king." She took his hand in hers and held it until the shaking stopped. Then she spoke evenly. "If Elijah prophesied your death he did so at the word of his god. Baal is stronger."

Ahaziah responded weakly. "You'll use my life to fight your battle, won't you, mother?"

"Not my battle, son, your battle. We are talking about your life."

"No, mother. You want me to live, but you want more to see Melkart beat Yahweh. My injury is your battleground."

Jezebel spoke carefully, realizing that her son had the power to order her death. She distrusted the weak spirit bound now to an injured body. "Yahweh has thrust forward the challenge, son, not I. Your injury is a battleground of the gods only because Baal must make it so for you to live."

The king pushed himself up painfully on his elbows. "Yahweh cursed my father and he died. Baal could not save him."

"Ahab was a great man," Jezebel entreated, "but he vacillated between Baal and Yahweh. He never truly gave Melkart a chance." The Queen Mother knelt beside the bed and kissed the back of her son's hand. "Please, Ahaziah. Fight." She spoke in a low, intense voice. "Fight for your life. Take up Yahweh's challenge."

The son gripped his mother's hand and sank deeper into the pillows. He looked at her. "All right. What shall we do?"

Jezebel smiled and reached to push a lock of hair from Ahaziah's forehead. "Select a captain who is fervent for Melkart," she said. "Explain to him the challenge of Yahweh. Send him with his fifty men to arrest Elijah. Then Yahweh will be in Baal's power."

Ahaziah nodded his assent, only half understanding the battle lines but glad for the hope his mother instilled. Jezebel left the room quietly and sent the doctors back to her son.

She walked more sprightly, a rekindled flame growing inside her bowels. Her hair had grayed in recent years and her skin had become a bit sallow. Yet she had guarded carefully against fleshiness, so that her stomach still was almost flat and her skin unusually smooth.

Meor-baal returned quickly with the information she sought. He had located the man she wanted, an ambitious, simple-minded captain who was slightly a fanatic toward Melkart and Asherah. He was a good leader who inspired his men to battle with promises of help and rewards from Baal.

"Delightful," Jezebel laughed. Meor-baal had not seen her so excited in a long time. Her zest was infectious, and soon he was laughing with her as she caricatured Elijah's wild hair and rustic dress.

She grew serious after a few moments. "Meor-baal," she instructed, "I want you to arrange for messengers to wait for the soldiers to return with Elijah. The moment they approach the gate I want criers to rush to their posts and announce to the city his capture. The people must know that Baal is stronger than Yahweh's curse."

Meor-baal bowed. He had aged more quickly than she, and had gained considerable weight. Still, their friendship had deepened over the years, even more since she had become Queen Mother rather than Queen.

The captain was outside the door when the priest made his exit. He entered Jezebel's conference room with a practiced but cautious air of confidence. A scar from a former battle ran from his forehead down the side of his nose very close to his left eye. The eye still was good, but the scar made it appear a bit larger than the other. He was dressed in a warrior's tunic and cradled his dress helmet in his arm. He bowed, "At your service, my Queen Mother."

"How strongly do you believe in Melkart?" Jezebel asked abruptly.

The soldier stood at attention. "He is the strongest of all the gods," he replied.

"Stronger than Yahweh?"

"Yes, honored Queen Mother." He laughed softly. "Much stronger."

"Then how do you account for Yahweh's victory years ago on Mount Carmel?" she pressed.

The captain considered the question carefully. "I have thought much about that contest," he responded. "I must admit that I do not know how Yahweh won. A weaker god wins an occasional battle. But if Yahweh were stronger his nation would be stronger. And he would not allow Baal in his domain."

Jezebel's inner smile did not appear on her face. The reasoning of rustic men amused her. What difference did it make what arguments the captain used, though, so long as his belief in Melkart was firm. Her next question was crucial, though, and she looked at him intently. "Are you afraid of Elijah?"

The warrior smiled, causing the scar on his face to deepen. "He is the prophet of Mount Carmel," he said. "Surely he is Yahweh's strongest prophet. But Baal is stronger. If I ever meet him, it will be in the strength of Melkart. Melkart is stronger, so Melkart will win."

"But what about Carmel? Melkart did not win there."

"Sometimes prophets lose touch with the gods."

"And you are in touch."

The captain fidgeted nervously, but only for a moment. "Yes," he said flatly.

"All right," Jezebel said. "I am giving you the most important assignment of your career." She stretched herself upright in her throne chair. "The prophet of Yahweh has pronounced that the king will die. You must find him so we may break his curse by the power of Baal."

The captain beamed. "His arrest will be my pleasure."

"He lives on a hill not far south of here," the Queen Mother continued. "Find out the location from one of the priests. Bring him to Ahaziah, but announce your arrival so I can be there. Treat Elijah as you please on the way, but I want him alive when I see him. Do you understand?"

"Yes, Queen Mother Jezebel." The captain bowed and turned.

He gathered his men quickly to brief them. Mounted, without chariots, the party circled Samaria's wall and turned south toward Mounts Ebal and Gerizim. The sky was bleak, overcast with a mottled blanket of dark gray high-topped clouds. The captain teased his men about needing such a large force to arrest one man, skillfully seeking to quiet the fears of those who knew of Elijah's power. They were going to a picnic, not to a battle. To emphasize the point, he stopped his contingent at Kozoh and again at Elmathan for wine. By the time he led his fifty down the steep wadi that passed at the foot of Elijah's hill the men were laughing and singing the robust songs of Asherah.

The captain gathered his men in a tight group around him so Elijah could note the force of the arresting party. He looked up the hill and called loudly, "Elijah!" The prophet did not immediately appear. The captain screamed the name louder, then turned and swore to his men. He hoped he could avoid climbing the steep hill.

Elisha looked toward his master. "The time has come, Elijah," he said.

Elijah threw on his mantle and walked slowly toward the crest of his hill, then stooped low behind a thick bush. He could hear clearly the raucous laughter of the soldiers, interspersed with insults toward the man they came to capture. He was not surprised by Ahaziah's action. The man was desperate. How much easier for him simply to call on Yahweh for help. Jezebel was the power, of course. She could never let such a challenge to Baal go unanswered.

The prophet rose and stepped to the crest so the soldiers could see him. The hill sloped too steeply for horses, so the soldiers would have to climb on foot. The men laughed louder now, pointing upward and joking about his appearance.

"Hey, Elijah," the captain called loudly, "you dervish."
The men roared. Elijah sat down on a rock to stare down
impassively onto the soldiers. "Elijah," the captain repeated, "you crazy man of a weak god. The king wants to
see you. Come with us."

Elijah's forearm rested easily on his knee. "What does
Ahaziah want?"

"What do you think, prophet of Yahweh?" The captain
spoke more sternly now. "You will learn to respect the king
and you will learn the power of Baal."

"If Baal can heal, let him heal. Or is he too weak to
break Yahweh's word?"

The captain motioned for his men to remain in their
places. He dismounted and stood in front of his horse.
Cupping his hands to his mouth, he shouted at the top of
his voice. "Elijah, you so-called man of a god, come down
or I will come and drag you down."

Elijah stood to his feet and looked down the long slope
toward the close-ranked warriors. He could see each face.
Some appeared amused, others were intense with anger.
He called back to the captain. "You would challenge the
power of Yahweh with the force of arms?"

The leader's face relaxed from its anger. He spoke taunt-
ingly. "Hey, Elijah, I wasn't on Mount Carmel. You're
talking to soldiers now, not prophets and priests. I warn
you. Come down now or you will wish you were dead."

Elijah recalled the derisive laughter of the salt diggers.
What of the gentle voice now? Should he become a pris-
oner of the soldiers the people would award Baal a great
victory. Even Ahaziah's death would not eclipse the significance of his capture.

He spoke in measured words. "You must know, Captain,
that Yahweh will not allow me to be captured. You will do
well to return to Samaria."

The captain slowly withdrew his sword from its sheath.
He gestured with his other hand for his men to dismount.
They gathered around him quickly, drawing their swords
as they moved.

Elijah held his hand outstretched toward them. "Yahweh has warned you, Captain. Now all Israel will know that the God who sent fire on Mount Carmel can meet on any god's battlefield. If I truly am a prophet of Yahweh, let fire come down from heaven to consume every one of you."

The captain's face was impassive. As if in common ritual, all fifty-one men raised their swords high, their points like lightning rods toward the slated sky. It happened then. Lightning streaked in blinding waves from the moisture-filled heavens to touch the tip of every sword. Thunder roared its deafening proclamation of disaster as brilliant light flashed through armor and men to sizzle on the earth. Warriors were thrown in wild heaps by the force, flung onto their backs and sides and chests, electricity crackling in their armor. The horses behind them reared up and neighed in terror. The nearer ones fell to the ground, some of them dead; the ones behind broke into frantic gallops up the narrow trail.

Not a man moved. Each hand held still to its sword, seared flesh welded to iron handles. Shreds of burnt, smoldering cloth lay on and around the blackened flesh of bodies lying promiscuously together, a center heap with straggled corpses flung around the perimeter.

Elijah stared at the scene, his horror mixed with anger. He was not repelled at the sight any more than at the slaughter on Carmel. He could understand God's vengeance better than God's gentle voice. And so could other men . . . and so could other men.

Elisha stood close behind him. As Elijah turned, his servant spread his arms to receive the prophet's embrace. A thrill of victory grew so fiercely in their breasts that they wept. Elisha spoke first. "Surely," he said ecstatically, "Ahaziah will repent now."

Elijah shook his head. "No. Ahaziah is too weak to repent. Especially with Jezebel at his side. But perhaps the next king will. Perhaps."

The horses scattered once they reached the road. Some ran into fields and stopped, snorting their fear, rearing and galloping away when villagers approached them. Some ran south, others north.

None of the horses returned to Samaria. The noon hour passed and the messengers stared with increasing nervousness down the road that ran along the city wall. A worried Meor-baal posted lookouts on the southeastern parapet.

At two o'clock, an hour before the afternoon sacrifice, Jezebel summoned her priest. "Perhaps," he ventured, "villagers faithful to Yahweh were able to overcome the contingent."

She shrieked. "Able to overcome fifty-one good fighting men?" Her face was flushed, her hands trembling with anger. She stepped down from her dais and walked to the statue of Melkart by the window. She stared at it for a long time. Her arms hung tight to her sides and she clenched and unclenched her fists repeatedly. Finally she turned. "Meor-baal, come here."

The priest immediately stepped close to her. Jezebel spoke directly into his face, loudly. "Order all of the standing army stationed in the city to the large courtyard immediately. I will give the orders to them myself. Move quickly. I want Elijah before nightfall."

Meor-baal bowed.

Word of the call to arms spread rapidly. Soldiers walked away from half-filled wine goblets and pseudo-worried prostitutes. Fathers and husbands quickly kissed their families. Religious soldiers interrupted their sacrifices and left their offerings behind. Within little more than an hour all but a few stragglers had gathered in the assembly area by the city gate.

Jezebel stood on a quickly-improvised podium. She was dressed in a purple robe trimmed in red, her Queen Mother headdress in place. She raised her chin a bit as she began. "I speak for the king. He has ordered a crucial mission for which only the bravest and most select soldiers should volunteer." She paused, watching the curious, rough faces staring at her in anticipation. "All of you who worship Melkart step forward. The rest of you fall back," she ordered. The shuffling began, but, to her surprise, fully two-thirds of the troops fell back. Yahweh had gained more ground than she thought. "You soldiers who do not worship Melkart are dismissed," she shouted.

Jezebel reweighed her plan carefully as the Yahweh worshipers moved away. Some five hundred soldiers would be left. She had intended to send all of the Melkart men after Elijah, but the surprising show of Yahweh's strength called for caution. The marginal believers would add weakness, not strength, to the battle of the gods.

"Now," she shouted at last, "who is the best among you?"

The soldiers looked around to find Baal-hanan. A shouting tumult, as his comrades raised his arms and shouted his name companionably, indicated him to be on the left side of the assembly.

"Come forward," Jezebel ordered.

Baal-hanan made his way to the podium.

"Come up here," she said softly.

He mounted the stand quickly, as muted exclamations of surprise swept through the crowd—surprise that a common soldier would be given such an honor.

The Queen Mother spoke quietly, making sure her instructions would be heard only by him. He was to select fifty of the best warriors, each one dedicated to Melkart, and order them to prepare to ride at once. When that was arranged, he was to meet her in her conference room.

She answered Meor-baal's quizzical look as they walked to Jezebel's chambers. "Melkart obviously has guarded the champion carefully in all his battles, my dear priest. I chose a man whom Melkart likes."

A half-hour later Baal-hanan was announced. Jezebel accepted his bow, then told him of the king's injury and Elijah's curse. The first contingent had not yet returned, she explained. She spoke with strained emotion. "Look toward the window at Melkart."

Baal-hanan obeyed. The stone god was caught in half-stride, a loin cloth coming to midthigh, a high turban on his head. He was bearded, with a large battleaxe on his shoulder. His eyes were large and staring.

"Walk closer," she ordered. "See what Melkart will say."

Baal-hanan walked self-consciously to the statue. He stared into the large eyes and studied the axe.

"Give your mind to Melkart," Jezebel said.

The soldier let his mind go, caught up in his conviction of Melkart's power. He stood for several minutes in complete silence, the Queen Mother behind him. When he turned, Jezebel searched his eyes with satisfaction. They were fierce with determination.

She walked slowly to her dais and pulled a heavy cloth away to uncover a captain's helmet. She picked it up and turned, holding it at her waist with both hands. "You are a captain now," she said.

Baal-hanan blinked, then walked to her and knelt. She placed the helmet on his head without a word.

"I will not fail you, my Queen Mother Jezebel."

"You will not fail Melkart," she responded.

By early evening the hand-picked troops stared in horror at the grotesque bodies of horses and men that lay stiffening in the wadi. Baal-hanan watched his men carefully. All of them had seen bodies before, scattered and bloody and decapitated across a battlefield. They were hardened men, knowing well the horrors of war yet captivated by the heroic glory of the conquest.

The new captain, still mounted, screamed Elijah's name with such force that his horse jumped forward nervously. Baal-hanan cursed and jerked the reins hard. "Elijah!" he repeated loudly.

A moment later the prophet appeared at the crest, Elisha close beside and slightly behind him. He stared down on the soldiers without speaking.

Baal-hanan, enraged at the sight of the blackened corpses of men he knew, rose up in his saddle and screamed at the prophet, his voice rasping from the loudness. "Elijah, you filthy prophet of a filthy god, obey your king and come down! Now!"

Elijah, his dark hair and mantle black and brown against a darkening gray sky, was indistinct on the crest.

The captain did not wait for the prophet to speak. Convulsed with rage, he screamed hoarsely at his men and jumped from his horse. He drew his sword and waved it, cursing his men to join him. Elijah watched them take the first few steps up the hill, shouting curses at him as they came. Lost in their violent fury, they did not hear him speak. "If I really am a man of God, then let fire from heaven consume all of you."

At dusk, one lone horse loped toward Samaria's city gate. The gatekeeper, on the watch for Baal-hanan and his men, ordered the gate open. Two men caught the horse's bridle and calmed him down, patting his shoulder and talking to him in ever more soothing tones.

Jezebel was mystified. Subdued, she had to force herself to order messengers to the villages near Elijah's hill to determine what happened. They returned near midnight to find her in Ahaziah's bedroom with the doctors. The king was deteriorating rapidly and with increasing pain.

There were eyewitnesses to both catastrophies, the messengers reported, curious men and boys who lived near Elijah. All of them told the same story. The bodies both of horses and men confirmed their words. The messengers had commandeered carts from the villages to bring back the bodies.

Jezebel was stoic. Her control, though, was the result of years of practice. She clasped her hands behind her back to keep them from trembling. She stared hard at the messengers as though the force of her will could change what had happened. Then, rather than risk the chance of a cracked voice, she jerked her head toward the door as a signal to empty the room.

Ahaziah coughed, a muffled sound that brought blood from his throat. He spit into the container. "So much for your Melkart," he choked bitterly.

Jezebel did not speak. Her jaw set hard against violent, angry tears, she knelt beside the bed. Ahaziah knew that she was more disturbed at losing to Elijah than by the approaching death of her son. Weakly, he pushed her away. "Call the attendants," he said.

The Queen Mother walked to the door and beckoned them in. Ahaziah gestured for them to come close.

"Send a contingent of soldiers for Elijah, but this time send Yahweh's men."

Jezebel gritted her teeth but said nothing.

Elijah arrived at the palace the next morning. The dead bodies had already been cleared away before the last contingent had arrived at his hill. The captain acknowledged Yahweh as the God of his troops and begged the prophet's mercy. "Please," the captain had said, "come with us to the king. Yahweh will protect you there as well as here."

The prophet knew they were right even before the voice from inside his breast told him he should go. Yahweh had won another great victory. The story would spread throughout the villages and cities of the land. Melkart's back was broken.

Ahaziah stared at the prophet through aching gray eyes. He was in constant pain now. "Is there no way to change the word of Yahweh?" he asked.

Elijah's voice was even, confident. "No, there is no hope. You would not change even if God were to spare your life. You placed yourself in Baal's hands—and lost. Now, because you sent messengers to Baal-zebub, as though there were no God in Israel, you shall die."

Ahaziah closed his eyes to stem the tears that slipped beneath his lids.

The king died without a son. His brother, Jehoram, an able military man, was anointed in his place. The new king was met with joy by the people and relief by the prophets.

Elijah did not go to the coronation, nor did Macaiah. They stayed at Gilgal to await news of the event from a company of younger prophets who represented the coenobia. Elisha listened silently as the older men talked of former days. They spoke as though a great bridge had been crossed. Elisha's heart pulsed with a sense of premonition.

At last, near midmorning, the prophets returned with their report. They burst through the door shouting, unable to contain their delight. "Jehoram has vowed to tear down the altars of Melkart and Asherah!" The prophets rose to meet the young emissaries with surprised joy, their faces wide with anticipation. "Are you sure? How do you know?" The questions came quick and confused, until Macaiah called the group to order and set the young men in front to tell their story more fully.

Only when the report was finished and the questions turned to prolonged comments did Elisha realize that his master was silent. He went to his side, his earlier prescience weighing heavily.

Elijah waited until his successor kneeled beside him before he spoke, as though he had bided his time until this moment. "Elisha," he said gently, "I must go to Bethel. Stay here."

The younger man, now in his middle years and a powerful prophet in his own right, refused. "No. I fear that I will not see you again. I will go with you."

"I want to go alone."

"You always want to be alone when you feel Yahweh speaking to you." Elisha's whisper became more urgent. He swore a double oath. "As Yahweh lives and as you live, I will not leave you."

Elijah glared at the man, slightly angered at his aggressiveness. He nodded, though, and the two men slipped unnoticed out of the house and away from Gilgal.

Bethel was seven miles to the south, up higher along the spine of the ridge and toward Jerusalem. They walked the distance in two hours.

A group of prophets stood outside the door of their coenobia house, waiting as though they expected the great prophet to come. They watched Elijah with curious interest as he neared them. One of them caught Elisha's sleeve. Quickly, the group surrounded him, whispering in urgent and painful tones. "Did you know that Yahweh is going to take your lord and master away?"

"Yes," Elisha replied, "I do know. Let's not talk about it." They sensed, as he did, that Jehoram's promise to remove the baals was the seal of Elijah's life. His work was done. The awareness struck the other prophets with the overwhelming sense of destiny that Elisha himself felt earlier in the morning. Yet their certainty made him light-headed. He felt as though he walked through a story already written.

Elijah talked with the coenobia for forty minutes. His speech, Elisha thought, was the best of his life. The prophets listened with awesome awareness that the great man of God soon would be gone.

The great mentor talked of the past and of the future, of the battle won and the war ahead, of the sense of lostness once that now was turned to victory. He talked of truth, of nearness to Yahweh, of listening for God's voice amid the din of religious chaos. He talked of a prophet's distinct and tailored call and how it is garbled when he listens more to other prophets than to God. He challenged them at last to ignore the thumping drumbeat of prophetic fame, so to hear the weeping wail of the wounded day.

Elijah finished and walked from the group that was left silent in the heavy air of signal truth. Elisha followed. Outside the door, he repeated his earlier plea. "Stay here, Elisha. Yahweh sends me to Jericho. I want to go alone."

"No," Elisha said flatly. "I meant what I said. I will stay with you."

Elijah chose not to respond. He wanted to be alone, yet he wanted Elisha with him. The two men took the southeast road toward the Michmash fortress, then turned east down the Way of the Border toward Jericho. They covered the fifteen-mile, downhill distance in three hours, running short distances as the older man was able.

The scene at Jericho was virtually a replay of the Bethel scene. A company of prophets waited expectantly at their door. They watched with deep, silent respect as the great prophet entered the house, then they surrounded Elisha with their concern.

"Yes," he answered. "I know. Yahweh will take him away. Please do not ask me about it."

As the great prophet spoke to the assembled coenobia, Elisha's mind was caught up in his own sense of destiny. Elijah, he knew, did not stand honored before the prophets because he was famous, but because he was faithful. Ironically, the famous man never had sought fame, only Yahweh's distinctive word. *To be like that at my life's end,* Elisha thought, *to be able to look back on life without regret, to have the assurance that life was handled well, faithful against the confusing call of the generation, that is life's greatest moment.*

A low murmur ran through the group to call Elisha back to the present. Elijah was through. The prophets bowed to their faces and did not rise until the great man was out the door.

"Yahweh calls me to the Jordan," he said to Elisha, and again he pled unconvincingly to go alone.

"You go to die," Elisha answered quietly.

"Yes," the prophet answered. "I go to be taken by Yahweh. Alone."

Elisha realized now that his master's reluctance was to test his disciple. His successor must not see him go unless he feels certain that Yahweh bids him to. "No," he answered firmly. "You shall not go alone. As God lives, I will stay with you to the end."

The road to the Jordan was bleak, the bleached soil spread flat and dismal beyond Jericho. The men walked in silence for nearly two hours. Then they stood on the bank of the river. It was low now, but still swift and thirty yards wide between its ugly mud banks.

The men watched the brown water. Five miles to the south the Dead Sea glistened a brilliant blue. To the north the mountain walls closed on either side to squeeze the valley tightly to its green ribbon. Here the wider flood bed was bare and gray, spotted with clumps of thorn bushes.

Elijah removed his mantle and rolled it tightly into a long bundle. He stepped to the slime-covered edge of the water. Grasping one end, he swung it in an arc over his head. The brown cloak splashed sharply against the brown water. The water began to churn. Backwards it rolled, turned up onto itself in a swirling moment, roaring against itself, clawing at the air, fighting against the unseen shield of God's breath, piling its brown-earthed fury into a standing wall of wetness.

The men walked through the corridor, the wild Jordan rearing high to their left, stretching shallow and receding to their right. They looked back from the other side. The water closed from the bottom, its high rippled hump dropping quickly in a racing flood to catch the shallowed south. The moment was done. Elisha stared at his master, open-mouthed.

The two men did not see the miracle alone. Across the Jordan were fifty prophets who had followed unseen from Bethel and Jericho. They fell to the ground and buried their faces in the dirt, shielding their sight against the moment when Yahweh himself might fill the valley with his blinding glory.

Elijah's gentle voice pulled his servant from his stunned silence. "Elisha, I will leave you in a while. What would you have me to do for you before I am taken?"

The servant's eyes were wide, his lips trembling. He clenched his teeth to still the tempest in his soul. Evenly, with conviction and strength, an edge of anticipation in his voice, he answered, "I have been your son. Give me an elder son's inheritance of the spirit that dwells within you."

The master turned toward the eastern mountains. Elisha fell into step beside him. They crossed the floodbed and climbed the rise to the valley plain. He answered finally, with measured caution, "My son, you ask a hard thing. My spirit is not mine to give. The gift must come from Yahweh."

Elisha did not answer, but in his tearing heart he prayed with all his strength. The two walked toward the hills in silence. They covered a quarter mile before Elijah spoke again. "Perhaps Yahweh will grant your wish. If you see me as I am taken from you, your wish will be granted. If you do not see me, your wish is denied."

Mount Nebo was ahead and to the north. The two men walked toward the high, jutting ridge. The plain still was level, stripped bare of its scattered barley, dusty and hot.

They were halfway across the plain when the sirocco hit. The eastern wind poured over the edge of the plateau, marking its approach with twisting devils of red,

2 9 8

spiraling dirt. The temperature rose rapidly, so quickly that the prophets felt their breath sucked away. They turned their backs against the onrush. The dust-filled wind attacked their nostrils, drying the membranes, making breath itself painful. The whirling wind snapped their clothing furiously. They shut their eyes against the wildness and pulled the ends of their turbans across their faces.

As the hot wind pulled the loose soil upward into its ever-thickening cloud, Elisha reached his hand toward his master. Elijah was not there. The servant spread his hands across his face for protection. Looking through the slits between his fingers, he turned full circle to search for his friend. The sound of a roaring wind pulled his eyes upward. In the dim, red-dirt sky Elijah's form mounted into flaming chariots drawn by flaming horses. The wheels were circles of fire, the carriages were rings of fire, the traces were streams of fire. The horses' manes were shooting flames, their thrashing hooves were flailing fire, their flashing eyes were furnaced coals. The sky was filled with them, with chariots and horses, mounted by fiery angels, pulling at fire-streaked reins.

Elisha screamed at his master. "My father, my father." His voice fought through the wind. "I see them! The chariots and horsemen of Israel! I see them!"

The red-dirt sky tore at Elisha's eyes. His hand held back its fury only for a moment. His tears fought against the siege of dust, and he could see no more. Still screaming at the sky, he fell to the ground and crouched his face into his knees, away from the wind.

The worst was over in a few minutes, though the hot sirocco wind still blew the desert dust with vengeance and wrung all moisture from the air. The dirty sky above held like a fog over the land. With his turban still wrapped around his face, he wiped his eyes and looked around. A dark, dust-covered cloth lay tangled on a bush a few steps away. He walked to it. Carefully, he extracted Elijah's mantle from the thin branches and shook the loose dust into the wind. He placed it over his shoulders and turned back toward the Jordan.

Epilogue

JEHORAM REIGNED for twelve years. He was an able king, but not as competent as his father. War was the pattern of his rule. The trouble with Syria continued, while Mesha of Moab took advantage of circumstances to capture much of Israel's territory that lay east of the Jordan.

Elisha became the most significant prophet in Israel. His fame spread beyond Israel's borders, and especially to Syria. He was aggressive, sometimes harsh, and heavily involved in the politics of the day. He established a school for prophets that became both community and seminary to them.

The prophet anointed Hazael to be king of Syria, in fulfillment of Elijah's charge, but he wept when he performed the act. He knew well the grief Ben-hadad's successor would bring to Israel. Hazael returned to the ailing Ben-hadad, smothered him with a wet blanket, and claimed the throne.

Jehu's anointing was postponed, since Jehoram showed some sympathy, perhaps mainly through political motives, for the Yahwist reforms. But Jezebel still was Queen

Mother and a power in Israel. So long as she lived, Jehoram's efforts could only be token, whatever his motives. At last, while the king recovered in Jezreel from wounds inflicted in yet another battle for Ramoth-gilead, Elisha sent one of his prophet sons to the battlefield to anoint Jehu.

The commander quickly was accepted by the officers under him. He instructed them not to allow anyone to get word to Jezreel. With a troop of chariots, he raced madly for the summer palace to carry out his coup. Jehoram spotted the speeding company while they were still a good way off. He sent a horseman to determine the nature of the party. The horseman joined with Jehu, and the next horseman sent out did the same. Jehoram himself then went to meet the company, but by that time Jehu was near Jezreel. They met in Naboth's field.

Jehu's accusations were stern. He accused Jehoram of allowing Jezebel to continue her obscene idol worship. The king, aware of Jehu's intentions and almost unprotected, tried to escape. Jehu shot an arrow through his heart. He commanded his men to leave the body where it lay, so to fulfill Elijah's prophecy. As soon as the troop left, wild dogs tore into Jehoram's body.

The new king rode quickly to the palace in Jezreel. News of the coup had reached Jezebel, and she leaned from a high window to shout her imprecations at the victorious Jehu. Ignoring her, he called out for any who supported his cause. Some eunuchs who attended the queen looked out from her window to shout their allegiance to Jehu. He commanded them to throw her out the window. They grabbed her with a vengeance and hurled her screaming to the pavement. Her body slammed onto the stones with such force that blood splattered onto the wall on one side and on the horses' legs on the other. Jehu reared his horses and guided their thrashing hooves to the queen's unconscious body. In a moment she was unrecognizable.

Jehu went into the palace to eat the necessary communal meal at which the court officials would have to determine their allegiance. Sometime later, he gave the command to bury the cursed woman, since she was a king's daughter. The men quickly returned, however, to inform Jehu that Jezebel's body had been torn to shreds by wild dogs, her clothing and bones ripped apart and carried away by the snarling beasts. Nothing remained of her but her skull, her feet, and the palms of her hands.

The new king moved quickly to consolidate his reign. As was the practice in that day, he slaughtered every kinsman of Ahab's, seventy of whom were royal princes, and every person considered a close friend to the royal family. Then he attacked Baalism with a fury. As a ruse, he announced a great sacrifice to Baal, so important that any Baal priest or minister who did not attend would be killed. Then, once the priests were gathered in a single large temple, Jehu had them slaughtered mercilessly.

The people were tired of the policies of Ahab and his successors. They rallied with enthusiasm to the new king, thrilled to claim a king once more who had the endorsement of the prophets. Jehu ruled for twenty-eight years, and his dynasty lasted for three generations after him.

Even with all the efforts of Jehu, Elisha, and their contemporaries, Baalism was not beaten. It remained a force in Israel, rising and falling in repute according to the sympathies of the kings, until the final destruction of the nation by Assyria in 721 B.C. Moreover, the practices of commerce and politics released by the Baal emphases permeated much of the life of Israel, even within the worship of Yahweh itself. Those emphases, the later prophets claimed, were the seeds of the final destruction of the nation. But through the almost single efforts of Elijah, the back of the Baal religion was broken. Never again did it threaten the religion of Yahweh with extinction.

And so, because of Elijah's single-minded commitment to his God, Yahweh worked through the genius of Israel to give to the world an ethical code that rose head, shoulders, chest, and waist above anything the world had known.

Other Living Books Bestsellers

THE MAN WHO COULD DO NO WRONG by Charles E. Blair with John and Elizabeth Sherrill. He built one of the largest churches in America . . . then he made a mistake. This is the incredible story of Pastor Charles E. Blair, accused of massive fraud. A book "for error-prone people in search of the Christian's secret for handling mistakes." 07-4002 $3.50.

GIVERS, TAKERS AND OTHER KINDS OF LOVERS by Josh McDowell. This book bypasses vague generalities about love and sex and gets right down to basic questions: Whatever happened to sexual freedom? What's true love like? What is your most important sex organ? Do men respond differently than women? If you're looking for straight answers about God's plan for love and sexuality then this book was written for you. 07-1023 $2.50.

MORE THAN A CARPENTER by Josh McDowell. This best selling author thought Christians must be "out of their minds." He put them down. He argued against their faith. But eventually he saw that his arguments wouldn't stand up. In this book, Josh focuses upon the person who changed his life—Jesus Christ. 07-4552 $2.50.

HIND'S FEET ON HIGH PLACES by Hannah Hurnard. A classic allegory which has sold more than a million copies! 07-1429 $3.50.

THE CATCH ME KILLER by Bob Erler with John Souter. Golden gloves, black belt, green beret, silver badge. Supercop Bob Erler had earned the colors of manhood. Now can he survive prison life? An incredible true story of forgiveness and hope. 07-0214 $3.50.

WHAT WIVES WISH THEIR HUSBANDS KNEW ABOUT WOMEN by Dr. James Dobson. By the best selling author of *DARE TO DISCIPLINE* and *THE STRONG-WILLED CHILD*, here's a vital book that speaks to the unique emotional needs and aspirations of today's woman. An immensely practical, interesting guide. 07-7896 $2.95.

PONTIUS PILATE by Dr. Paul Maier. This fascinating novel is about one of the most famous Romans in history—the man who declared Jesus innocent but who nevertheless sent him to the cross. This powerful biblical novel gives you a unique insight into the life and death of Jesus. 07-4852 $3.50.

BROTHER OF THE BRIDE by Donita Dyer. This exciting sequel to *THE BRIDE'S ESCAPE* tells of the faith of a proud, intelligent Armenian family whose Christian heritage stretched back for centuries. A story of suffering, separation, valor, victory, and reunion. 07-0179 $2.95.

LIFE IS TREMENDOUS by Charlie Jones. Believing that enthusiasm makes the difference, Jones shows how anyone can be happy, involved, relevant, productive, healthy, and secure in the midst of a high-pressure, commercialized, automated society. 07-2184 $2.50.

HOW TO BE HAPPY THOUGH MARRIED by Dr. Tim LaHaye. One of America's most successful marriage counselors gives practical, proven advice for marital happiness. 07-1499 $2.95.

The books listed are available at your bookstore. If unavailable, send check with order to cover retail price plus 10% for postage and handling to:

Tyndale House Publishers, Inc.
Box 80
Wheaton, Illinois 60189

Prices and availability subject to change without notice. Allow 4-6 weeks for delivery.